AWS Machine Learning Engineer Associate Complete Study Guide

450+ Practice Questions with Real-World MLOps Projects for MLA-C01

Abrielle Wang Perkins

Disclaimer:

This book is an independent study guide and is not affiliated with, endorsed by, or sponsored by Amazon Web Services, Inc. or any of its affiliates. AWS, Amazon SageMaker, and all related trademarks and service marks are the property of Amazon Web Services, Inc. or its affiliates.

The information contained in this book is provided for educational and informational purposes only. While every effort has been made to ensure accuracy, the author and publisher make no warranties or representations regarding the completeness, accuracy, or suitability of the information contained herein. The author and publisher shall not be liable for any loss or damage arising from the use of this book.

The practice questions and scenarios presented in this book are created for educational purposes and may not reflect the exact format, content, or difficulty level of the actual AWS Machine Learning Engineer Associate certification exam. Readers should refer to official AWS certification documentation and resources for the most current and accurate exam information.

All company names, product names, and service names mentioned in this book are used for identification purposes only and may be trademarks or registered trademarks of their respective owners. The use of these names does not imply any affiliation with or endorsement by these companies.

The case studies and examples presented in this book are fictional or based on publicly available information. Any resemblance to actual companies, organizations, or individuals is purely coincidental.

The author and publisher disclaim any liability for any actions taken based on the information provided in this book. Readers should always verify information and consult official AWS documentation before implementing any solutions or strategies discussed in this book.

By using this book, you acknowledge that you have read this disclaimer and agree to its terms.

ISBN: 978-1-7641942-2-8
Isohan Publishing

Table of Contents

Chapter 1: The AWS ML Ecosystem and Career Landscape

The machine learning profession stands at an unprecedented crossroads. Organizations worldwide struggle to bridge the gap between theoretical knowledge and practical implementation, creating a skills shortage that translates into extraordinary career opportunities for those who understand both the technical foundations and business applications of ML systems.

Amazon Web Services has positioned itself as the dominant force in cloud-based machine learning, offering a comprehensive suite of tools that spans from data ingestion to model deployment. Understanding this ecosystem requires more than memorizing service names—it demands practical knowledge of how these components work together to solve real business problems.

AWS ML Certification Paths and Career Trajectories

The AWS certification structure follows a logical progression that mirrors real-world career development. At the foundational level, the **AWS Certified Cloud Practitioner** establishes basic cloud literacy. This certification covers fundamental concepts like the shared responsibility model, basic pricing structures, and core service categories (1).

Moving into specialized territory, the **AWS Certified Machine Learning Engineer - Associate** represents the newest addition to the certification family. Launched in 2024, this certification addresses the growing demand for professionals who can implement production-ready ML systems rather than just theoretical models (2). The certification focuses on four key domains:

1. **Data Engineering for ML** (28% of exam)
2. **Exploratory Data Analysis and Feature Engineering** (24% of exam)
3. **Model Development** (26% of exam)
4. **MLOps Implementation** (22% of exam)

The **AWS Certified Machine Learning - Specialty** serves as the advanced tier, requiring deeper technical knowledge and broader experience across the AWS ML ecosystem. This certification demands understanding of complex scenarios involving multiple services, cost optimization strategies, and enterprise-scale implementations (3).

Case Example 1: Career Progression at FinTech Startup

Sarah began as a data analyst at a financial technology company with a computer science background but limited cloud experience. She started with the Cloud Practitioner certification to understand AWS fundamentals, spending three months building basic familiarity with core services like EC2, S3, and IAM.

After six months of hands-on experience with SageMaker for fraud detection models, Sarah pursued the ML Engineer Associate certification. The practical focus aligned perfectly with her daily responsibilities—building data pipelines for real-time transaction processing, implementing feature stores for customer behavior patterns, and deploying models that processed thousands of transactions per minute.

Eighteen months later, with successful production deployments under her belt, Sarah tackled the ML Specialty certification. This advanced credential opened doors to senior ML engineer positions, resulting in a 45% salary increase and responsibilities spanning multiple business units. Her progression demonstrates how strategic certification planning accelerates career advancement when combined with practical experience.

Case Example 2: Enterprise Migration Specialist

Marcus worked as a traditional software developer at a large insurance company when the organization decided to modernize its underwriting processes using machine learning. His initial role involved migrating legacy risk assessment models from on-premises infrastructure to AWS.

Starting with the Solutions Architect Associate certification, Marcus gained broad AWS knowledge before specializing in machine learning. The ML Engineer Associate certification provided the specific skills needed for his migration projects—understanding how to optimize data pipelines for cost efficiency, implement proper model monitoring, and ensure compliance with financial regulations.

Within two years, Marcus became the lead ML architect for the entire underwriting division. His unique combination of domain knowledge and AWS ML expertise made him indispensable during the company's digital transformation. The certifications validated his skills and provided structured learning paths for technologies he encountered daily.

Case Example 3: Independent Consultant Success

Lisa leveraged AWS ML certifications to establish a successful consulting practice specializing in retail analytics. Her strategy involved earning multiple certifications rapidly—completing the ML Engineer Associate within four months, followed by the ML Specialty six months later.

The certifications provided credibility when approaching potential clients, but more importantly, they ensured she understood the full range of AWS ML services available for different use cases. Her first major project involved implementing a demand forecasting system for a regional grocery chain, utilizing Amazon Forecast, SageMaker, and custom models for seasonal adjustment.

The success of that initial project, built on solid certification knowledge, led to contracts with three additional retail clients within the first year. Lisa's consulting revenue exceeded her previous corporate salary by 200%, demonstrating how certifications can enable entrepreneurial success in the ML field.

MLOps Market Overview and Salary Expectations

The MLOps market represents one of the fastest-growing segments in technology, with compound annual growth rates exceeding 35% according to multiple industry analyses (4). This growth stems from organizations recognizing that building models represents only 20% of the challenge—the remaining 80% involves deployment, monitoring, and maintenance in production environments.

Salary Expectations by Role and Experience:

Entry-level ML engineers with AWS certifications typically start between $85,000-$120,000 annually, depending on geographic location and industry sector. The ML Engineer Associate certification can add $15,000-$25,000 to base compensation for candidates with relevant experience (5).

Mid-level positions (3-5 years experience) with AWS ML certifications command $120,000-$180,000, with total compensation often reaching $200,000+ when including equity and bonuses. The combination of practical experience and validated skills creates significant negotiating power in today's competitive market.

Senior ML engineers and architects with multiple AWS certifications regularly earn $180,000-$280,000 in base salary, with total compensation packages exceeding $350,000 at major technology companies. The ML Specialty certification particularly correlates with higher compensation levels due to its advanced technical requirements (6).

Geographic variations significantly impact compensation levels. San Francisco Bay Area positions typically offer 40-60% premiums over national averages, while remote positions have narrowed geographic disparities as companies compete for scarce talent.

Industry sectors also influence compensation patterns. Financial services and healthcare organizations often pay premiums for ML professionals due to regulatory complexity and high stakes associated with model accuracy. Technology companies may offer lower base salaries but compensate through equity participation and comprehensive benefits packages.

Book Navigation: Certification Prep vs Implementation Tracks

This book adopts a dual-track approach recognizing that readers have different primary objectives. Some focus primarily on certification success, while others prioritize practical implementation skills. Most benefit from both perspectives integrated thoughtfully.

Certification Track Elements:

Each chapter includes exam-specific practice questions aligned with the actual AWS ML Engineer Associate exam format. These questions test both conceptual understanding and practical application scenarios typical of real-world implementations.

Key exam topics receive special attention through dedicated sections that explain not just what services do, but why specific approaches work better in different scenarios. The AWS exam emphasizes decision-making skills rather than rote memorization.

Common exam pitfalls receive explicit coverage based on analysis of student performance patterns and feedback from recent exam takers. Understanding why incorrect answers seem plausible helps build the analytical skills needed for exam success.

Implementation Track Elements:

Hands-on projects in each chapter build progressively complex systems using real AWS services. These projects simulate actual business scenarios rather than artificial academic exercises.

Code repositories accompany each project, providing working examples that readers can modify and extend for their specific needs. All code follows AWS best practices for security, cost optimization, and scalability.

Architecture diagrams and cost analysis help readers understand the business implications of technical decisions. Understanding the financial impact of different implementation choices is essential for professional success.

Integration Strategy:

The most effective approach combines both tracks, using certification preparation to ensure broad knowledge coverage while projects provide hands-on experience with core concepts. The exam questions test understanding of scenarios that mirror the project implementations.

Setting Up Your Learning Environment

Effective AWS ML learning requires a properly configured environment that balances hands-on experience with cost control. The following setup provides production-like capabilities while minimizing expenses for individual learners.

AWS Account Configuration:

Start with a new AWS account dedicated to learning activities. This separation prevents accidental interference with existing work environments and provides clean cost tracking for educational expenses.

Enable AWS Organizations even for single-account setups to establish good governance habits from the beginning. Future multi-account architectures become easier when proper organizational structures exist from the start (7).

Configure billing alerts immediately, setting conservative thresholds that trigger notifications before significant costs accumulate. A $50 monthly alert provides sufficient warning for most learning activities while allowing meaningful experimentation.

Identity and Access Management Setup:

Create separate IAM users for different types of activities rather than using root account credentials for daily work. This practice mirrors enterprise security requirements and builds proper security habits.

Establish least-privilege access policies that grant only the permissions needed for specific learning modules. Start with restricted access and expand permissions as needed rather than beginning with broad administrative rights.

Enable CloudTrail logging from the beginning to understand what actions generate costs and how different services interact. This visibility becomes essential when troubleshooting issues or optimizing expenses.

Regional Selection Strategy:

Choose a primary region based on service availability and pricing rather than geographic proximity. US East (N. Virginia) offers the broadest service selection and often the lowest pricing for ML services.

Understand data transfer costs between regions before implementing multi-region architectures. Educational projects rarely require global distribution, and cross-region data transfer can generate unexpected expenses.

Consider compliance requirements if working with real data rather than synthetic datasets. Some industries restrict data storage to specific geographic regions, affecting regional selection decisions.

Project: Configure Multi-Account AWS MLOps Sandbox

This foundational project establishes the infrastructure foundation for all subsequent learning activities. The multi-account structure mirrors enterprise patterns while remaining manageable for individual learners.

Account Structure Design:

Create three linked accounts within an AWS Organization structure:

1. **Security Account**: Centralized logging, monitoring, and identity management
2. **Development Account**: Experimentation, model development, and testing
3. **Production Account**: Stable deployments and production-like environments

This structure allows realistic simulation of enterprise deployment patterns while maintaining clear separation between different types of activities.

Cross-Account Access Configuration:

Establish cross-account roles that allow controlled access between accounts without sharing credentials. The security account maintains audit logs and monitoring data from all accounts, while development and production accounts handle their respective workloads.

Configure AWS Single Sign-On (SSO) to manage access across accounts efficiently. This setup provides experience with enterprise identity management patterns while simplifying day-to-day access management.

Cost Management Implementation:

Deploy AWS Cost Explorer and Budgets across all accounts to monitor spending patterns. Set up automated alerts that trigger when spending exceeds predetermined thresholds in any account.

Implement tagging strategies that enable cost allocation by project, learning module, or experiment type. Consistent tagging from the beginning enables detailed cost analysis as projects become more complex.

Monitoring and Logging Foundation:

Configure CloudWatch across all accounts with centralized log aggregation in the security account. This setup provides visibility into system behavior and enables troubleshooting when experiments don't work as expected.

Deploy AWS Config to track resource configurations and changes over time. Understanding how configurations affect system behavior becomes essential when working with complex ML pipelines.

Data Storage Architecture:

Establish S3 buckets with proper naming conventions and access policies that support cross-account data sharing when needed. Design bucket structures that support both raw data storage and processed results from ML experiments.

Configure S3 lifecycle policies to automatically transition data to less expensive storage classes as datasets age. This cost optimization becomes important as projects generate large amounts of intermediate data.

Security Baseline Implementation:

Enable GuardDuty across all accounts to detect potential security issues early. ML environments often contain sensitive data, making security monitoring essential even in learning environments.

Configure AWS Systems Manager for patch management and compliance monitoring. Establishing good security hygiene during learning prevents bad habits that cause problems in production environments.

Networking Foundation:

Deploy VPC structures that support both public and private subnet configurations. ML workloads often require internet access for downloading models and datasets while maintaining security for sensitive processing.

Configure VPC endpoints for commonly used services like S3 and SageMaker to reduce data transfer costs and improve security posture. Understanding the cost implications of different networking patterns helps optimize production deployments.

Documentation and Knowledge Management:

Establish documentation repositories using AWS CodeCommit or external systems like GitHub. Documenting configurations and decisions during learning creates valuable reference materials for future projects.

Create runbooks for common tasks like account setup, permission management, and cost monitoring. These documents become essential when collaborating with others or returning to projects after extended breaks.

Practical Insights

The AWS ML ecosystem continues expanding rapidly, with new services and capabilities announced regularly. Successful professionals maintain currency through continuous learning rather than attempting to master everything before beginning practical work.

Certification provides structure and validation, but real expertise develops through solving actual problems with production constraints. The combination of theoretical knowledge and hands-on experience creates the most valuable skill set in today's market.

Cost management skills often distinguish successful ML practitioners from those who struggle with practical implementations. Understanding the financial implications of technical decisions enables sustainable long-term success in ML engineering roles.

Looking Forward

The foundation established in this chapter supports all subsequent learning activities. Proper account setup, security configuration, and cost management create the stable platform needed for complex ML implementations.

The next chapter builds on this foundation by examining MLOps fundamentals and how they differ from traditional machine learning approaches. Understanding these differences is essential for success in production ML environments.

Key Learning Outcomes

- AWS ML certification paths provide structured career advancement opportunities with significant salary premiums
- Multi-account architectures support realistic learning while maintaining proper security and cost control
- Cost management skills are essential for practical ML implementation success
- Hands-on experience combined with certification knowledge creates the most valuable professional skill set
- Proper foundational setup enables complex implementations without unnecessary technical debt

Chapter 2: MLOps Fundamentals for AWS

Machine learning operations represents a paradigm shift from traditional software development practices, requiring new approaches to testing, deployment, and monitoring that account for the unique characteristics of ML systems. Unlike traditional applications where code behavior remains predictable given the same inputs, ML systems introduce data dependencies that create additional complexity layers requiring specialized management approaches.

The fundamental challenge of MLOps lies in managing the intersection of code, data, and models as interdependent components that must evolve together while maintaining system reliability and performance. This complexity multiplies in cloud environments where infrastructure costs, security requirements, and scalability demands add additional constraints to system design decisions.

Traditional ML vs MLOps Approaches

Traditional machine learning development typically follows an experimental workflow focused on model accuracy optimization within controlled environments. Data scientists work with fixed datasets, iterating through different algorithms and hyperparameters until achieving satisfactory performance metrics. This approach works well for research and proof-of-concept projects but fails when transitioning to production systems that must handle real-world variability.

Traditional ML Workflow Limitations:

The conventional approach treats model development as a linear process culminating in a final model artifact that gets deployed once and remains static. This perspective ignores the dynamic nature of real-world data where distributions shift, new patterns emerge, and business requirements evolve continuously.

Manual processes dominate traditional workflows, with data scientists performing ad-hoc data preprocessing, feature engineering, and model evaluation steps that resist automation and scaling. These manual interventions create bottlenecks that prevent rapid iteration and introduce opportunities for human error in production systems.

Model deployment often occurs through informal handoffs between data science teams and infrastructure teams, lacking the automated testing and validation processes that ensure reliable software releases. This disconnect frequently results in models that perform well in development environments but fail when confronted with production data characteristics.

MLOps Operational Philosophy:

MLOps treats machine learning as an operational system requiring continuous monitoring, automated testing, and systematic improvement processes. Models become living components that must adapt to changing conditions while maintaining performance standards and business value delivery.

Automation replaces manual processes wherever possible, enabling rapid experimentation cycles and reducing the time between model improvements and production deployment. Automated pipelines handle data preprocessing, feature engineering, model training, and deployment processes with minimal human intervention.

Version control extends beyond code to include data, models, and infrastructure configurations, enabling reproducible experiments and rollback capabilities when issues arise. This comprehensive versioning approach provides the foundation for debugging production issues and maintaining system reliability over time.

Case Example 1: Financial Services Risk Assessment Transformation

A regional bank initially deployed credit risk models using traditional approaches where data scientists developed models quarterly using historical loan data, manually generating feature sets, and deploying updated models through lengthy approval processes involving multiple departments.

The traditional process required six weeks from data extraction to model deployment, during which market conditions often changed significantly. Model performance degraded between deployments as data distributions shifted, but monitoring capabilities were limited to basic accuracy metrics checked monthly.

The MLOps transformation introduced automated data pipelines that processed loan applications in real-time, continuously monitored model performance against business metrics, and enabled rapid model updates when performance degradation was detected. Feature engineering became automated, incorporating external data sources like economic indicators and market trends.

The new system reduced deployment time from six weeks to two days while improving model accuracy by 15% through more frequent updates and broader data incorporation.

Automated monitoring detected data drift issues within hours rather than weeks, enabling proactive responses to changing market conditions.

Case Example 2: E-commerce Recommendation System Evolution

An online retailer operated recommendation systems using batch processing approaches where models were retrained weekly using the previous month's transaction data. The manual process involved data scientists extracting purchase histories, computing item similarities, and deploying updated recommendation matrices to production servers.

Customer behavior changed rapidly, especially during seasonal periods and promotional campaigns, but the weekly update cycle meant recommendations often reflected outdated preferences. Model performance measurement focused on offline metrics that didn't necessarily correlate with business outcomes like conversion rates and revenue.

The MLOps implementation created real-time data streams that captured customer interactions continuously, enabling dynamic model updates that reflected immediate behavior changes. A/B testing frameworks allowed systematic evaluation of different recommendation strategies against business metrics rather than just technical accuracy measures.

Online model serving capabilities enabled personalized recommendations that incorporated real-time customer context, improving click-through rates by 23% and conversion rates by 18%. Automated feature stores ensured consistent data representations across different model types while enabling rapid experimentation with new recommendation approaches.

Case Example 3: Healthcare Diagnostic Support System

A medical device company developed diagnostic support algorithms using traditional research workflows where models were trained on curated datasets and validated through offline testing procedures. Model updates required extensive regulatory review processes that typically took months to complete.

The traditional approach created fixed models that couldn't adapt to new diagnostic patterns or incorporate emerging medical knowledge without lengthy revalidation procedures. Performance monitoring relied on periodic audits rather than continuous assessment, making it difficult to detect gradual performance degradation.

The MLOps transformation maintained regulatory compliance while enabling more responsive model improvement through automated validation pipelines that ensured consistent testing protocols. Continuous monitoring tracked model performance across different patient populations and diagnostic scenarios, identifying potential bias issues before they affected patient care.

Automated documentation generation ensured regulatory submissions included complete audit trails of model development and validation processes. The new approach reduced time from model improvement to deployment from eight months to six weeks while maintaining full regulatory compliance and improving diagnostic accuracy.

AWS Well-Architected Framework for ML

The AWS Well-Architected Framework provides structured guidance for building reliable, secure, efficient, and cost-effective systems in the cloud. The Machine Learning Lens extends these principles to address the unique challenges of ML workloads, providing specific guidance for each pillar of the framework (8).

Operational Excellence for ML Systems:

ML systems require operational practices that account for the complexity of managing code, data, and models as interdependent components. Traditional software operations focus primarily on code deployment and infrastructure management, while ML operations must also consider data quality, model performance, and business metric alignment.

Automation becomes essential for ML operational excellence due to the complexity and frequency of updates required across multiple system components. Manual processes that work for traditional software become bottlenecks when applied to ML systems that may require daily or hourly updates based on changing data patterns.

Monitoring and alerting must extend beyond traditional infrastructure metrics to include data quality, model performance, and business impact measures. Technical teams need visibility into how model changes affect business outcomes, not just system performance metrics.

Security Considerations for ML Workloads:

ML systems often process sensitive data requiring protection throughout the entire pipeline from data ingestion through model serving. Traditional security approaches focused on network and application security must expand to include data privacy, model security, and inference protection.

Data governance becomes particularly important in ML systems where training data quality directly affects model behavior and potential bias issues. Access controls must balance data scientist productivity needs with security requirements for sensitive information.

Model security considerations include protecting intellectual property embedded in trained models, preventing adversarial attacks that could manipulate model behavior, and ensuring model outputs don't leak sensitive training data information.

Reliability Patterns for ML Systems:

ML system reliability requires addressing failure modes that don't exist in traditional software systems. Model performance can degrade gradually due to data drift without triggering traditional error conditions, requiring specialized monitoring and response procedures.

Backup and recovery procedures must account for data dependencies and model state in addition to traditional infrastructure components. Model rollback capabilities require maintaining previous versions along with their associated data preprocessing and feature engineering configurations.

Testing strategies must include data validation, model performance testing, and business impact assessment in addition to traditional software testing approaches. ML system failures often manifest as gradual performance degradation rather than obvious errors, requiring more sophisticated detection mechanisms.

Performance Efficiency in ML Workloads:

ML workloads exhibit different performance characteristics than traditional applications, with training workloads requiring intensive compute resources for relatively short periods while inference workloads need consistent low-latency responses with varying throughput demands.

Cost optimization requires understanding the trade-offs between training frequency, model complexity, and infrastructure costs. More frequent training may improve model accuracy but increases computational expenses, while more complex models may provide better performance but require more expensive infrastructure.

Resource allocation strategies must account for the bursty nature of ML training workloads while maintaining cost-effective inference serving capabilities. Auto-scaling policies need to consider both technical performance requirements and business cost constraints.

Cost Optimization Strategies:

ML workloads can generate significant costs if not managed carefully, particularly for training large models or processing high-volume data streams. Understanding cost drivers enables informed decisions about architecture trade-offs and resource allocation strategies.

Data storage costs often represent a significant portion of ML system expenses, especially when maintaining multiple versions of large datasets for experimentation and training purposes. Lifecycle management policies can reduce storage costs while maintaining necessary data access for ML workflows.

Compute cost optimization requires balancing training frequency, model complexity, and performance requirements against available budget constraints. Spot instances can reduce training costs significantly but require fault-tolerant training procedures that can handle instance interruptions.

Cost Optimization Strategies from Day One

Successful ML implementations require cost management strategies integrated from the beginning rather than addressed as an afterthought when bills become problematic. Understanding cost drivers and implementing appropriate controls enables sustainable scaling of ML operations within budget constraints.

Data Storage Cost Management:

S3 storage costs can accumulate rapidly when storing multiple versions of large datasets along with intermediate processing results and model artifacts. Implementing intelligent tiering policies automatically moves infrequently accessed data to less expensive storage classes while maintaining immediate access to actively used datasets.

Data lifecycle policies should reflect actual usage patterns rather than theoretical retention requirements. Training datasets older than six months rarely provide value for model improvement but continue generating storage costs if not managed properly.

Compression strategies can reduce storage costs significantly for datasets that aren't accessed frequently. Modern compression algorithms achieve substantial size reductions with minimal impact on processing time when data needs to be accessed.

Compute Resource Optimization:

Training workloads represent the largest variable cost component in most ML systems, making compute optimization essential for budget management. Spot instances can reduce training costs by 70-90% compared to on-demand pricing but require fault-tolerant training procedures.

Instance type selection should match workload characteristics rather than defaulting to general-purpose instances. GPU instances provide better cost-performance ratios for deep learning workloads, while high-memory instances work better for large dataset processing.

Auto-scaling policies should consider both performance requirements and cost constraints when determining resource allocation. Aggressive scaling policies may improve performance but can generate unnecessary costs during low-demand periods.

Model Serving Cost Management:

Inference serving costs depend heavily on traffic patterns and latency requirements, requiring different optimization strategies for different use cases. Batch inference often provides better cost efficiency for scenarios that don't require real-time responses.

Multi-model endpoints enable cost sharing across multiple models when serving requirements allow shared infrastructure. This approach works particularly well for scenarios with multiple small models rather than few large models.

Auto-scaling configurations should account for cold start latencies and scaling delays when determining minimum instance counts. Over-provisioning for peak loads generates unnecessary costs, while under-provisioning affects user experience during traffic spikes.

Security and Compliance Foundations

ML systems require security approaches that address traditional application security concerns while adding protections for data privacy, model intellectual property, and inference integrity. Regulatory compliance adds additional requirements that must be integrated into system architecture from the beginning.

Data Protection Throughout the ML Pipeline:

Encryption at rest and in transit protects sensitive data throughout the ML pipeline, but key management becomes complex when data flows through multiple processing stages and storage systems. AWS Key Management Service provides centralized key management that integrates with all ML services.

Data access controls must balance security requirements with data scientist productivity needs. Overly restrictive access policies impede experimentation and model development, while insufficient controls create compliance risks and potential data breaches.

Data anonymization and pseudonymization techniques can reduce privacy risks while maintaining data utility for ML applications. These approaches require careful implementation to prevent re-identification attacks while preserving statistical properties needed for model training.

Model Security Considerations:

Trained models contain valuable intellectual property that requires protection from unauthorized access and reverse engineering attacks. Model serving architectures should prevent direct access to model artifacts while maintaining necessary inference capabilities.

Adversarial attack protection requires implementing input validation and anomaly detection systems that identify potentially malicious inputs before they reach trained models. These protections must balance security concerns with inference latency requirements.

Model output filtering can prevent unintended information disclosure through inference results while maintaining model utility for legitimate use cases. This protection becomes particularly important for models trained on sensitive data.

Compliance Framework Implementation:

Regulatory compliance requirements vary significantly across industries and geographies, requiring flexible security frameworks that can adapt to different regulatory environments. GDPR, HIPAA, SOX, and other regulations impose specific requirements for data handling and audit trail maintenance.

Audit trail generation must capture all data access, model training, and inference activities with sufficient detail to support compliance reporting and security investigations. Automated audit log aggregation and analysis capabilities reduce compliance overhead while improving security monitoring.

Data residency requirements may restrict where data can be stored and processed, affecting architecture decisions and service selection options. Understanding these requirements early prevents costly architecture changes later in the development process.

Project: Build Cost-Aware ML Development Environment

This project establishes a production-ready ML development environment that incorporates cost monitoring, security best practices, and operational efficiency from the beginning. The environment supports both experimentation and production deployment while maintaining visibility into cost drivers and performance characteristics.

Infrastructure as Code Foundation:

Deploy all infrastructure components using AWS CloudFormation or AWS CDK to ensure reproducible and version-controlled environment setup. Infrastructure as code enables rapid environment recreation and reduces configuration drift over time.

Template parameterization allows customization for different environments (development, staging, production) while maintaining consistent security and monitoring configurations across all deployments.

Cost Monitoring and Alerting Implementation:

Configure AWS Cost Explorer with custom cost allocation tags that track expenses by project, experiment type, and resource category. This granular cost tracking enables informed decisions about resource allocation and experiment prioritization.

Deploy custom CloudWatch metrics that track ML-specific cost drivers like training time, data processing volume, and inference request counts. These metrics provide leading indicators of cost trends before they appear in billing reports.

Implement automated cost alerts that trigger when spending exceeds predetermined thresholds for different cost categories. Separate alerts for training costs, inference costs, and storage costs enable targeted responses to different types of cost increases.

Security Configuration:

Establish IAM roles and policies that implement least-privilege access for different types of users and applications. Data scientists need different permissions than production inference systems, requiring role-based access control that matches actual usage patterns.

Configure VPC endpoints for commonly used services to reduce data transfer costs while improving security posture. Private connectivity to S3, SageMaker, and other ML services eliminates internet gateway dependencies and associated costs.

Deploy AWS Config rules that monitor compliance with security best practices and organizational policies. Automated compliance monitoring reduces administrative overhead while ensuring consistent security standards across all environments.

Data Management Architecture:

Implement S3 bucket structures that support data versioning, lifecycle management, and cross-region replication for disaster recovery scenarios. Proper bucket organization enables efficient data discovery and access control implementation.

Configure S3 Intelligent Tiering to automatically optimize storage costs based on access patterns without manual intervention. This automatic optimization reduces storage costs while maintaining data availability when needed.

Deploy AWS Glue Data Catalog to maintain metadata about datasets, enabling data discovery and lineage tracking throughout the ML pipeline. Centralized metadata management improves collaboration and reduces duplicate data storage.

Model Development and Deployment Infrastructure:

Configure SageMaker Studio with custom instance types and auto-shutdown policies that balance productivity and cost control. Automatic shutdown of idle instances prevents unnecessary compute costs while maintaining development environment availability.

Establish SageMaker model registry with approval workflows that ensure proper testing and validation before production deployment. Automated deployment pipelines reduce manual effort while maintaining quality control.

Deploy SageMaker endpoints with auto-scaling configurations that respond to traffic patterns while maintaining cost efficiency. Traffic-based scaling policies prevent over-provisioning during low-demand periods while ensuring adequate capacity during peak usage.

Monitoring and Observability:

Implement comprehensive logging that captures all ML pipeline activities including data processing, model training, and inference serving. Centralized log aggregation enables troubleshooting and performance analysis across all system components.

Deploy custom CloudWatch dashboards that provide visibility into system performance, cost trends, and business metrics. Real-time monitoring enables proactive responses to issues before they affect users or generate excessive costs.

Configure automated alerts for data quality issues, model performance degradation, and infrastructure problems that could affect system reliability or cost efficiency.

Understanding the ML Engineering Discipline

Machine learning engineering represents a distinct professional discipline that combines traditional software engineering practices with specialized knowledge of ML systems, data management, and statistical modeling. This discipline requires different skills and approaches than traditional data science or software development roles.

The ML engineer focuses on system reliability, scalability, and maintainability rather than maximizing model accuracy in isolation. Understanding business requirements and translating them into technical architectures that can scale sustainably becomes more important than achieving marginal improvements in offline model metrics.

Successful ML engineers develop intuition for the trade-offs between model complexity, infrastructure costs, and business value that enables practical decision-making in resource-constrained environments. This business-technical perspective distinguishes effective practitioners from those who struggle with production implementations.

Establishing Professional Foundations

The journey toward ML engineering expertise requires systematic skill development across multiple domains including cloud infrastructure, data management, statistical modeling, and business analysis. Building competency in each area while understanding their interactions creates the foundation for successful practice.

Continuous learning becomes essential due to the rapid pace of change in both ML techniques and cloud services capabilities. Staying current requires ongoing investment in skill development and practical experimentation with new technologies and approaches.

Professional networks and communities provide valuable resources for learning best practices, troubleshooting complex issues, and staying informed about industry trends. Active participation in these communities accelerates learning and career development.

Key Learning Outcomes

- MLOps fundamentals require different approaches than traditional ML development focused on production reliability and business value
- AWS Well-Architected Framework provides structured guidance for building reliable, secure, and cost-effective ML systems
- Cost optimization strategies must be integrated from the beginning rather than addressed after systems become expensive
- Security and compliance requirements add complexity that must be considered throughout system architecture
- Proper foundational setup enables sustainable scaling while maintaining cost control and operational efficiency

Chapter 3: Statistical Foundations and ML Mathematics

Mathematical foundations form the bedrock upon which all machine learning systems rest, yet many practitioners attempt to build production systems without sufficient understanding of the statistical principles governing model behavior. This knowledge gap creates vulnerabilities that manifest as poor model performance, unreliable predictions, and systems that fail when confronted with real-world data variations.

Understanding statistical concepts enables informed decisions about algorithm selection, hyperparameter tuning, and performance evaluation that distinguish competent practitioners from those who rely on trial-and-error approaches. The AWS ecosystem provides tools that implement these statistical foundations, but using them effectively requires understanding the underlying mathematical principles.

Essential Statistics for ML Practitioners

Statistical literacy begins with understanding data distributions and their properties, which directly influence algorithm selection and model performance expectations. Most machine learning algorithms make implicit assumptions about data characteristics that must be validated before applying specific techniques to real datasets.

Central Tendency and Variability Measures:

Mean, median, and mode provide different perspectives on data center points, with each measure appropriate for different data characteristics and use cases. The arithmetic mean works well for normally distributed data but becomes misleading when outliers or skewed distributions are present.

Median values provide robust measures of central tendency that resist outlier influence, making them more appropriate for analyzing features with extreme values or non-normal distributions. Understanding when to use median versus mean affects feature engineering decisions and model interpretation.

Standard deviation and variance quantify data spread around central values, providing essential information for normalization procedures and algorithm selection. Algorithms like linear regression assume homoscedasticity (constant variance), while others like decision trees handle variable variance naturally.

Correlation and Covariance Analysis:

Pearson correlation coefficients measure linear relationships between variables but miss non-linear associations that may be important for model performance. Understanding correlation limitations prevents overlooking important feature relationships that require different analytical approaches.

Spearman correlation captures monotonic relationships that don't follow linear patterns, providing better insights for ordinal variables and non-linear associations. This distinction becomes important when analyzing customer behavior data or time-series patterns that exhibit non-linear trends.

Covariance matrices provide foundation for dimensionality reduction techniques like Principal Component Analysis, but understanding eigenvalue decomposition enables proper interpretation of results and appropriate application to different data types.

Distribution Properties and Testing:

Normal distribution assumptions underlie many statistical tests and machine learning algorithms, making distribution testing essential for proper technique selection. The Shapiro-Wilk test and Anderson-Darling test provide formal methods for evaluating normality assumptions.

Skewness and kurtosis measurements quantify distribution asymmetry and tail thickness, indicating whether transformations may improve model performance. Log transformations often normalize right-skewed distributions common in financial and user behavior data.

Q-Q plots provide visual methods for comparing observed distributions against theoretical distributions, enabling intuitive assessment of distribution assumptions before applying specific algorithms or statistical tests.

Case Example 1: Customer Lifetime Value Modeling

A subscription software company attempted to predict customer lifetime value using linear regression models that assumed normal distribution of revenue data. Initial models performed poorly because customer revenue followed a heavily right-skewed distribution with many low-value customers and few high-value outliers.

Statistical analysis revealed that log transformation of revenue values produced approximately normal distributions more suitable for linear modeling approaches. However, business stakeholders required predictions in original dollar amounts, necessitating careful back-transformation procedures that accounted for bias introduced by log-normal distributions.

The final approach combined multiple techniques: log transformation for model training, bias correction during back-transformation, and confidence intervals calculated using bootstrap methods that didn't assume normal distributions. This statistically principled approach improved prediction accuracy by 35% compared to naive linear regression applications.

Case Example 2: Manufacturing Quality Control

An electronics manufacturer implemented anomaly detection systems to identify defective products using sensor data from production lines. Initial approaches used simple threshold-based rules that generated excessive false alarms because they didn't account for natural process variation.

Statistical process control principles guided development of more sophisticated detection algorithms that considered normal process variation while identifying genuine anomalies. Control charts helped establish appropriate thresholds based on historical process capability rather than arbitrary cutoffs.

Implementation of multivariate statistical process control using Hotelling's T-squared statistic enabled simultaneous monitoring of multiple sensor readings while accounting for correlations between different measurements. This approach reduced false alarm rates by 70% while improving detection of actual quality issues.

Linear Algebra Concepts in Practice

Linear algebra provides the mathematical foundation for most machine learning algorithms, from simple linear regression to complex deep neural networks. Understanding these concepts enables optimization of algorithm performance and interpretation of model behavior in ways that black-box approaches cannot achieve.

Matrix Operations and Properties:

Matrix multiplication rules govern how data flows through machine learning algorithms, particularly neural networks where each layer represents matrix operations applied to input data. Understanding these operations enables optimization of computational efficiency and memory usage.

Matrix inversion operations appear in many analytical solutions to machine learning problems, but numerical stability issues require careful implementation. The Moore-Penrose pseudoinverse provides robust solutions for cases where standard matrix inversion fails due to singularity or near-singularity conditions.

Eigenvalue decomposition underlies Principal Component Analysis and many other dimensionality reduction techniques used for feature engineering and data visualization. Understanding eigenvalue interpretation enables proper selection of principal components and assessment of information loss during dimensionality reduction.

Vector Spaces and Transformations:

Feature spaces represent data points as vectors in high-dimensional spaces where distance and angle measurements enable similarity calculations and clustering operations. Understanding vector space properties helps optimize feature selection and engineering procedures.

Linear transformations preserve vector space structure while enabling data normalization, rotation, and scaling operations that improve algorithm performance. These transformations form the basis for many preprocessing techniques used in production ML pipelines.

Orthogonality concepts enable understanding of feature independence and correlation structures that affect algorithm performance and interpretation. Gram-Schmidt orthogonalization procedures can create independent feature sets when algorithm assumptions require uncorrelated inputs.

Optimization Foundations:

Gradient-based optimization algorithms rely on partial derivatives and linear approximations to find optimal model parameters. Understanding these concepts enables proper learning rate selection and convergence troubleshooting.

Convex optimization theory provides guarantees about global optimum discovery that apply to many machine learning problems. Understanding convexity enables selection of appropriate optimization algorithms and assessment of convergence reliability.

Lagrange multipliers enable constrained optimization problems common in support vector machines and regularized regression models. Understanding these techniques enables proper hyperparameter tuning and constraint specification.

Case Example 3: Recommendation System Optimization

An e-commerce platform implemented collaborative filtering recommendation systems using matrix factorization techniques to predict customer preferences for products they hadn't purchased. Initial implementations used standard alternating least squares algorithms but suffered from convergence issues and poor performance on sparse data.

Linear algebra analysis revealed that the customer-product interaction matrix had poor conditioning due to extreme sparsity (less than 0.1% of entries were non-zero). Standard matrix factorization approaches struggled with this sparsity, requiring specialized techniques for sparse matrix operations.

Implementation of randomized singular value decomposition techniques enabled efficient processing of sparse matrices while maintaining numerical stability. This approach reduced computation time by 80% while improving recommendation accuracy through better handling of data sparsity characteristics.

Probability Distributions in Real Scenarios

Probability theory provides the foundation for understanding uncertainty in machine learning predictions and enables proper statistical inference from model results. Different probability distributions model different types of real-world phenomena, making distribution selection crucial for accurate modeling.

Discrete Probability Distributions:

Bernoulli distributions model binary outcomes common in classification problems, click prediction, and A/B testing scenarios. Understanding Bernoulli properties enables proper modeling of success rates and conversion probabilities.

Poisson distributions model count data like website visits, customer calls, or defect rates where events occur independently at constant average rates. Many business metrics follow Poisson patterns, making this distribution essential for forecasting and capacity planning.

Multinomial distributions extend Bernoulli concepts to multi-class scenarios common in text classification, customer segmentation, and recommendation systems. Understanding multinomial properties enables proper handling of categorical outcomes with more than two classes.

Continuous Probability Distributions:

Normal distributions appear frequently in natural phenomena and measurement error, making them fundamental for many statistical tests and modeling approaches. Central Limit Theorem ensures that sample means approach normal distributions regardless of underlying population distributions.

Exponential distributions model time-to-event data like customer churn, equipment failure, and response times. Understanding exponential properties enables proper survival analysis and reliability modeling for business applications.

Beta distributions provide flexible models for proportions and probabilities that must remain between zero and one. Beta distributions often serve as prior distributions in Bayesian analysis and model parameters that represent rates or percentages.

Distribution Parameter Estimation:

Maximum likelihood estimation provides principled methods for estimating distribution parameters from observed data. Understanding likelihood concepts enables proper model fitting and parameter uncertainty quantification.

Method of moments estimation offers alternative approaches that may be more robust in small sample situations or when likelihood functions are complex. These methods often provide good initial parameter estimates for more sophisticated optimization procedures.

Bayesian parameter estimation incorporates prior knowledge about parameter values while updating beliefs based on observed data. This approach provides natural uncertainty quantification and enables incorporation of domain expertise into statistical models.

AWS-Specific Statistical Tools and Services

Amazon Web Services provides numerous tools that implement statistical analyses and machine learning algorithms, but using them effectively requires understanding their underlying mathematical foundations and appropriate application scenarios.

Amazon QuickSight ML Insights:

QuickSight automatically detects anomalies in time-series data using sophisticated statistical methods including seasonal decomposition and robust statistical estimators. Understanding these techniques enables proper interpretation of detected anomalies and adjustment of sensitivity parameters.

Forecasting capabilities implement multiple statistical methods including ARIMA models, exponential smoothing, and Prophet algorithm variants. Comparing these approaches requires understanding their different assumptions about data characteristics and trend patterns.

Narrative insights automatically generate natural language descriptions of statistical patterns in data, but understanding the underlying statistical tests enables validation of automated insights and identification of limitations.

SageMaker Built-in Statistical Functions:

Random Cut Forest algorithm implements unsupervised anomaly detection using statistical properties of random forest models. Understanding this approach enables proper threshold setting and interpretation of anomaly scores.

Statistical feature preprocessing functions implement standardization, normalization, and transformation procedures that improve algorithm performance. Understanding these transformations enables proper selection and sequencing of preprocessing steps.

Automatic model tuning uses Bayesian optimization techniques to efficiently explore hyperparameter spaces. Understanding these methods enables better initial parameter ranges and convergence assessment.

AWS Glue DataBrew Statistical Operations:

Profile generation automatically computes statistical summaries including distribution parameters, correlation matrices, and data quality metrics. Understanding these statistics enables proper data assessment and cleaning procedures.

Outlier detection implements multiple statistical methods including z-score, interquartile range, and isolation forest approaches. Comparing these methods requires understanding their different assumptions and performance characteristics.

Data transformation recipes implement statistical transformations like Box-Cox normalization and percentile scaling that improve data quality for machine learning applications.

Mathematical Foundations for Model Selection

Choosing appropriate machine learning algorithms requires understanding their mathematical foundations and assumptions about data characteristics. This knowledge enables informed decisions that consider both technical performance and business requirements.

Bias-Variance Tradeoff Analysis:

Model complexity affects the balance between bias (systematic error) and variance (sensitivity to training data variations). Understanding this tradeoff enables optimal model selection that minimizes total prediction error.

Cross-validation procedures provide empirical methods for estimating bias and variance components of prediction error. Understanding these decompositions enables principled model comparison and selection.

Regularization techniques like L1 and L2 penalties provide mathematical methods for controlling model complexity and managing bias-variance tradeoffs. Understanding regularization theory enables proper hyperparameter selection and model tuning.

Information Theory Applications:

Entropy measurements quantify information content in datasets and model predictions, providing theoretical foundations for feature selection and model evaluation. Understanding entropy enables optimization of information extraction from available data.

Mutual information measures dependency between variables without assuming linear relationships, enabling detection of complex feature interactions that correlation analysis might miss.

Kullback-Leibler divergence quantifies differences between probability distributions, providing foundations for many machine learning algorithms and model comparison techniques.

Statistical Learning Theory:

PAC learning theory provides theoretical guarantees about model generalization performance based on training sample sizes and model complexity. Understanding these concepts enables proper sample size planning and generalization assessment.

Rademacher complexity measurements provide data-dependent bounds on generalization error that can guide model selection decisions. These concepts help assess whether observed performance differences reflect genuine model superiority or statistical noise.

VC dimension theory provides model-independent bounds on generalization performance that help assess algorithm appropriateness for different problem sizes and complexities.

Practical Implementation Strategies

Applying statistical foundations in production machine learning systems requires balancing theoretical rigor with practical constraints including computation time, data availability, and business requirements.

Statistical Validation Procedures:

Hypothesis testing provides formal methods for assessing model performance differences and feature importance, but multiple testing corrections become necessary when evaluating many comparisons simultaneously.

Bootstrap procedures enable confidence interval estimation and significance testing without distributional assumptions, providing robust alternatives to parametric statistical tests.

Permutation tests provide exact significance testing for complex statistics where theoretical distributions are unknown or difficult to compute.

Performance Monitoring:

Statistical process control techniques enable monitoring of model performance over time while accounting for natural variation in prediction accuracy. Control charts help distinguish genuine performance degradation from random fluctuations.

Sequential testing procedures enable early stopping of A/B tests when sufficient evidence accumulates, reducing opportunity costs associated with prolonged testing periods.

Change point detection algorithms identify when model performance characteristics shift significantly, triggering appropriate responses like model retraining or feature engineering updates.

Bridging Theory and Practice

The path forward requires integrating statistical foundations with practical implementation skills that address real-world constraints and business requirements. Mathematical understanding enables optimization of system performance while avoiding common pitfalls that arise from insufficient theoretical grounding.

Understanding statistical foundations also enables effective communication with stakeholders who need to understand model capabilities and limitations without detailed technical knowledge. This communication skill becomes essential for successful deployment and adoption of machine learning systems.

Key Learning Outcomes

- Statistical foundations enable informed algorithm selection and proper model interpretation in production systems
- Linear algebra concepts underlie most machine learning algorithms and optimization procedures used in practice
- Probability distributions provide frameworks for modeling uncertainty and making statistical inferences from data
- AWS statistical tools implement sophisticated methods but require understanding of underlying principles for effective use
- Mathematical foundations enable optimization of system performance while avoiding common implementation pitfalls

Practice Questions: AWS ML Engineer Associate Exam Preparation

Question 1: A data scientist notices that their linear regression model performs poorly on a dataset with customer purchase amounts. Statistical analysis shows the purchase amounts follow a heavily right-skewed distribution. What preprocessing approach would be most appropriate?

A) Apply standardization to center the data around zero B) Use min-max scaling to normalize values between 0 and 1
C) Apply log transformation to reduce skewness D) Remove outliers using the interquartile range method

Correct Answer: C - Log transformation is the appropriate technique for right-skewed distributions as it compresses large values more than small values, often resulting in approximately normal distributions suitable for linear regression.

Question 2: When implementing anomaly detection for IoT sensor data, which statistical approach would be most appropriate for identifying multivariate outliers?

A) Z-score calculation for each sensor independently B) Mahalanobis distance considering sensor correlations C) Simple threshold rules based on historical averages D) Percentile-based outlier detection for each sensor

Correct Answer: B - Mahalanobis distance accounts for correlations between multiple sensors and provides a unified metric for multivariate anomaly detection, unlike approaches that treat sensors independently.

Question 3: A recommendation system uses matrix factorization to predict user preferences. The user-item interaction matrix is 99.8% sparse. Which mathematical approach would best handle this sparsity?

A) Standard singular value decomposition (SVD) B) Randomized SVD with truncated eigenvalue computation C) Complete matrix inversion using Moore-Penrose pseudoinverse D) Principal component analysis on the full matrix

Correct Answer: B - Randomized SVD efficiently handles sparse matrices by focusing computational effort on the most significant eigenvalues, avoiding the computational challenges of processing mostly-zero matrices.

Question 4: When evaluating model performance using cross-validation, what statistical principle ensures that performance estimates are unbiased?

A) The training and validation sets must have identical distributions B) Each data point appears in exactly one validation fold C) The model must be retrained on each fold's training data D) All features must be standardized before cross-validation

Correct Answer: C - Retraining the model on each fold's training data ensures that performance estimates reflect the model's ability to generalize to truly unseen data, preventing data leakage that would bias results.

Question 5: A time-series forecasting model needs to account for seasonal patterns in retail sales data. Which probability distribution would best model the seasonal component?

A) Normal distribution with constant variance B) Poisson distribution with time-varying rate C) Exponential distribution with seasonal parameters D) Beta distribution constrained between seasonal bounds

Correct Answer: B - Poisson distributions naturally model count data like sales transactions, and time-varying rate parameters can capture seasonal fluctuations in average sales levels.

Question 6: When implementing Bayesian hyperparameter optimization in SageMaker, what statistical principle guides the selection of the next hyperparameter configuration to evaluate?

A) Random sampling from uniform distributions B) Grid search over predefined parameter ranges C) Acquisition function optimization balancing exploration and exploitation D) Gradient descent on validation loss surface

Correct Answer: C - Bayesian optimization uses acquisition functions that balance exploring uncertain regions of hyperparameter space with exploiting areas that show promise for good performance.

Question 7: A classification model shows perfect accuracy on training data but poor performance on validation data. What statistical concept best explains this behavior?

A) High bias due to underfitting B) High variance due to overfitting C) Inadequate feature normalization D) Insufficient training data quantity

Correct Answer: B - Perfect training accuracy with poor validation performance indicates high variance (overfitting), where the model memorizes training data but fails to generalize to new examples.

Question 8: When analyzing customer churn data, which probability distribution would be most appropriate for modeling the time until a customer cancels their subscription?

A) Normal distribution for continuous time values B) Exponential distribution for memoryless failure processes C) Binomial distribution for binary churn outcomes D) Uniform distribution for equally likely churn times

Correct Answer: B - Exponential distributions naturally model time-to-event data like customer churn, especially when the hazard rate remains approximately constant over time.

Question 9: A feature engineering pipeline needs to detect and handle outliers in financial transaction data. Which statistical approach provides the most robust outlier detection?

A) Standard deviation-based z-scores B) Interquartile range (IQR) method C) Mean absolute deviation from median D) Percentile-based thresholds

Correct Answer: B - The IQR method uses median and quartiles, which are robust to outliers themselves, making it more reliable for outlier detection in financial data that often contains extreme values.

Question 10: When implementing dimensionality reduction using Principal Component Analysis, how should the number of components be selected based on statistical principles?

A) Always use exactly half of the original features B) Select components explaining at least 95% of variance C) Choose the number that minimizes reconstruction error D) Use cross-validation to optimize downstream task performance

Correct Answer: D - While variance explained provides useful information, the optimal number of components depends on the specific downstream task, making cross-validation the most principled selection approach.

Question 11: A machine learning model needs to handle missing data in customer demographics. Which statistical principle should guide the choice between different imputation methods?

A) Always use mean imputation for simplicity B) Missing at random (MAR) assumptions determine appropriate methods C) Mode imputation works best for all data types D) Forward-fill imputation preserves temporal relationships

Correct Answer: B - Understanding whether data is missing completely at random (MCAR), missing at random (MAR), or missing not at random (MNAR) determines which imputation methods will produce unbiased results.

Question 12: When evaluating A/B test results for a new recommendation algorithm, what statistical consideration is most important for determining test duration?

A) Equal sample sizes in both groups B) Statistical power to detect meaningful effect sizes C) Normal distribution of outcome metrics D) Independence of user interactions

Correct Answer: B - Statistical power analysis determines the sample size needed to reliably detect effect sizes that matter for business decisions, ensuring tests run long enough to produce meaningful results.

Question 13: A natural language processing model uses term frequency-inverse document frequency (TF-IDF) features. What statistical principle underlies the inverse document frequency component?

A) Words appearing in many documents carry less information B) Rare words should be completely removed from analysis C) Document length normalization improves comparisons D) Frequency distributions should be standardized

Correct Answer: A - IDF is based on information theory principles: words appearing in many documents provide less discriminatory information than words that appear in few documents.

Question 14: When implementing ensemble methods like Random Forest, what statistical principle explains why averaging multiple models often improves performance?

A) Central Limit Theorem ensures normal prediction distributions B) Variance reduction through averaging independent estimators C) Bias reduction through model combination D) Increased sample size through bootstrap aggregation

Correct Answer: B - Ensemble methods primarily reduce variance by averaging predictions from multiple independent models, while individual model bias remains approximately unchanged.

Question 15: A computer vision model needs to handle images with varying lighting conditions. Which statistical preprocessing approach would be most appropriate?

A) Histogram equalization to normalize brightness distributions B) Z-score standardization of pixel values C) Min-max scaling to [0,1] range D) Logarithmic transformation of pixel intensities

Correct Answer: A - Histogram equalization specifically addresses brightness variation by transforming the image intensity distribution to achieve more uniform brightness levels across different images.

Question 16: When monitoring model performance in production, what statistical approach helps distinguish between normal performance variation and genuine model degradation?

A) Simple threshold-based alerts on accuracy metrics B) Statistical process control with control charts C) Daily comparison with training set performance D) Linear trend analysis of prediction accuracy

Correct Answer: B - Statistical process control techniques account for natural variation in performance metrics while providing principled methods for detecting significant changes that indicate model degradation.

Question 17: A clustering algorithm needs to determine the optimal number of clusters for customer segmentation. Which statistical criterion provides the best guidance?

A) Always use exactly 5 clusters for interpretability B) Silhouette analysis measuring within and between cluster distances C) Maximum number of clusters that fit in memory D) Equal-sized clusters for balanced analysis

Correct Answer: B - Silhouette analysis provides statistical measures of cluster quality by comparing within-cluster cohesion to between-cluster separation, enabling objective cluster number selection.

Question 18: When implementing regularized regression models, what statistical principle guides the selection of regularization strength?

A) Larger penalties always improve generalization B) Cross-validation to optimize prediction performance C) Theoretical optimal values from statistical literature D) Trial and error with business stakeholder feedback

Correct Answer: B - Cross-validation provides empirical estimates of generalization performance for different regularization strengths, enabling data-driven optimization of the bias-variance tradeoff.

Question 19: A time-series anomaly detection system generates many false alarms. What statistical adjustment would most likely improve performance?

A) Increase detection sensitivity to catch more anomalies B) Apply multiple hypothesis testing corrections C) Use longer time windows for anomaly assessment D) Implement ensemble voting across multiple detection methods

Correct Answer: B - Multiple testing corrections account for the increased probability of false positives when performing many statistical tests, reducing false alarm rates in anomaly detection systems.

Question 20: When implementing feature selection for high-dimensional data, which statistical approach provides the most principled variable selection?

A) Correlation-based filtering using Pearson coefficients B) Mutual information to capture non-linear relationships C) Variance thresholding to remove low-variation features D) Random selection to avoid selection bias

Correct Answer: B - Mutual information captures both linear and non-linear relationships between features and target variables, providing more comprehensive dependence measurement than correlation-based approaches.

Question 21: A recommendation system experiences the "cold start" problem for new users with no historical data. What statistical approach would be most appropriate for initial recommendations?

A) Use global popularity rankings based on frequency statistics B) Apply collaborative filtering with similarity metrics C) Implement content-based filtering using user demographics D) Random recommendations to gather initial preference data

Correct Answer: A - Global popularity statistics provide the most reliable information available for new users, representing the best estimate of preferences before individual user data becomes available.

Question 22: When implementing gradient-based optimization for neural networks, what statistical property of the loss function landscape affects convergence behavior?

A) Function smoothness and Lipschitz continuity B) Global minimum uniqueness C) Convexity throughout the parameter space D) Linear separability of the optimization problem

Correct Answer: A - Lipschitz continuity ensures that gradients don't change too rapidly, enabling stable optimization algorithms with appropriate learning rates for reliable convergence.

Question 23: A fraud detection model needs to balance false positive and false negative rates. What statistical framework provides optimal threshold selection?

A) Receiver Operating Characteristic (ROC) analysis B) Equal error rate minimization C) Business cost-weighted optimization D) Accuracy maximization on balanced datasets

Correct Answer: C - Optimal threshold selection requires incorporating the actual business costs of false positives versus false negatives, which typically differ significantly in fraud detection scenarios.

Question 24: When analyzing experimental results from model comparisons, what statistical consideration is most important for valid conclusions?

A) Large sample sizes guarantee statistical significance B) Multiple comparison corrections for simultaneous tests C) Normal distribution assumptions for all performance metrics D) Equal computational resources for all models tested

Correct Answer: B - Multiple comparison procedures prevent inflated Type I error rates when testing several models simultaneously, ensuring that observed performance differences represent genuine effects rather than statistical noise.

Question 25: A reinforcement learning system needs to balance exploration and exploitation in decision-making. What statistical principle guides this balance?

A) Central Limit Theorem for action value estimation B) Confidence interval width for uncertainty quantification C) Maximum likelihood estimation of optimal actions D) Hypothesis testing for action superiority

Correct Answer: B - Confidence intervals quantify uncertainty about action values, enabling principled exploration strategies that balance trying uncertain actions (wide intervals) with exploiting known good actions (narrow intervals).

Chapter 4: Building Scalable Data Pipelines

Data pipelines form the backbone of every successful machine learning system, yet most organizations struggle with architectures that break under production loads or consume budgets faster than they deliver business value. The difference between systems that scale gracefully and those that fail catastrophically often comes down to architectural decisions made during the initial design phase—decisions that become increasingly expensive to change as systems mature.

Modern ML systems demand data architectures that can handle diverse data sources, varying processing requirements, and unpredictable scaling demands while maintaining cost efficiency and operational simplicity. Amazon Web Services provides the building blocks for these architectures, but assembling them effectively requires understanding both the technical capabilities and the cost implications of different design choices.

S3 Data Lake Architectures for ML

Amazon S3 serves as the foundation for data lake architectures that support machine learning workloads at scale. Unlike traditional data warehouses with rigid schemas and expensive scaling characteristics, data lakes enable storage of raw data in its original format while providing flexible processing options that adapt to changing analytical requirements (9).

Foundational Architecture Principles:

Data lakes organize information using a zone-based approach that separates raw data, processed data, and curated datasets into distinct storage areas with appropriate access controls and lifecycle policies. The raw zone stores data exactly as received from source systems, preserving complete historical records for future analysis needs that may not be apparent today.

The processed zone contains cleaned and standardized data that's been validated for quality issues and transformed into formats optimized for analytical workloads. This zone serves as the primary source for feature engineering and model training activities, reducing processing time and improving consistency across different ML projects.

The curated zone houses datasets that have been specifically prepared for business consumption, including feature stores, model training datasets, and analytical reports. This zone maintains the highest data quality standards and provides the most predictable performance characteristics for production ML workflows.

Storage Class Optimization Strategies:

S3 storage classes enable cost optimization by automatically transitioning data to less expensive storage tiers based on access patterns. Standard storage provides immediate access for frequently used datasets, while Intelligent Tiering automatically optimizes costs for data with changing access patterns without manual intervention.

Infrequent Access storage reduces costs for data accessed less than monthly, such as historical training datasets or backup copies of processed data. Glacier storage classes provide even lower costs for long-term archival needs, though retrieval times increase significantly.

Storage optimization requires understanding actual access patterns rather than theoretical requirements. Many organizations discover that 80% of their analytical queries access data created in the last 30 days, enabling significant cost savings through proper tier selection.

Partitioning and Organization Schemes:

Effective partitioning strategies dramatically improve query performance while reducing costs by limiting the amount of data scanned for typical analytical queries. Time-based partitioning works well for event data and logging information, enabling efficient filtering by date ranges common in ML feature engineering.

Geographic partitioning helps when data processing regulations require regional data isolation or when analytical workloads focus on specific geographic regions. Customer-based partitioning can optimize performance for segmentation analyses and personalization models that process data for specific customer cohorts.

Hive-style partitioning provides compatibility with multiple analytical tools while maintaining human-readable directory structures. The format enables automatic partition discovery by services like AWS Glue and Amazon Athena, reducing administrative overhead.

Case Example 1: Financial Services Transaction Processing

A digital payment processor needed to build ML models for fraud detection that could analyze transaction patterns in real-time while maintaining historical data for regulatory compliance. The initial architecture stored all transaction data in a single S3 bucket without partitioning, leading to expensive queries and slow model training processes.

The redesigned data lake architecture implemented time-based partitioning by day and geographic partitioning by processing region. Raw transaction data landed in the ingest zone with automatic classification and tagging based on transaction types and risk levels. Streaming data from Kinesis Data Firehose wrote compressed Parquet files every five minutes to optimize both storage costs and query performance.

The processed zone contained standardized transaction records with enriched metadata from external fraud intelligence sources. Feature engineering pipelines generated rolling aggregations and behavioral patterns that updated hourly, providing near real-time features for fraud detection models. Cost optimization through storage tiering reduced monthly storage expenses by 60% while improving query performance by 400%.

Case Example 2: Retail Customer Analytics Platform

A multinational retailer consolidated customer data from online stores, physical locations, and mobile applications into a unified data lake supporting personalization and inventory optimization models. The original system used separate databases for each channel, creating data silos that prevented effective cross-channel analytics.

The new architecture ingested data from all touchpoints into a common S3-based data lake with standardized customer identifiers and event schemas. Raw data preservation enabled reprocessing of historical information when new analytical requirements emerged. Automated data quality checks validated schema compliance and flagged anomalies before data entered the processed zone.

Customer behavior features were computed daily for batch recommendation models and updated continuously for real-time personalization systems. The architecture supported both structured POS data and unstructured social media content, enabling sentiment analysis and trend detection that improved inventory planning. Storage lifecycle policies reduced long-term storage costs by 45% while supporting new analytical use cases that weren't possible with the previous siloed approach.

Case Example 3: Healthcare Research Data Platform

A medical research organization created a data lake supporting clinical trial analytics and drug discovery research across multiple therapeutic areas. Patient privacy requirements demanded strict access controls and audit capabilities while enabling collaborative research across different study teams.

The architecture implemented dataset-level encryption with fine-grained access controls based on study participation and role-based permissions. Raw clinical data remained in encrypted format with automatic key rotation, while processed datasets used column-level encryption for personally identifiable information.

Research-ready datasets in the curated zone supported both traditional statistical analyses and machine learning model development for biomarker discovery. Automated anonymization pipelines created de-identified datasets suitable for broader research collaboration while maintaining statistical validity. The platform reduced data preparation time for new studies from weeks to days while ensuring full regulatory compliance.

Real-time vs Batch Processing Decisions

Choosing between real-time and batch processing approaches significantly impacts system architecture, cost structure, and operational complexity. Understanding the trade-offs enables informed decisions that balance business requirements with technical and financial constraints.

Business Requirements Analysis:

Real-time processing becomes necessary when business decisions depend on immediate data insights and delayed processing creates measurable negative impacts. Fraud detection systems require real-time processing because delayed detection enables fraudulent transactions to complete, causing direct financial losses.

Batch processing suffices when analytical insights support longer-term decision making and processing delays don't affect business outcomes. Monthly customer segmentation analyses or quarterly demand forecasting can utilize batch processing without sacrificing business value while achieving significant cost savings.

Mixed architectures often provide optimal solutions by implementing real-time processing for time-sensitive decisions while using batch processing for complex analytical workloads that don't require immediate results. This approach minimizes costs while ensuring critical business needs receive appropriate responsiveness.

Cost-Performance Trade-offs:

Real-time processing typically costs 3-5 times more than equivalent batch processing due to infrastructure overhead required for low-latency operations. Streaming systems require continuous resource allocation even during low-traffic periods, while batch systems can utilize spot instances and scheduled scaling to minimize costs.

Processing complexity affects cost differentials more dramatically. Simple aggregations and filtering operations show smaller cost differences between real-time and batch approaches, while complex machine learning inference and multi-stage transformations show larger cost gaps.

Latency requirements drive architectural complexity and associated costs. Near real-time processing (sub-minute latency) can often utilize micro-batch approaches that provide significant cost savings compared to true streaming architectures while meeting business requirements.

Hybrid Architecture Patterns:

Lambda architectures combine batch and streaming processing to provide both real-time responsiveness and comprehensive analytical capabilities. Streaming layers handle immediate processing needs while batch layers process complete datasets for accuracy and completeness.

Kappa architectures simplify operational complexity by using streaming systems for all processing while maintaining reprocessing capabilities for historical data. This approach reduces architectural complexity but may increase costs for workloads that don't require real-time processing.

Event-driven architectures enable flexible processing patterns that adapt to different data types and business requirements within the same platform. Critical events trigger real-time processing while routine data flows through batch pipelines, optimizing costs while maintaining responsiveness for important scenarios.

Kinesis, MSK, and Streaming Architectures

AWS provides multiple streaming platforms with different characteristics suited for various use cases and performance requirements. Understanding these differences enables selection of appropriate technologies that balance functionality, cost, and operational complexity.

Amazon Kinesis Ecosystem:

Kinesis Data Streams provides managed streaming infrastructure with automatic scaling and built-in integration with other AWS services. The service handles infrastructure management while providing fine-grained control over stream configuration and processing logic.

Kinesis Data Firehose simplifies data ingestion by providing managed delivery to storage and analytical services without requiring custom processing logic. The service automatically handles batching, compression, and error handling while supporting real-time transformation through Lambda functions.

Kinesis Analytics enables real-time analytical processing using SQL queries against streaming data. The service supports complex analytical operations including windowing, aggregations, and anomaly detection without requiring custom streaming applications.

Amazon MSK for Enterprise Streaming:

Managed Streaming for Apache Kafka (MSK) provides enterprise-grade Kafka infrastructure with automatic patching, monitoring, and scaling capabilities. The service maintains compatibility with existing Kafka applications while reducing operational overhead.

MSK supports higher throughput and more complex routing patterns than Kinesis, making it appropriate for enterprise architectures with multiple consumers and complex data flow requirements. The service provides detailed monitoring and logging capabilities essential for production environments.

Cost structures differ significantly between MSK and Kinesis based on usage patterns and cluster sizing requirements. MSK provides better cost efficiency for sustained high-throughput workloads, while Kinesis offers advantages for variable or lower-volume streaming scenarios.

Streaming Architecture Design Patterns:

Producer-consumer patterns enable loose coupling between data sources and processing applications, improving system resilience and enabling independent scaling of different components. Proper partitioning strategies ensure even load distribution and optimal processing performance.

Multi-consumer architectures allow different applications to process the same data streams for various purposes without impacting each other's performance. Real-time dashboards, ML feature engineering, and data archival can all consume the same stream independently.

Error handling and dead letter queue patterns provide resilience against processing failures and data quality issues. Failed messages require systematic handling to prevent data loss while avoiding infinite retry loops that can overwhelm downstream systems.

Cost-Performance Optimization Patterns

Effective cost optimization requires understanding the relationship between architectural choices and ongoing operational expenses while maintaining performance standards that support business requirements.

Resource Scaling Strategies:

Auto-scaling configurations should account for both performance requirements and cost constraints when determining resource allocation policies. Aggressive scaling improves performance but can generate unnecessary costs during low-demand periods.

Predictive scaling uses historical patterns to pre-allocate resources before demand increases, reducing latency while optimizing costs through better resource utilization. This approach works particularly well for predictable workloads like daily ETL processing or weekly model training.

Mixed instance types enable cost optimization by using appropriate compute resources for different processing stages. Memory-optimized instances work well for large dataset processing, while compute-optimized instances provide better value for CPU-intensive transformations.

Data Movement Optimization:

Regional placement strategies minimize data transfer costs by co-locating processing resources with data storage. Cross-region data movement generates significant expenses that can exceed processing costs for large datasets.

Compression and data format optimization reduce both storage and transfer costs while improving processing performance. Parquet format provides significant compression benefits and enables efficient columnar processing for analytical workloads.

Processing locality ensures that data transformation occurs near data storage rather than moving large datasets to distant processing resources. AWS Glue and EMR automatically optimize job placement to minimize data movement costs.

Storage Lifecycle Management:

Automated tiering policies transition data to appropriate storage classes based on access patterns and retention requirements. Manual storage management becomes impractical for data lakes containing millions of objects with varying access patterns.

Data lifecycle policies should consider both storage costs and retrieval costs when determining appropriate storage classes. Infrequently accessed data that requires immediate availability when needed may warrant Standard-IA storage despite higher per-GB costs.

Deletion policies for temporary and intermediate data prevent storage cost accumulation for data that doesn't provide ongoing business value. ETL intermediate files and failed processing outputs often accumulate without proper cleanup procedures.

Project: Multi-source Data Ingestion Pipeline

This project builds a production-ready data ingestion pipeline that handles multiple data sources with different characteristics while optimizing costs and maintaining data quality standards.

Architecture Design and Planning:

The pipeline architecture supports structured database exports, semi-structured API responses, and unstructured file uploads through a unified ingestion framework. Each data source requires different handling strategies while maintaining consistent data quality and metadata management.

Source system integration points require error handling and retry logic that accounts for different reliability characteristics and rate limiting constraints. Database exports provide reliable batch data while API sources may experience rate limits and temporary failures.

Data landing zones separate raw ingestion from processed data to enable reprocessing and quality validation without impacting source systems. This separation provides operational flexibility while maintaining data lineage and audit capabilities.

Real-time Ingestion Implementation:

Kinesis Data Streams capture high-frequency event data from web applications and mobile clients with automatic partitioning based on customer identifiers to ensure even load distribution. Stream configuration balances latency requirements with cost optimization through appropriate shard sizing.

API Gateway integration enables secure and scalable REST endpoints for data submission with automatic request validation and rate limiting. Lambda functions provide lightweight transformation and routing logic while maintaining cost efficiency for variable workloads.

Database Change Data Capture (CDC) implementations use AWS Database Migration Service to capture real-time changes from operational databases without impacting production performance. CDC streams feed into Kinesis for immediate processing while maintaining complete audit trails.

Batch Processing Pipeline Development:

AWS Glue jobs handle large-scale data transformation and quality validation with automatic scaling based on data volume and processing complexity. Job configuration optimizes costs through appropriate instance sizing and spot instance utilization where appropriate.

Step Functions coordinate complex multi-stage processing workflows with error handling and retry logic that ensures reliable processing while minimizing resource waste. Workflow orchestration enables parallel processing where possible while maintaining data dependencies.

S3 event triggers initiate processing automatically when new data arrives, reducing latency and operational overhead compared to scheduled polling approaches. Event-driven processing ensures timely handling of urgent data while maintaining cost efficiency.

Data Quality and Monitoring Framework:

Automated data profiling identifies statistical properties and quality issues in ingested data before it enters downstream processing systems. Quality metrics include completeness, uniqueness, validity, and consistency checks that adapt to different data source characteristics.

AWS Glue Data Quality provides built-in validation rules and custom quality checks that flag potential issues before they affect analytical workloads. Quality dashboards provide visibility into data health across all ingestion sources.

CloudWatch monitoring captures processing metrics, error rates, and performance characteristics that enable proactive system management. Custom metrics track business-relevant quality indicators alongside technical performance measures.

Cost Optimization Implementation:

Resource tagging strategies enable detailed cost allocation and optimization by tracking expenses across different data sources, processing stages, and business units. Granular cost visibility supports informed decisions about processing trade-offs and resource allocation.

Spot instance utilization reduces batch processing costs by 60-70% for workloads that can tolerate interruptions. Processing job design incorporates checkpointing and recovery mechanisms that enable efficient use of spot capacity.

Storage lifecycle automation implements intelligent tiering policies that balance access requirements with cost optimization. Frequently accessed landing zone data transitions to infrequent access storage after 30 days, while processed data moves to Glacier after 90 days unless flagged for retention.

Practical Implementation Guidance

Building successful data pipelines requires balancing theoretical best practices with practical constraints including budget limitations, skill availability, and organizational requirements. Start with simple architectures that address immediate needs while establishing foundations for future growth.

Monitoring and alerting systems become essential for production pipelines that process business-critical data. Invest in observability from the beginning rather than adding monitoring after problems arise in production environments.

Documentation and runbook development enable efficient troubleshooting and knowledge transfer as teams grow and change. Capture architectural decisions, configuration details, and operational procedures to reduce dependency on individual team members.

Building for the Future

Data pipeline architectures must balance current requirements with anticipated future needs while avoiding over-engineering that increases complexity without delivering value. Focus on modularity and standardization that enables growth without requiring complete architecture rebuilds.

The next building blocks involve data transformation and feature engineering capabilities that turn raw data into ML-ready features. These transformation systems build upon the ingestion pipelines established in this foundation.

Essential Takeaways

- S3 data lake architectures provide scalable foundations for ML workloads with proper partitioning and lifecycle management
- Real-time versus batch processing decisions significantly impact costs and architectural complexity
- Kinesis and MSK offer different streaming capabilities suited for various enterprise requirements
- Cost optimization requires systematic approaches to resource scaling, data movement, and storage management
- Multi-source ingestion pipelines need unified frameworks that handle diverse data characteristics while maintaining quality standards

Chapter 5: Data Transformation at Scale

Data transformation represents the most computationally intensive and cost-significant phase of most machine learning pipelines. Raw data rarely exists in formats suitable for direct model consumption, requiring sophisticated processing systems that can handle terabytes of information while maintaining both performance standards and budget constraints. The AWS ecosystem provides multiple transformation platforms, each optimized for different scenarios and data characteristics.

Understanding the capabilities and cost implications of different transformation approaches enables informed architectural decisions that balance processing performance with operational expenses. The wrong choice can lead to systems that either fail to meet performance requirements or consume budgets at unsustainable rates, while optimal selections provide both technical success and financial efficiency.

AWS Glue for ML Preprocessing

AWS Glue serves as a managed ETL (Extract, Transform, Load) service that handles the operational complexity of running distributed data processing jobs while providing flexible programming interfaces for custom transformation logic. The service automatically manages infrastructure scaling, job monitoring, and error handling, enabling teams to focus on business logic rather than operational details (10).

Serverless ETL Capabilities:

Glue's serverless architecture eliminates infrastructure management overhead while providing automatic scaling based on data volume and processing complexity. Jobs start within minutes and scale to hundreds of workers when processing large datasets, then scale down to zero when complete to minimize costs.

The service provides both visual ETL interfaces for non-technical users and full Python/Scala programming environments for complex transformation logic. Visual interfaces enable rapid development of standard transformation patterns, while custom code handles specialized business logic and advanced analytics requirements.

Dynamic frame abstraction simplifies schema evolution handling by automatically adapting to changing data structures without requiring code modifications. This capability becomes essential when processing data from evolving source systems that add new fields or modify data types over time.

Data Catalog Integration:

Glue Data Catalog provides centralized metadata management that enables automatic schema discovery and evolution tracking across all data sources. Catalog integration eliminates manual schema maintenance while providing data lineage tracking essential for debugging and compliance.

Automatic schema inference analyzes data files to detect structure, data types, and partitioning patterns without manual configuration. The catalog updates automatically when new data arrives with different characteristics, maintaining current metadata without administrative overhead.

Cross-service integration enables other AWS services likc Athena, EMR, and SageMaker to automatically discover and utilize cataloged datasets without additional configuration. This integration reduces development time while ensuring consistent data access patterns across different analytical tools.

Cost Optimization Strategies:

Glue pricing includes both job execution time and Data Processing Unit (DPU) allocation, making job optimization essential for cost control. Right-sizing DPU allocation based on data volume and complexity prevents over-provisioning while ensuring adequate performance.

Development endpoints enable code development and testing without running full production jobs, reducing development costs while providing realistic testing environments. These endpoints support interactive development workflows that improve code quality and reduce debugging time.

Job bookmark functionality prevents reprocessing of previously handled data, reducing both processing time and costs for incremental update scenarios. Bookmarks track processing progress automatically, enabling efficient handling of slowly changing data sources.

Case Example 1: E-commerce Customer Data Unification

An online retailer needed to combine customer data from web analytics, mobile applications, email marketing systems, and customer service interactions into unified customer profiles for personalization models. Each source system used different customer identifiers and data formats, requiring complex transformation and matching logic.

The Glue-based solution implemented fuzzy matching algorithms using Python libraries to link customer records across systems based on email addresses, phone numbers, and behavioral patterns. Custom transformation logic handled data quality issues like duplicate records, missing values, and inconsistent formatting across source systems.

Processing pipeline automatically detected new data files from each source system and triggered appropriate transformation jobs using S3 event notifications. The unified customer profiles updated daily, providing fresh data for recommendation systems and marketing automation while maintaining complete audit trails for privacy compliance.

Performance optimization through proper partitioning and DPU sizing reduced processing costs by 40% while improving data freshness from weekly to daily updates. The solution processed 500GB of source data daily, producing 50GB of clean customer profiles ready for ML model training.

Case Example 2: Financial Risk Data Processing

A regional bank implemented credit risk modeling that required combining internal loan data with external economic indicators, credit bureau information, and real estate market data. Regulatory requirements demanded complete audit trails and data lineage documentation for all transformations.

AWS Glue handled complex data validation rules that checked for regulatory compliance, data quality issues, and consistency across multiple data sources. Custom Python scripts implemented risk calculation logic while maintaining compliance with banking regulations and audit requirements.

The processing pipeline generated both detailed transaction-level data for regulatory reporting and aggregated risk metrics for model training. Automatic job scheduling ensured daily updates while bookmark functionality prevented reprocessing of historical data, optimizing both costs and processing time.

Integration with AWS Glue Data Quality enabled automated monitoring of data completeness, accuracy, and consistency across all processing stages. Quality metrics dashboards provided real-time visibility into data health while automated alerts flagged potential issues before they affected downstream models.

EMR and Spark for Distributed Processing

Amazon EMR (Elastic MapReduce) provides managed big data processing using Apache Spark, Hadoop, and other distributed computing frameworks. EMR offers fine-grained control over cluster configuration and processing logic while handling infrastructure management and scaling complexity (11).

Spark Processing Capabilities:

Apache Spark on EMR enables in-memory distributed processing that dramatically improves performance for iterative algorithms and complex transformations compared to traditional MapReduce approaches. Memory caching reduces data access latency while distributed processing scales across hundreds of compute nodes.

Spark SQL provides familiar SQL interfaces for data transformation while leveraging Spark's distributed processing capabilities. DataFrames and Datasets APIs offer type-safe programming interfaces for complex transformation logic that combines SQL operations with custom functions.

MLlib integration enables distributed machine learning algorithms that process datasets too large for single-machine implementations. Feature engineering, model training, and batch inference can all execute within the same Spark environment, reducing data movement and improving processing efficiency.

Cluster Configuration and Optimization:

Instance type selection significantly impacts both performance and costs for EMR clusters. Memory-optimized instances work well for Spark applications that cache large datasets, while compute-optimized instances provide better value for CPU-intensive transformations.

Auto-scaling configurations enable dynamic cluster sizing based on processing demands while maintaining cost efficiency. EMR automatically adds or removes nodes based on workload characteristics, ensuring adequate performance while minimizing unnecessary capacity.

Spot instance integration reduces compute costs by 50-70% for fault-tolerant workloads that can handle node interruptions. EMR automatically handles spot instance management and task redistribution when interruptions occur.

Advanced Processing Patterns:

Structured Streaming enables real-time data processing using familiar batch processing APIs, simplifying development while providing low-latency processing capabilities. Streaming applications can combine real-time data with historical datasets for context-aware processing.

Delta Lake implementation provides ACID transactions and versioning for data lakes, enabling reliable data pipelines that handle concurrent access and provide rollback capabilities. This reliability becomes essential for production ML pipelines that require consistent data states.

Custom library integration allows use of specialized ML libraries and algorithms not available in standard distributions. Docker-based custom images enable deployment of complex dependencies while maintaining reproducible environments across development and production.

Case Example 3: Telecommunications Network Analytics

A mobile network operator needed to process call detail records (CDRs) to detect network anomalies, optimize capacity planning, and identify customer usage patterns. The system processed 10TB of CDR data daily while providing real-time alerts for network issues.

EMR clusters with Spark Streaming processed CDRs in real-time to detect anomalous traffic patterns that could indicate network problems or security threats. Complex event processing logic identified patterns spanning multiple cell towers and time periods while maintaining sub-minute latency for critical alerts.

Batch processing jobs performed deeper analytics on daily CDR datasets to identify long-term trends, capacity bottlenecks, and customer behavior patterns. Machine learning models trained on historical data predicted future capacity needs while clustering algorithms identified unusual usage patterns for investigation.

Cost optimization through mixed instance types and spot instances reduced processing costs by 60% while maintaining performance requirements. Auto-scaling policies ensured adequate capacity during peak processing periods while minimizing costs during low-demand hours.

Lambda-based Transformation Patterns

AWS Lambda provides serverless computing for lightweight data transformations that don't require persistent infrastructure. Lambda functions excel at event-driven processing, simple transformations, and integration between different AWS services (12).

Event-driven Processing Architecture:

S3 event triggers enable automatic processing when new data files arrive, reducing latency and eliminating polling overhead. Lambda functions can process files immediately upon arrival while scaling automatically based on concurrent file uploads.

Kinesis integration enables real-time stream processing for simple transformations and routing logic. Lambda functions process streaming data records individually or in batches, providing flexible processing patterns for different latency and throughput requirements.

API Gateway integration creates REST endpoints for data submission with automatic validation, transformation, and routing. Lambda functions handle authentication, data validation, and initial processing before routing data to appropriate storage systems.

Transformation Logic Implementation:

Python and Node.js runtime environments support extensive libraries for data processing, enabling complex transformations within Lambda's execution constraints. JSON processing, data validation, and simple analytics work well within Lambda's memory and execution time limits.

Layer functionality enables sharing of common libraries and utility functions across multiple Lambda functions, reducing deployment package sizes while ensuring consistent transformation logic. Layers simplify dependency management for complex processing pipelines.

Environment variable configuration enables flexible function behavior without code changes, supporting different processing logic for development, staging, and production environments. Parameter Store integration provides secure management of configuration data and sensitive information.

Cost-Performance Optimization:

Memory allocation directly affects both performance and cost for Lambda functions. Higher memory allocation provides more CPU power and may reduce execution time, potentially reducing total costs despite higher per-second pricing.

Provisioned concurrency eliminates cold start latency for time-sensitive applications while providing predictable performance characteristics. This feature works well for real-time processing scenarios that require consistent response times.

Step Functions integration coordinates complex multi-step transformations while maintaining cost efficiency through appropriate function sizing and execution patterns. Workflow orchestration enables parallel processing where possible while maintaining data dependencies.

Data Quality and Validation Frameworks

Data quality directly impacts machine learning model performance, making systematic validation essential for production ML systems. AWS provides multiple tools for implementing data quality frameworks that detect issues before they affect downstream processing.

AWS Glue Data Quality Implementation:

Built-in quality rules provide standard checks for completeness, uniqueness, validity, and statistical properties without requiring custom code development. Rules adapt to different data types and business requirements while providing consistent quality assessment across all datasets.

Custom quality rules enable business-specific validation logic that checks domain constraints, referential integrity, and complex relationships between fields. Python-based rule definitions provide flexibility for sophisticated validation requirements.

Quality result integration with monitoring systems enables automated alerting when data quality issues are detected. CloudWatch integration provides dashboards and notifications that support proactive quality management.

Real-time Quality Monitoring:

Kinesis Analytics enables real-time quality assessment for streaming data, detecting anomalies and quality issues as data arrives. SQL-based quality rules provide immediate feedback on data characteristics while maintaining low processing latency.

Lambda-based validation functions process individual records or small batches to provide immediate quality feedback for API-submitted data. Validation logic can reject poor-quality data before it enters processing pipelines, preventing downstream issues.

QuickSight anomaly detection automatically identifies unusual patterns in data quality metrics, enabling proactive response to emerging quality issues. Automated analysis reduces manual monitoring overhead while improving issue detection speed.

Quality Metrics and Reporting:

Statistical profiling generates detailed quality reports that track completeness, uniqueness, validity, and consistency metrics over time. Trend analysis identifies gradual quality degradation that might not trigger threshold-based alerts.

Data lineage tracking enables impact analysis when quality issues are detected, showing which downstream processes and models might be affected. This visibility supports efficient incident response and quality issue resolution.

Quality scorecards provide executive-level visibility into data health across all sources and processing stages. Standardized quality metrics enable comparison between different data sources and processing pipelines.

Project: Automated Feature Engineering Pipeline

This project builds a production-ready feature engineering pipeline that automatically generates ML-ready features from raw data while maintaining quality standards and cost efficiency.

Pipeline Architecture Design:

The feature engineering pipeline processes multiple data sources with different update frequencies and characteristics while maintaining consistent feature definitions and quality standards. Event-driven processing ensures timely feature updates while batch processing handles complex aggregations efficiently.

Feature definitions use configuration-driven approaches that enable rapid development of new features without code changes. JSON or YAML configuration files define feature logic, data sources, and update schedules, enabling non-technical stakeholders to contribute to feature development.

Version control integration tracks feature definition changes and enables rollback capabilities when feature modifications cause model performance issues. Git-based workflows provide collaboration capabilities while maintaining audit trails for regulatory compliance.

Real-time Feature Generation:

Kinesis Data Streams capture real-time events that trigger immediate feature updates for time-sensitive applications like fraud detection and real-time personalization. Stream processing logic computes rolling aggregations and trend indicators with sub-minute latency.

Lambda functions handle simple feature transformations and routing logic while maintaining cost efficiency for variable workloads. Functions scale automatically based on event volume while providing consistent processing logic across different event types.

DynamoDB integration provides low-latency storage for real-time features that require immediate access during model inference. Automatic scaling handles varying read/write loads while maintaining consistent performance characteristics.

Batch Feature Processing:

AWS Glue jobs handle complex feature engineering that requires large-scale data processing, including customer lifetime value calculations, seasonal trend analysis, and multi-table joins. Job scheduling ensures features update according to business requirements while optimizing processing costs.

Spark-based processing enables distributed computation of features that require complex algorithms or large dataset processing. Feature engineering logic combines multiple data sources while handling data quality issues and missing value imputation.

S3-based feature storage provides cost-effective storage for batch-computed features with automatic lifecycle management. Partitioning strategies optimize query performance while reducing storage costs through appropriate tier selection.

Feature Store Integration:

SageMaker Feature Store provides centralized feature management with automatic versioning, metadata tracking, and discovery capabilities. Integration enables consistent feature access across different models and development teams while maintaining feature lineage.

Feature validation ensures all generated features meet quality standards before entering the feature store. Automated testing checks feature distributions, completeness, and consistency with historical patterns to prevent quality issues.

Access control implementation ensures appropriate feature access based on data sensitivity and business requirements. Role-based permissions combined with data classification enable secure feature sharing while maintaining compliance requirements.

Monitoring and Quality Assurance:

CloudWatch monitoring tracks feature generation performance, quality metrics, and processing costs across all pipeline components. Custom metrics provide business-relevant insights alongside technical performance indicators.

Automated quality testing validates feature values against expected ranges, distributions, and business rules. Quality checks run automatically after each feature update, flagging potential issues before they affect model performance.

Feature drift detection compares current feature distributions with historical patterns to identify potential data quality issues or changing business conditions. Drift alerts trigger investigation workflows while maintaining feature quality standards.

Production Deployment Considerations

Successful feature engineering pipelines require careful attention to operational aspects including error handling, monitoring, and cost management. Production systems must handle failures gracefully while maintaining data quality and processing schedules.

Security considerations include protecting sensitive data throughout the processing pipeline while enabling appropriate access for authorized users and systems. Encryption, access controls, and audit logging provide comprehensive security coverage.

Change management processes ensure feature modifications don't break existing models or violate compliance requirements. Testing procedures validate feature changes before production deployment while maintaining system stability.

Strategic Implementation Approach

Feature engineering represents a significant investment in data infrastructure that pays dividends across multiple ML projects and business initiatives. Focus on building reusable capabilities that serve multiple use cases rather than point solutions for individual models.

The foundation established here supports the advanced feature management and model development capabilities covered in subsequent sections. Proper feature engineering infrastructure accelerates model development while ensuring consistent data quality across all ML initiatives.

Essential Takeaways

- AWS Glue provides managed ETL capabilities with automatic scaling and metadata management for most transformation needs
- EMR and Spark enable complex distributed processing for large-scale feature engineering and advanced analytics
- Lambda functions excel at event-driven transformations and lightweight processing with cost-efficient scaling
- Data quality frameworks prevent issues from propagating through ML pipelines and affecting model performance
- Automated feature engineering pipelines accelerate model development while ensuring consistent feature quality and availability

Chapter 6: Feature Stores and Data Management

Feature stores represent one of the most significant advances in ML infrastructure, solving the persistent challenges of feature sharing, versioning, and consistency that plague production ML systems. Organizations that implement feature stores properly experience dramatic improvements in model development velocity, feature reuse, and system reliability, while those that treat them as simple data storage often struggle with increased complexity without corresponding benefits.

The fundamental value proposition of feature stores lies not in data storage capabilities—which existing data warehouses and lakes provide adequately—but in the operational frameworks that enable consistent feature definitions, automated quality monitoring, and seamless integration between offline training and online serving environments. Understanding these operational benefits guides effective implementation decisions.

SageMaker Feature Store Implementation

Amazon SageMaker Feature Store provides a fully managed service that addresses the unique requirements of ML feature management while integrating seamlessly with other AWS services. The service handles both offline storage for model training and online serving for real-time inference, eliminating the architectural complexity of maintaining separate systems for different access patterns (13).

Foundational Architecture Components:

Feature groups serve as logical containers that organize related features while maintaining consistent schema definitions and access patterns. Each feature group contains multiple features with defined data types, enabling automatic validation and type checking during feature ingestion and retrieval.

Offline store implementation uses S3 storage with automatic partitioning and indexing that optimizes query performance for training dataset generation. The offline store supports complex analytical queries across large historical datasets while maintaining cost efficiency through intelligent storage tiering.

Online store provides low-latency feature retrieval for real-time inference scenarios using DynamoDB as the underlying storage mechanism. Automatic scaling handles varying read loads while maintaining consistent single-digit millisecond response times essential for real-time applications.

Feature Definition and Schema Management:

Schema registration enables explicit feature type definitions that prevent data quality issues and ensure consistent feature interpretation across different models and teams. Strong typing catches errors early in the development process while enabling automatic validation during feature ingestion.

Feature metadata tracking captures business context, data lineage, and quality metrics that enable effective feature discovery and governance. Rich metadata helps teams find relevant features while understanding their business meaning and quality characteristics.

Evolution support enables schema changes while maintaining backward compatibility with existing models and applications. Versioning capabilities allow teams to modify feature definitions without breaking existing dependencies while providing migration paths for system updates.

Integration with ML Workflows:

SageMaker Processing integration enables automated feature ingestion from batch processing jobs while maintaining feature quality and consistency. Processing jobs can validate feature values, handle missing data, and ensure feature store updates complete successfully.

Training job integration simplifies feature retrieval for model training by providing automatic dataset generation from feature store contents. Time travel capabilities enable consistent training datasets that reflect feature values at specific points in time, essential for reproducible model development.

Inference integration provides SDKs and APIs that enable real-time feature retrieval during model serving with optimized performance characteristics. Batch prediction integration supports efficient feature retrieval for large-scale inference scenarios.

Case Example 1: Financial Services Credit Scoring

A credit card company implemented a feature store to standardize credit risk features across multiple business units that previously maintained separate risk models with inconsistent feature definitions. The fragmented approach led to conflicting risk assessments and made regulatory compliance difficult to demonstrate.

The SageMaker Feature Store implementation established standardized definitions for customer financial metrics, payment histories, and external credit bureau data. Feature groups organized features by data source and update frequency, with customer financial features updating daily and credit bureau features updating monthly.

Automated feature validation prevented data quality issues that previously caused model performance degradation during economic changes. Quality rules checked for expected value ranges, completeness requirements, and consistency with historical patterns. The feature store reduced model development time by 60% while improving model performance through better feature quality and more comprehensive feature sets.

Real-time credit decisions retrieved features from the online store with sub-10ms latency while maintaining consistent feature definitions with batch training processes. The unified feature infrastructure supported both individual credit applications and portfolio risk analytics using identical feature calculations.

Case Example 2: E-commerce Personalization Platform

An online marketplace needed to serve personalized product recommendations across web, mobile, and email channels using consistent customer behavior features. The previous system maintained separate feature calculations for each channel, leading to inconsistent customer experiences and duplicated development effort.

Feature groups organized customer behavior data by interaction type (browsing, purchasing, reviewing) and temporal characteristics (hourly, daily, weekly aggregations). Real-time streaming ingestion updated behavioral features continuously while batch processing computed longer-term trends and seasonal patterns.

Cross-channel consistency improved recommendation quality by providing unified customer views across all touchpoints. A/B testing showed 18% improvement in click-through rates and 23% improvement in conversion rates compared to the previous channel-specific approach.

Feature sharing between recommendation, search ranking, and marketing automation systems eliminated duplicate feature engineering effort while ensuring consistent customer treatment across all customer-facing systems. Development velocity increased 40% while maintaining higher feature quality standards.

Feature Versioning and Governance

Effective feature versioning enables controlled evolution of ML systems while maintaining reproducibility and backwards compatibility. Governance frameworks ensure feature quality and compliance while enabling productive collaboration across different teams and business units.

Version Control Strategies:

Semantic versioning provides structured approaches to feature evolution that communicate the impact of changes on existing dependencies. Major version increments indicate breaking changes that require code updates, while minor versions add functionality without breaking existing interfaces.

Immutable feature versions ensure reproducible model training by preventing modification of feature definitions after they're used in production models. Immutability enables confident model rollbacks and debugging while supporting regulatory requirements for audit trails.

Branching strategies enable parallel feature development and testing without affecting production systems. Development branches allow experimentation while main branches maintain stable feature definitions for production use.

Data Lineage and Impact Analysis:

Automatic lineage tracking captures dependencies between features, data sources, and models to enable impact analysis when changes are proposed. Understanding downstream dependencies prevents changes that could break existing models or violate compliance requirements.

Change impact assessment identifies all systems and models that would be affected by proposed feature modifications. Impact analysis enables informed decisions about change timing and coordination across different teams and systems.

Rollback capabilities provide safety nets when feature changes cause unexpected issues in production systems. Automated rollback procedures minimize downtime while providing learning opportunities for future change management improvements.

Quality and Compliance Frameworks:

Feature quality standards establish consistent expectations for completeness, accuracy, and timeliness across all feature groups. Standardized quality metrics enable comparison between different features and identification of improvement opportunities.

Compliance monitoring ensures feature usage adheres to data governance policies, privacy regulations, and business rules. Automated compliance checking prevents policy violations while reducing manual oversight requirements.

Access control implementation provides appropriate feature access based on data sensitivity, business requirements, and regulatory constraints. Role-based permissions combined with feature-level access controls enable secure collaboration while maintaining compliance.

Online vs Offline Feature Serving

The distinction between online and offline feature serving reflects different performance requirements and usage patterns that drive architectural decisions and cost optimization strategies. Understanding these differences enables appropriate technology selection and system design.

Performance Characteristics Analysis:

Online serving requires single-digit millisecond response times to support real-time inference scenarios without adding noticeable latency to user-facing applications. Low latency demands specialized storage and caching strategies that prioritize speed over cost efficiency.

Offline serving supports analytical workloads and batch training processes that can tolerate higher latency in exchange for better cost efficiency and support for complex analytical queries. Offline systems optimize for throughput and cost rather than latency.

Consistency requirements differ between online and offline scenarios. Online serving often accepts eventual consistency to achieve low latency, while offline analytics typically require strong consistency for accurate historical analysis.

Architecture Design Patterns:

Dual-write patterns maintain both online and offline feature stores simultaneously during feature ingestion, ensuring consistency between training and serving environments. Synchronization logic handles potential inconsistencies while maintaining system performance.

Cache-aside patterns populate online caches from offline storage on demand, reducing storage costs while maintaining acceptable performance for frequently accessed features. Cache eviction policies balance memory usage with performance requirements.

Lambda architecture separates real-time and batch processing paths while providing unified interfaces for feature access. This separation enables optimization of each path for its specific performance and cost requirements while maintaining consistent feature access patterns.

Cost Optimization Strategies:

Feature access patterns drive cost optimization decisions between online and offline storage systems. Frequently accessed features justify online storage costs, while infrequently accessed features work better with offline storage and cache-on-demand patterns.

TTL (Time To Live) policies for online features prevent storage of stale data while optimizing costs for features with predictable refresh cycles. Automatic cleanup reduces storage costs while ensuring feature freshness for real-time applications.

Tiered storage strategies use different storage systems for features with different access patterns and performance requirements. Hot features remain in low-latency storage while warm and cold features use more cost-effective storage with higher latency.

Feature Sharing Across Teams

Effective feature sharing multiplies the value of feature engineering investments while reducing duplication and improving consistency across different ML initiatives. Organizational and technical frameworks enable productive collaboration while maintaining appropriate access controls and quality standards.

Discovery and Documentation Frameworks:

Feature catalogs provide searchable interfaces that enable teams to find relevant features based on business context, data sources, or statistical characteristics. Rich metadata and documentation help teams understand feature meaning and appropriate usage patterns.

Usage analytics track feature adoption and popularity across different teams and applications, identifying highly valuable features and optimization opportunities. Analytics also reveal unused features that may be candidates for deprecation.

Community contribution models enable teams to share feature engineering expertise while maintaining quality standards. Code review processes and feature validation ensure contributed features meet organizational standards while encouraging broader participation.

Collaboration Patterns:

Feature ownership models establish clear responsibilities for feature maintenance, quality monitoring, and evolution while enabling shared usage across teams. Ownership clarity prevents features from becoming orphaned while ensuring appropriate maintenance resources.

Service level agreements (SLAs) for shared features establish expectations for availability, latency, and quality that enable teams to depend on shared infrastructure. Clear SLAs enable planning and accountability while supporting collaborative development.

Change coordination processes ensure feature modifications consider impact on all consuming teams and applications. Communication frameworks and approval processes prevent breaking changes while enabling necessary evolution.

Case Example 3: Multi-Brand Retail Analytics

A retail conglomerate with multiple brands needed to share customer analytics features across different business units while maintaining brand-specific customizations and compliance requirements. Each brand previously maintained separate analytics capabilities, leading to duplicated effort and inconsistent insights.

The shared feature store implemented hierarchical feature organization with common customer demographics and behavior features available to all brands, while brand-specific features remained accessible only to appropriate business units. Access controls ensured data privacy compliance while enabling valuable feature sharing.

Standardized feature definitions enabled cross-brand analytics and customer journey analysis that revealed valuable insights about multi-brand customers. Shared feature infrastructure reduced overall analytics costs by 45% while improving feature quality through concentrated expertise and resources.

Brand-specific feature groups enabled customization for different customer segments and business models while leveraging shared infrastructure and governance frameworks. The hybrid approach balanced collaboration benefits with business unit autonomy and compliance requirements.

Project: Production Feature Store with Monitoring

This project implements a production-ready feature store with automated monitoring, quality assurance, and governance capabilities that support multiple teams and use cases while maintaining performance and cost efficiency.

Infrastructure Setup and Configuration:

Feature store architecture supports both real-time and batch feature ingestion while maintaining consistency between offline training and online serving environments. Infrastructure as code deployment ensures reproducible environments across development, staging, and production.

Network configuration optimizes data transfer costs while maintaining security requirements through VPC endpoints and private connectivity. Regional deployment strategies minimize latency for real-time applications while complying with data residency requirements.

Security implementation includes encryption at rest and in transit, fine-grained access controls, and audit logging that supports compliance requirements. Identity and access management integration provides seamless authentication while maintaining security standards.

Feature Group Design and Implementation:

Customer feature groups organize demographic, behavioral, and preference features with appropriate update frequencies and access patterns. Schema definitions include business metadata, data quality constraints, and lineage information that supports governance requirements.

Product feature groups capture inventory, pricing, and performance metrics with real-time updates for dynamic features and batch updates for analytical features. Time-based partitioning optimizes query performance while managing storage costs.

Transaction feature groups handle high-volume event data with streaming ingestion and configurable retention policies. Event deduplication and ordering ensure data quality while managing storage costs for high-frequency data.

Automated Quality Monitoring:

Quality rule implementation validates feature values against business constraints, statistical expectations, and historical patterns. Rules adapt to different feature types while providing consistent quality assessment across all feature groups.

Drift detection monitors feature distributions over time to identify potential data quality issues or changing business conditions. Statistical tests automatically flag significant distribution changes while accounting for normal business variation.

Alerting systems notify appropriate teams when quality issues are detected while providing sufficient context for efficient issue resolution. Integration with incident management systems ensures proper escalation and tracking of quality issues.

Performance Optimization:

Caching strategies balance performance requirements with cost efficiency for different feature access patterns. Intelligent cache warming ensures frequently accessed features remain readily available while minimizing cache storage costs.

Query optimization techniques including appropriate indexing, partitioning, and compression reduce both query latency and storage costs. Performance monitoring identifies optimization opportunities while ensuring SLA compliance.

Auto-scaling configuration handles varying load patterns while maintaining cost efficiency during low-demand periods. Predictive scaling uses historical patterns to pre-allocate capacity during anticipated high-demand periods.

Governance and Compliance Framework:

Feature lifecycle management includes automated testing, approval workflows, and deprecation procedures that ensure controlled evolution while maintaining system stability. Change management processes coordinate updates across all consuming systems.

Access audit logging captures all feature access patterns and provides detailed trails for compliance reporting and security analysis. Log aggregation and analysis identify unusual access patterns while supporting regulatory requirements.

Data classification and sensitivity labeling enable appropriate access controls and handling procedures for different types of sensitive information. Automated policy enforcement reduces manual oversight requirements while ensuring compliance.

Operational Excellence in Practice

Feature stores require ongoing operational attention including performance monitoring, cost optimization, and user support to maintain their value proposition. Establish clear operational procedures and metrics that support continuous improvement and user satisfaction.

Change management becomes particularly important for shared infrastructure that supports multiple teams and critical business processes. Implement processes that balance agility with stability while ensuring appropriate stakeholder communication.

User training and documentation enable effective feature store adoption while reducing support overhead. Invest in user experience improvements that encourage adoption and productive usage patterns.

The Path Forward

Feature stores represent foundational infrastructure that enables advanced ML capabilities including automated model training, real-time personalization, and cross-functional analytics. The investment in proper implementation pays dividends across multiple initiatives while reducing overall system complexity.

The data management capabilities established here provide the foundation for exploratory data analysis and advanced feature engineering covered in the next section. Quality data management enables more sophisticated analytical capabilities and better business insights.

Essential Takeaways

- SageMaker Feature Store provides managed infrastructure for both offline training and online serving with automatic scaling and integration
- Feature versioning and governance frameworks enable controlled evolution while maintaining reproducibility and compliance
- Online versus offline serving requires different architectural approaches optimized for latency versus cost efficiency
- Feature sharing across teams multiplies engineering investments while requiring appropriate discovery and collaboration frameworks
- Production feature stores need automated monitoring, quality assurance, and governance to maintain their value proposition over time

Practice Questions: AWS ML Engineer Associate Exam Preparation

Question 26: A company wants to implement a feature store that serves both real-time inference and batch training workloads. Which SageMaker Feature Store capability addresses this requirement?

A) Feature groups with offline storage only B) Online store with DynamoDB backend C) Dual storage with both online and offline stores D) S3-based storage with caching layers

Correct Answer: C - SageMaker Feature Store provides both online and offline storage capabilities, with online stores for low-latency serving and offline stores for batch training and analytics.

Question 27: A machine learning team needs to ensure that features used for model training are identical to those used during inference. What feature store capability best addresses this requirement?

A) Feature versioning with immutable versions B) Real-time feature computation during inference C) Separate feature stores for training and inference D) Manual feature synchronization processes

Correct Answer: A - Feature versioning with immutable versions ensures that the same feature definitions and values are used consistently between training and inference.

Question 28: When implementing feature sharing across multiple teams, what governance mechanism helps prevent unauthorized access to sensitive features?

A) Feature group documentation requirements B) Role-based access control with feature-level permissions C) Manual approval processes for feature access D) Team-based feature group isolation

Correct Answer: B - Role-based access control with feature-level permissions provides automated, scalable access management that ensures appropriate feature access based on user roles and data sensitivity.

Question 29: A feature store contains customer behavioral features that update hourly and demographic features that update monthly. What optimization strategy would best serve real-time inference requirements?

A) Cache all features in memory regardless of update frequency B) Implement TTL policies based on feature update frequencies C) Store all features in offline storage with batch retrieval D) Use separate storage systems for each feature type

Correct Answer: B - TTL policies based on update frequencies optimize storage costs while ensuring feature freshness, with shorter TTLs for frequently updated features and longer TTLs for slowly changing features.

Question 30: A company needs to track which models are using specific features to assess the impact of feature changes. What feature store capability provides this functionality?

A) Feature usage analytics and dependency tracking B) Model performance monitoring integration C) Automated feature validation rules D) Feature group metadata management

Correct Answer: A - Feature usage analytics and dependency tracking provide visibility into which models and applications use specific features, enabling impact analysis for proposed changes.

Question 31: When designing feature groups for a recommendation system, what partitioning strategy would optimize query performance for user-based features?

A) Time-based partitioning by feature creation date B) User ID-based partitioning for even distribution C) Feature type partitioning by category D) Random partitioning for load balancing

Correct Answer: B - User ID-based partitioning enables efficient retrieval of all features for specific users, which is the most common access pattern for recommendation systems.

Question 32: A feature store needs to support both high-frequency streaming ingestion and complex analytical queries. What architecture pattern best addresses these requirements?

A) Single storage system optimized for streaming B) Lambda architecture with separate streaming and batch layers C) Real-time processing with immediate analytical availability D) Batch-only processing with near real-time updates

Correct Answer: B - Lambda architecture separates streaming ingestion from analytical processing, allowing optimization of each component for its specific performance requirements.

Question 33: What quality monitoring approach helps detect when feature distributions change significantly over time?

A) Schema validation during feature ingestion B) Statistical drift detection comparing current and historical distributions C) Business rule validation against expected ranges D) Manual quality audits performed monthly

Correct Answer: B - Statistical drift detection automatically identifies significant changes in feature distributions that could indicate data quality issues or changing business conditions.

Question 34: A feature store serves multiple applications with different latency requirements. How should feature caching be optimized?

A) Cache all features with identical TTL settings B) Implement application-specific caching strategies based on latency requirements C) Disable caching to ensure data freshness D) Use database-level caching only

Correct Answer: B - Application-specific caching strategies optimize the balance between latency and cost for different use cases, with aggressive caching for latency-sensitive applications and more conservative caching for cost-sensitive workloads.

Question 35: When implementing feature store access controls, what principle should guide permission design?

A) Grant broad access to simplify management B) Implement least privilege access based on business needs C) Use team-based permissions only D) Require manual approval for all feature access

Correct Answer: B - Least privilege access ensures users and applications receive only the minimum permissions necessary for their specific business requirements, improving security while maintaining productivity.

Question 36: A company needs to maintain feature store compliance with GDPR requirements. What capability is most important for supporting data subject deletion requests?

A) Feature versioning with historical tracking B) Data lineage tracking with deletion propagation C) Regular feature store backups D) Access logging for audit purposes

Correct Answer: B - Data lineage tracking with deletion propagation enables identification and removal of all data related to specific individuals, supporting GDPR compliance requirements.

Question 37: What feature store design pattern best supports A/B testing of new feature definitions?

A) Separate feature stores for each test variant B) Feature versioning with branch-based development C) Real-time feature computation during experiments D) Manual feature switching based on experiment assignment

Correct Answer: B - Feature versioning with branch-based development allows parallel development and testing of different feature definitions while maintaining production stability.

Question 38: A feature store experiences high query latency during peak business hours. What optimization approach should be implemented first?

A) Increase compute capacity for all queries B) Implement query result caching for frequently accessed features C) Move all features to in-memory storage D) Redesign feature groups with better partitioning

Correct Answer: B - Query result caching provides immediate latency improvements for frequently accessed features while being more cost-effective than increasing compute capacity or moving to expensive in-memory storage.

Question 39: When designing feature groups for time-series forecasting, what storage optimization provides the best balance of cost and query performance?

A) Store all historical data in online storage B) Implement time-based partitioning with lifecycle policies C) Use compression for all time-series data D) Maintain separate storage for each time period

Correct Answer: B - Time-based partitioning with lifecycle policies enables efficient queries on recent data while automatically moving older data to more cost-effective storage tiers.

Question 40: A feature store needs to support both individual feature lookup and bulk feature retrieval for batch processing. What API design pattern accommodates both use cases efficiently?

A) Single API with automatic batch optimization B) Separate APIs optimized for each access pattern C) Batch-only API with caching for individual requests D) Individual lookup API with client-side batching

Correct Answer: B - Separate APIs optimized for each access pattern provide the best performance and cost efficiency, with individual lookup APIs optimized for latency and bulk APIs optimized for throughput.

Question 41: What monitoring metric is most important for detecting feature store performance issues before they affect applications?

A) Storage utilization percentages B) Query latency percentiles (P95, P99) C) Feature ingestion rates D) User access frequency

Correct Answer: B - Query latency percentiles provide early warning of performance degradation, with P95 and P99 metrics showing when a significant portion of queries experience unacceptable latency.

Question 42: A feature store serves features with different sensitivity levels requiring different retention policies. How should this be implemented?

A) Single retention policy applied to all features B) Feature-level metadata with automated retention enforcement C) Manual deletion processes based on feature type D) Separate feature stores for each sensitivity level

Correct Answer: B - Feature-level metadata with automated retention enforcement provides flexible, scalable retention management that adapts to different data sensitivity requirements while maintaining operational efficiency.

Question 43: When implementing cross-region feature store deployment, what consideration is most important for maintaining consistency?

A) Identical hardware configuration in all regions B) Asynchronous replication with eventual consistency C) Synchronous replication with strong consistency D) Independent feature stores in each region

Correct Answer: B - Asynchronous replication with eventual consistency provides acceptable consistency for most ML applications while maintaining performance and cost efficiency across regions.

Question 44: A feature store needs to support rapid experimentation with new features while maintaining production stability. What development workflow best supports this requirement?

A) Direct production feature modification with rollback capabilities B) Branch-based development with staging environment validation C) Separate experimental feature stores D) Feature flags for runtime feature switching

Correct Answer: B - Branch-based development with staging environment validation enables safe experimentation while providing pathways to production that maintain system stability and quality standards.

Question 45: What feature store capability helps teams discover and reuse existing features rather than creating duplicates?

A) Automated feature generation recommendations B) Searchable feature catalog with rich metadata C) Feature usage monitoring and alerts D) Mandatory feature review processes

Correct Answer: B - Searchable feature catalog with rich metadata enables teams to discover existing features based on business context, data sources, or statistical characteristics, reducing duplication and improving collaboration.

Chapter 7: EDA in the AWS Ecosystem

Data tells stories, but those stories remain hidden until you ask the right questions in the right ways. Exploratory Data Analysis represents the detective work of machine learning—the systematic investigation that reveals patterns, anomalies, and relationships that guide every subsequent modeling decision. The AWS ecosystem provides powerful tools for this investigation, but using them effectively requires understanding both their capabilities and their appropriate application scenarios.

Most organizations approach EDA as a preliminary step to rush through before "real" machine learning begins. This perspective misses the fundamental truth that quality analysis determines model success more than algorithm selection or hyperparameter tuning. Poor understanding of data characteristics leads to models that perform well in development but fail catastrophically in production when confronted with real-world data variations.

Athena and QuickSight for Data Exploration

Amazon Athena provides serverless query capabilities that enable SQL-based analysis of data stored in S3 without requiring infrastructure management or data movement. This serverless approach eliminates the overhead of maintaining analytical databases while providing familiar SQL interfaces that enable rapid exploration of large datasets (14).

Serverless Query Advantages:

Athena's pay-per-query pricing model aligns costs with actual usage, making exploratory analysis economically efficient even for large datasets. You pay only for the data scanned during queries, encouraging efficient query design while eliminating fixed infrastructure costs.

Automatic scaling handles queries ranging from small explorations to large analytical workloads without requiring capacity planning or configuration management. The service provisions resources automatically based on query complexity and data volume, ensuring consistent performance across different workload types.

Integration with AWS Glue Data Catalog provides automatic schema discovery and metadata management that simplifies data exploration workflows. Catalog integration enables immediate querying of new datasets without manual schema definition or data loading procedures.

Advanced Query Patterns:

Partition pruning dramatically reduces query costs and improves performance by limiting data scanning to relevant subsets. Effective partitioning strategies based on common query patterns can reduce costs by 90% while improving query response times significantly.

Columnar storage formats like Parquet enable efficient analytical queries by scanning only required columns rather than entire rows. Combined with compression, columnar formats reduce both storage costs and query execution time while maintaining full analytical capabilities.

Query optimization techniques including proper WHERE clause placement, efficient JOIN operations, and appropriate aggregation strategies minimize data scanning while maximizing analytical value. Understanding query execution plans enables optimization that balances cost with performance requirements.

Case Example 1: Retail Customer Behavior Analysis

A multi-channel retailer needed to analyze customer shopping patterns across online, mobile, and physical store channels to identify cross-channel behavior and optimization opportunities. Traditional analytics infrastructure required complex ETL processes and maintained expensive always-on infrastructure for sporadic analytical queries.

The Athena-based solution enabled direct analysis of transaction logs, web analytics data, and point-of-sale records stored in S3 without data movement or transformation. SQL queries analyzed customer journey patterns, identified high-value customer segments, and detected seasonal trends across all channels simultaneously.

Query optimization through proper partitioning (by date and store region) reduced analysis costs by 85% while enabling real-time exploration of customer behavior patterns. The team discovered that mobile users who visited physical stores within 24 hours had 3x higher conversion rates, leading to targeted marketing campaigns that increased revenue by 12%.

Advanced analytical queries using window functions and statistical aggregations identified customer lifetime value patterns that weren't visible in traditional reporting systems. These insights enabled personalized marketing strategies and inventory optimization that improved both customer satisfaction and profitability.

Amazon QuickSight for Visual Data Exploration

QuickSight provides managed business intelligence capabilities with automatic scaling, embedded analytics, and machine learning-powered insights that enable self-service analytics for business users. The service combines traditional dashboard capabilities with advanced analytical features including forecasting, anomaly detection, and natural language querying (15).

Machine Learning-Enhanced Analytics:

Automatic anomaly detection identifies unusual patterns in business metrics without requiring statistical expertise or manual threshold configuration. ML algorithms continuously learn normal patterns and flag deviations that merit investigation, reducing manual monitoring overhead while improving issue detection speed.

Forecasting capabilities provide statistical predictions for key business metrics using sophisticated time-series algorithms that handle seasonality, trends, and external factors automatically. Business users can generate forecasts without understanding underlying statistical methods while maintaining control over forecast parameters and assumptions.

Natural language query interfaces enable business users to ask questions using everyday language rather than learning SQL or dashboard navigation. This accessibility democratizes data analysis while maintaining accuracy through intelligent query interpretation and suggestion systems.

Dashboard Design and User Experience:

Interactive visualizations enable drill-down analysis and dynamic filtering that supports exploratory workflows rather than static reporting. Users can investigate anomalies, test hypotheses, and discover patterns through intuitive interactions without requiring technical assistance.

Mobile-responsive design ensures analytical capabilities remain available across devices and usage contexts. Field teams, executives, and remote workers can access critical insights regardless of location or device limitations, improving decision-making speed and accuracy.

Embedded analytics capabilities enable integration of QuickSight dashboards into custom applications and workflows. This integration provides analytical capabilities within existing business processes rather than requiring separate analytical tools and context switching.

Case Example 2: Healthcare Provider Performance Analytics

A regional health system needed to analyze patient care quality, operational efficiency, and financial performance across multiple hospitals and clinics. Traditional reporting systems provided historical views but lacked real-time insights and predictive capabilities needed for proactive management.

QuickSight dashboards integrated data from electronic health records, financial systems, and operational databases to provide unified views of organizational performance. Automatic anomaly detection identified unusual patterns in patient readmission rates, treatment costs, and staffing levels that required investigation.

Interactive analysis enabled department managers to explore performance trends, identify improvement opportunities, and track the impact of operational changes. Drill-down capabilities allowed investigation from high-level organizational metrics to specific patient encounters and treatment protocols.

Machine learning insights detected seasonal patterns in patient volumes, enabling proactive staffing adjustments and resource allocation. Forecasting capabilities predicted demand for different services, supporting capacity planning and budget development processes.

SageMaker Data Wrangler Workflows

SageMaker Data Wrangler provides visual data preparation capabilities that combine the flexibility of custom code with the accessibility of point-and-click interfaces. The service enables rapid data exploration, quality assessment, and transformation without requiring extensive programming knowledge while maintaining the ability to export workflows as production-ready code (16).

Visual Data Exploration Interface:

Automatic data profiling generates statistical summaries, distribution visualizations, and quality assessments for all dataset columns without manual configuration. Profiling results highlight potential issues including missing values, outliers, and unexpected distributions that require attention.

Interactive visualization tools enable exploration of relationships between variables through scatter plots, correlation matrices, and distribution comparisons. Visual exploration often reveals patterns that aren't apparent in statistical summaries while enabling rapid hypothesis testing and validation.

Built-in transformation suggestions recommend appropriate preprocessing steps based on data characteristics and common ML preparation patterns. Suggestions accelerate data preparation while educating users about best practices for different data types and analytical scenarios.

Automated Quality Assessment:

Data quality reports identify completeness, consistency, and validity issues across all dataset features while providing detailed statistics about each quality dimension. Quality assessment adapts to different data types while providing standardized metrics for comparison across datasets.

Outlier detection algorithms identify unusual values that may represent data quality issues or interesting analytical opportunities. Multiple detection methods including statistical and ML-based approaches provide different perspectives on data anomalies.

Schema validation compares actual data characteristics with expected schemas, identifying deviations that could affect downstream processing. Validation results highlight type mismatches, unexpected null values, and format inconsistencies that require resolution.

Workflow Export and Productionization:

Code generation creates Python scripts or Jupyter notebooks that reproduce Data Wrangler transformations in production environments. Generated code follows best practices while remaining readable and modifiable for custom requirements.

SageMaker Processing integration enables automated execution of Data Wrangler workflows at scale without manual intervention. Scheduled execution supports regular data preparation while maintaining consistency with exploratory analysis results.

Pipeline integration incorporates Data Wrangler workflows into complete ML pipelines that include data preparation, model training, and deployment steps. This integration ensures consistency between exploratory analysis and production implementations.

Statistical Analysis with EMR Notebooks

Amazon EMR provides managed Jupyter notebook environments with pre-configured Spark clusters that enable large-scale statistical analysis using familiar Python and R interfaces. This combination provides both the accessibility of notebook environments and the scalability of distributed computing (17).

Distributed Statistical Computing:

Spark DataFrames enable statistical analysis of datasets that exceed single-machine memory limitations while providing familiar programming interfaces. Distributed computing capabilities scale from gigabytes to petabytes while maintaining consistent programming patterns.

Statistical libraries including MLlib, scipy, and specialized packages provide sophisticated analytical capabilities that run efficiently on distributed infrastructure. Library integration combines ease of use with computational scalability for complex analytical workloads.

Interactive development environments enable iterative analysis and visualization workflows that support exploratory data science while maintaining access to production-scale computing resources. Notebooks provide documentation and reproducibility while supporting collaborative development.

Advanced Statistical Techniques:

Sampling strategies enable analysis of large datasets through representative subsets that maintain statistical validity while reducing computational requirements. Stratified sampling and other advanced techniques ensure analytical results generalize to complete datasets.

Hypothesis testing capabilities support formal statistical inference while handling multiple testing corrections and power analysis automatically. Statistical rigor prevents false discoveries while enabling confident decision-making based on analytical results.

Time-series analysis tools provide specialized capabilities for temporal data including seasonality detection, trend analysis, and forecasting. Distributed implementations enable analysis of high-frequency data streams that exceed traditional analytical tool capabilities.

Case Example 3: Financial Risk Analysis

A investment management firm needed to analyze portfolio risk across thousands of securities and market conditions while maintaining real-time risk monitoring capabilities. Traditional risk systems required expensive infrastructure and lengthy processing times that limited analytical agility.

EMR notebooks enabled interactive analysis of historical market data, portfolio positions, and risk factor exposures using distributed Spark computing. Statistical analysis identified risk concentrations, correlation patterns, and scenario-based loss projections that informed investment decisions.

Advanced statistical techniques including Monte Carlo simulation and stress testing ran efficiently on EMR clusters while maintaining notebook-based accessibility for risk analysts. Complex scenarios that previously required overnight processing completed in minutes, enabling dynamic risk management.

Real-time integration with market data feeds enabled continuous risk monitoring and automated alerting when portfolio characteristics exceeded predefined thresholds. The analytical infrastructure supported both interactive exploration and automated production monitoring within the same environment.

Identifying Data Quality Issues at Scale

Data quality problems multiply exponentially with dataset size, making automated detection and remediation essential for large-scale ML systems. AWS provides multiple tools and techniques for systematic quality assessment that scales from gigabytes to petabytes while maintaining consistency and reliability.

Systematic Quality Assessment Framework:

Completeness analysis identifies missing data patterns, including systematic gaps that may indicate upstream issues or business process changes. Understanding missingness patterns guides appropriate imputation strategies while highlighting potential data collection problems.

Consistency checking validates data against business rules, referential integrity constraints, and expected value ranges. Automated consistency checks prevent quality issues from propagating through analytical pipelines while identifying data source problems early.

Accuracy assessment compares data against external sources, historical patterns, and business logic to identify potential errors or anomalies. Accuracy metrics provide confidence indicators for analytical results while guiding data improvement investments.

Automated Detection and Alerting:

Statistical process control techniques identify when data characteristics deviate significantly from historical patterns, indicating potential quality issues or changing business conditions. Control charts and trend analysis distinguish normal variation from genuine problems.

Machine learning-based anomaly detection identifies complex patterns of unusual data that traditional rule-based systems miss. ML approaches adapt to changing data characteristics while reducing false positive rates compared to static threshold systems.

Real-time monitoring capabilities provide immediate feedback on data quality issues as they occur, enabling rapid response and preventing quality problems from affecting downstream systems. Streaming quality assessment maintains analytical reliability in real-time environments.

Quality Remediation Strategies:

Automated data cleaning procedures handle common quality issues including format standardization, duplicate removal, and obvious error correction. Automated cleaning improves data consistency while reducing manual processing overhead.

Imputation strategies for missing data consider data characteristics, missingness patterns, and business requirements to select appropriate replacement values. Advanced imputation techniques maintain statistical properties while providing complete datasets for analysis.

Quality scorecards provide standardized metrics that enable comparison across different datasets and time periods. Scorecard tracking identifies quality trends while supporting continuous improvement in data collection and processing systems.

Project: Automated EDA Report Generation

This project builds a production system that automatically generates exploratory data analysis reports for new datasets while maintaining quality standards and providing actionable insights for data science teams.

Architecture Design and Implementation:

Serverless architecture using Lambda functions, Step Functions, and managed services provides scalable EDA report generation without infrastructure management overhead. Event-driven processing triggers analysis automatically when new datasets arrive while managing computational resources efficiently.

Template-based reporting enables standardized analysis patterns while supporting customization for different data types and business requirements. Report templates balance consistency with flexibility while ensuring comprehensive coverage of analytical best practices.

Multi-format output generation produces reports in multiple formats including HTML dashboards, PDF documents, and JSON summaries that serve different stakeholder needs. Format variety enables integration with different workflows and consumption patterns.

Automated Analysis Pipeline:

Data profiling stage generates statistical summaries, distribution analysis, and quality assessments for all dataset features automatically. Profiling adapts to different data types while providing standardized metrics for comparison across datasets.

Relationship analysis identifies correlations, dependencies, and interaction patterns between variables using both statistical and visual techniques. Automated relationship detection guides feature selection and engineering decisions while revealing unexpected data patterns.

Quality assessment stage implements systematic checks for completeness, consistency, accuracy, and validity while generating detailed quality reports. Quality metrics provide confidence indicators for subsequent analytical work while identifying improvement opportunities.

Visualization and Reporting:

Interactive dashboard generation creates web-based reports that enable exploration and investigation of analytical findings. Dashboards combine automated insights with user-driven exploration capabilities while maintaining professional presentation standards.

Automated insight generation uses machine learning to identify notable patterns, anomalies, and relationships that merit investigation. Natural language summaries explain findings in business terms while providing technical details for data science teams.

Distribution and alerting systems ensure reports reach appropriate stakeholders while providing notifications when significant issues or opportunities are detected. Automated distribution improves analytical turnaround time while ensuring consistent communication.

Quality Control and Validation:

Report validation ensures generated analyses meet quality standards and provide actionable insights before distribution. Validation checks prevent publication of incomplete or misleading analyses while maintaining report consistency.

Performance monitoring tracks report generation time, resource utilization, and user engagement to optimize system performance and user experience. Monitoring enables continuous improvement while ensuring reliable service delivery.

Feedback integration enables users to provide input on report quality and usefulness, supporting iterative improvement of analysis templates and insight generation algorithms. User feedback drives system evolution while maintaining analytical value.

Building Analytical Foundations

Effective exploratory data analysis requires combining technical capabilities with business understanding to generate insights that drive better decisions. The AWS ecosystem provides powerful tools, but using them effectively requires systematic approaches that balance automation with human expertise.

Data quality assessment becomes increasingly important as dataset sizes grow and analytical complexity increases. Invest in systematic quality frameworks that scale with your data while maintaining reliability and consistency across different analytical scenarios.

Visualization and communication skills often determine the business impact of analytical work more than technical sophistication. Focus on developing capabilities that translate analytical findings into actionable business insights that drive measurable improvements.

The Foundation for Advanced Analytics

The exploratory analysis capabilities established in this section provide the foundation for advanced feature engineering and model development covered in subsequent sections. Quality data understanding enables better feature engineering decisions while identifying potential modeling challenges early in the development process.

Essential Takeaways

- Athena and QuickSight provide serverless analytical capabilities that scale from exploration to production analytics without infrastructure overhead
- SageMaker Data Wrangler combines visual interfaces with code generation to accelerate data preparation while maintaining production readiness
- EMR notebooks enable large-scale statistical analysis using familiar programming interfaces with distributed computing scalability

- Systematic data quality assessment prevents issues from propagating through ML pipelines while ensuring reliable analytical foundations
- Automated EDA report generation scales analytical best practices while ensuring consistent quality and stakeholder communication

Chapter 8: Advanced Feature Engineering

Feature engineering represents the art and science of transforming raw data into representations that enable machine learning algorithms to discover patterns and make accurate predictions. While automated feature selection and engineering tools have advanced significantly, understanding the underlying principles and techniques remains essential for building robust ML systems that perform reliably across diverse scenarios and changing conditions.

The gap between theoretical knowledge and practical implementation becomes most apparent in feature engineering, where textbook techniques often fail when confronted with real-world data characteristics like missing values, outliers, and distribution shifts. Successful practitioners develop intuition for selecting appropriate techniques based on data characteristics, business requirements, and computational constraints.

Handling Imbalanced Datasets

Class imbalance represents one of the most common challenges in real-world machine learning, where majority classes dominate datasets and minority classes—often the most important for business decisions—receive insufficient representation for reliable model training. Understanding the relationship between class distribution, algorithm behavior, and business impact guides selection of appropriate mitigation strategies.

Understanding Imbalance Impact:

Traditional accuracy metrics become misleading in imbalanced scenarios where a classifier can achieve high accuracy by simply predicting the majority class for all examples. A fraud detection model that predicts "no fraud" for every transaction might achieve 99% accuracy in a dataset with 1% fraud rate while providing zero business value.

Algorithm sensitivity to class imbalance varies significantly across different approaches. Tree-based algorithms often handle moderate imbalance naturally, while linear models and neural networks typically require explicit handling through resampling, weighting, or threshold adjustment techniques.

Business cost considerations should drive imbalance handling strategies rather than purely technical metrics. Missing fraudulent transactions often costs significantly more than false fraud alerts, requiring asymmetric approaches that prioritize recall over precision while maintaining acceptable overall performance.

Resampling Strategies:

Random oversampling duplicates minority class examples to balance class distributions but risks overfitting when datasets are small or minority class examples are not representative of the true population distribution. Simple duplication provides baseline performance improvement while introducing potential bias.

SMOTE (Synthetic Minority Oversampling Technique) generates synthetic minority class examples by interpolating between existing examples in feature space. This approach increases minority class representation without exact duplication while maintaining neighborhood relationships in the feature space.

Random undersampling removes majority class examples to balance distributions but discards potentially valuable information. Undersampling works well when majority class examples are redundant but can hurt performance when removing informative examples.

Informed undersampling techniques like Edited Nearest Neighbors or Tomek Links remove only majority class examples that are likely noise or borderline cases. These approaches maintain majority class information while improving class boundary definition and reducing training time.

Cost-Sensitive Learning:

Class weighting assigns different costs to misclassification errors based on business impact rather than treating all errors equally. Higher weights for minority class errors force algorithms to pay more attention to underrepresented examples during training.

Threshold optimization adjusts decision boundaries after training to optimize business-relevant metrics like F1-score or cost-weighted accuracy. Threshold tuning provides fine-grained control over precision-recall trade-offs without retraining models.

Algorithm-specific techniques like cost-sensitive SVM or weighted loss functions integrate business costs directly into the learning objective. These approaches optimize for business outcomes rather than technical metrics while maintaining algorithmic efficiency.

Case Example 1: Medical Diagnostic System

A healthcare provider needed to develop automated screening systems for rare diseases where positive cases represented less than 0.5% of patient encounters. Traditional models achieved high accuracy by predicting negative for all cases while missing critical positive diagnoses that required immediate intervention.

The feature engineering approach combined multiple resampling techniques with domain-specific feature creation. Clinical expertise guided synthetic example generation using SMOTE variants that respected medical constraints and physiological relationships between symptoms.

Cost-sensitive learning incorporated actual medical costs including delayed diagnosis impacts, unnecessary testing expenses, and patient outcome considerations. The final model achieved 85% recall for positive cases while maintaining acceptable false positive rates that balanced diagnostic accuracy with resource utilization.

Ensemble approaches combined models trained on different balanced subsets of the data, providing robust predictions that maintained performance across different patient populations and clinical scenarios. Model diversity improved generalization while reducing sensitivity to specific resampling strategies.

Dimensionality Reduction Techniques

High-dimensional data presents computational and statistical challenges that require systematic reduction approaches to maintain model performance while reducing computational complexity. Understanding the trade-offs between information preservation and computational efficiency guides selection of appropriate dimensionality reduction techniques for different scenarios.

Principal Component Analysis Applications:

PCA transforms correlated features into uncorrelated principal components that capture maximum variance in the original data. The technique works well for datasets with linear relationships and continuous features while providing interpretable variance explanation for component selection.

Component selection requires balancing information retention with dimensionality reduction goals. Cumulative variance plots and scree plots guide selection of component counts that preserve essential information while achieving desired dimensionality reduction.

Kernel PCA extends linear PCA to capture non-linear relationships by applying PCA in transformed feature spaces. This approach handles complex relationships while maintaining PCA's interpretability and efficiency characteristics.

Incremental PCA enables dimensionality reduction for datasets that exceed memory limitations by processing data in batches while maintaining mathematical equivalence to batch PCA. This scalability enables PCA application to large datasets without infrastructure limitations.

Advanced Reduction Techniques:

t-SNE (t-Distributed Stochastic Neighbor Embedding) preserves local neighborhood relationships during dimensionality reduction, making it excellent for visualization and exploratory analysis. The non-linear technique reveals cluster structures that linear methods like PCA might miss.

UMAP (Uniform Manifold Approximation and Projection) provides faster and more scalable non-linear dimensionality reduction compared to t-SNE while maintaining better global structure preservation. UMAP works well for both visualization and feature engineering applications.

Linear Discriminant Analysis (LDA) reduces dimensionality while maximizing class separability, making it particularly useful for classification problems. LDA combines dimensionality reduction with supervised learning to create features optimized for classification performance.

Independent Component Analysis (ICA) separates mixed signals into independent components, working well for source separation problems like audio processing or sensor data analysis. ICA assumptions about statistical independence guide appropriate application scenarios.

Feature Selection vs Feature Extraction:

Feature selection chooses subsets of original features while maintaining interpretability and domain meaning. Selection techniques include statistical tests, recursive feature elimination, and regularization-based approaches that identify most informative features.

Feature extraction creates new features through mathematical transformations that may lose direct interpretability but often improve model performance. Extraction techniques include PCA, autoencoder representations, and domain-specific transformations.

Hybrid approaches combine selection and extraction to achieve benefits of both interpretability and performance improvement. Sequential application of selection followed by extraction often provides optimal results for complex analytical problems.

Case Example 2: Customer Behavior Analytics

An e-commerce platform collected thousands of behavioral features for each customer including page views, click patterns, purchase history, and engagement metrics. The high-dimensional feature space created computational challenges while many features contained redundant information.

PCA analysis revealed that 200 components captured 95% of variance in the original 2,000 features, enabling significant dimensionality reduction without substantial information loss. Component analysis identified major behavioral patterns including browsing intensity, purchase frequency, and seasonal engagement.

Feature importance analysis using tree-based methods identified the most predictive original features for different business outcomes. This analysis guided creation of interpretable feature subsets for business users while maintaining predictive performance.

UMAP visualization revealed distinct customer segments with different behavioral patterns that weren't apparent in original feature analysis. These segments informed targeted marketing strategies and personalization algorithms that improved customer engagement.

Time-Series Feature Extraction

Time-series data requires specialized feature engineering approaches that capture temporal patterns, seasonality, and trend information that traditional feature engineering techniques miss. Understanding time-series characteristics guides selection of appropriate transformation and feature creation techniques.

Temporal Pattern Recognition:

Lag features capture relationships between current values and historical observations at specific time intervals. Multiple lag values provide different temporal perspectives while enabling models to learn complex time-dependent patterns.

Rolling statistics including means, standard deviations, and percentiles summarize recent historical behavior while adapting to changing conditions. Window size selection balances responsiveness to recent changes with stability of statistical estimates.

Seasonal decomposition separates time-series into trend, seasonal, and residual components that can be analyzed independently. Decomposition enables specialized modeling of different temporal patterns while improving interpretability of results.

Fourier transforms identify frequency domain patterns that reveal periodic behaviors not apparent in time domain analysis. Frequency analysis helps detect cycles, rhythms, and periodic anomalies in complex time-series data.

Technical Indicators and Domain Features:

Moving averages smooth short-term fluctuations while preserving longer-term trends, providing stable features for model training. Different moving average types (simple, exponential, weighted) capture different aspects of temporal behavior.

Rate of change and momentum indicators capture trend strength and direction changes that predict future behavior. These features work particularly well for financial and economic forecasting applications.

Volatility measures including standard deviation and average true range quantify uncertainty and risk levels that affect decision-making. Volatility features enable models to adapt predictions based on uncertainty levels.

Domain-specific indicators leverage business knowledge to create features that capture relevant patterns for specific applications. Financial indicators, weather patterns, and operational metrics provide business-relevant temporal features.

Multi-scale Temporal Features:

Hierarchical time representations capture patterns at multiple time scales simultaneously, enabling models to learn both short-term fluctuations and long-term trends. Multi-scale features improve model robustness across different prediction horizons.

Wavelet transforms provide time-frequency analysis that captures localized temporal patterns and anomalies. Wavelets work particularly well for non stationary time-series with changing statistical properties over time.

Change point detection identifies structural breaks and regime changes that affect model behavior. Change point features enable models to adapt to shifting conditions while maintaining predictive accuracy.

Text and Image Preprocessing

Unstructured data requires specialized preprocessing approaches that convert text and images into numerical representations suitable for machine learning algorithms.

Understanding the relationship between preprocessing choices and model performance guides selection of appropriate techniques for different applications.

Text Preprocessing Pipelines:

Tokenization breaks text into individual words or subword units while handling punctuation, capitalization, and special characters appropriately. Tokenization choices affect vocabulary size and model complexity while influencing downstream performance.

Normalization techniques including stemming and lemmatization reduce words to root forms while preserving meaning. These approaches reduce vocabulary size and improve generalization while potentially losing nuanced semantic information.

Stop word removal eliminates common words that provide little discriminative information while reducing feature dimensionality. Stop word lists should be customized for specific domains and applications rather than using generic lists.

N-gram features capture local context and phrase information that individual words miss. Bigrams and trigrams provide phrasal context while higher-order n-grams capture longer dependencies at the cost of increased sparsity.

Advanced Text Representations:

TF-IDF (Term Frequency-Inverse Document Frequency) weights word importance based on frequency within documents and rarity across the corpus. TF-IDF provides better feature representations than simple word counts while remaining interpretable.

Word embeddings like Word2Vec and GloVe capture semantic relationships between words through dense vector representations. Pre-trained embeddings provide rich semantic features while domain-specific training adapts to specialized vocabularies.

Document embeddings including Doc2Vec and BERT representations capture document-level semantic meaning that word-level features miss. Document embeddings enable similarity analysis and semantic search capabilities.

Sentence transformers provide specialized embeddings for sentence-level analysis that capture semantic meaning across different sentence structures and vocabularies. These models work particularly well for text similarity and classification tasks.

Image Preprocessing Foundations:

Image normalization standardizes pixel values and image dimensions while preserving essential visual information. Normalization choices affect model training stability and convergence speed while influencing feature quality.

Augmentation techniques including rotation, scaling, and color adjustment increase training data diversity while improving model robustness. Augmentation strategies should match anticipated real-world variations while avoiding unrealistic transformations.

Feature extraction using pre-trained CNN models provides rich visual representations without requiring large-scale image training datasets. Transfer learning enables effective image analysis for specialized domains with limited training data.

Object detection and segmentation provide structural information about image content that enables more sophisticated analysis. These techniques identify relevant image regions while providing spatial relationship information.

Case Example 3: Social Media Sentiment Analysis

A marketing agency needed to analyze customer sentiment across social media platforms to guide brand management and campaign optimization. The unstructured text data contained informal language, emotions, slang, and platform-specific conventions that challenged traditional text analysis approaches.

Text preprocessing addressed social media characteristics including hashtag handling, emoji interpretation, and abbreviation expansion. Domain-specific tokenization preserved meaningful social media conventions while standardizing text for analysis.

Feature engineering combined traditional text features with social media-specific indicators including posting frequency, engagement metrics, and network characteristics. Multi-modal features captured both content and context information for improved sentiment prediction.

Real-time processing capabilities enabled immediate sentiment monitoring during marketing campaigns and crisis management situations. Streaming text analysis provided actionable insights while maintaining low latency for time-sensitive responses.

Project: Multi-modal Feature Pipeline

This project builds a production feature engineering system that handles diverse data types including structured data, text, images, and time-series information while maintaining consistency and quality across all feature types.

Architecture Design and Data Flow:

Modular pipeline architecture enables independent processing of different data types while maintaining consistent feature management and quality standards. Separate processing modules handle structured, text, image, and time-series data with appropriate transformations and validations.

Feature store integration provides centralized management of multi-modal features while supporting both batch and real-time feature serving. Unified feature access enables models to combine information from multiple data modalities seamlessly.

Quality monitoring ensures consistent feature quality across all data types while providing specialized validation for different modalities. Quality metrics adapt to data type characteristics while maintaining standardized reporting and alerting.

Structured Data Processing:

Automated feature selection identifies most informative features while handling correlation and redundancy issues systematically. Selection algorithms adapt to different target types while providing interpretable explanations for feature choices.

Categorical encoding handles high-cardinality and rare categories through appropriate encoding strategies including target encoding, embedding approaches, and regularized techniques. Encoding choices balance model performance with overfitting risks.

Numerical feature transformations including scaling, binning, and polynomial features improve model performance while maintaining interpretability. Transformation selection adapts to feature distributions and business requirements.

Text Processing Implementation:

Scalable text preprocessing handles large document collections using distributed computing while maintaining processing consistency. Pipeline optimization balances processing speed with feature quality for production requirements.

Multi-language support enables text analysis across different languages and character sets while maintaining consistent feature representations. Language detection and appropriate preprocessing ensure reliable cross-language analysis.

Topic modeling and semantic analysis provide document-level features that capture thematic content beyond individual word features. Advanced text features enable more sophisticated content analysis and categorization.

Image Processing Capabilities:

Batch image processing handles large image collections efficiently while maintaining quality and consistency. Processing pipelines optimize for both speed and memory usage while supporting different image formats and sizes.

Feature extraction using pre-trained models provides rich visual representations while enabling customization for specific domains and use cases. Transfer learning approaches adapt general visual features to specialized applications.

Metadata extraction captures technical image characteristics including EXIF data, color profiles, and quality metrics that provide additional features for analysis. Metadata features complement visual features for comprehensive image analysis.

Time-Series Feature Engineering:

Multi-scale temporal features capture patterns at different time horizons while enabling models to learn both short-term and long-term dependencies. Hierarchical feature organization supports different modeling approaches and business requirements.

Seasonal and trend analysis provides specialized features for time-series forecasting while handling business calendars and domain-specific temporal patterns. Domain adaptation improves feature relevance for specific business applications.

Real-time feature computation enables streaming analysis while maintaining consistency with batch processing results. Stream processing optimizations balance latency requirements with computational efficiency.

Production Considerations and Best Practices

Feature engineering pipelines require careful attention to reproducibility, scalability, and maintainability to ensure reliable performance in production environments. Version control, testing, and monitoring become essential for complex multi-modal pipelines that support critical business processes.

Performance optimization balances feature quality with computational efficiency while ensuring pipelines meet latency and throughput requirements. Optimization strategies include caching, parallel processing, and intelligent resource allocation based on workload characteristics.

Error handling and recovery procedures ensure pipeline reliability while providing visibility into processing issues and quality problems. Robust error handling prevents complete pipeline failures while enabling rapid diagnosis and resolution of issues.

Moving Forward with Confidence

Advanced feature engineering provides the foundation for building robust machine learning models that perform reliably across diverse scenarios and changing conditions. The techniques and frameworks established here enable creation of rich feature representations that capture complex patterns while remaining computationally efficient.

The multi-modal feature engineering capabilities developed in this section support advanced visualization and analytics covered in the next section. Quality feature engineering enables more sophisticated analytical insights while improving model performance and business impact.

Essential Takeaways

- Imbalanced dataset handling requires business-aware approaches that balance technical metrics with real-world costs and constraints
- Dimensionality reduction techniques provide computational efficiency while requiring careful trade-offs between information preservation and complexity reduction
- Time-series feature extraction captures temporal patterns and dependencies that traditional techniques miss
- Text and image preprocessing converts unstructured data into numerical representations while preserving essential semantic and visual information
- Multi-modal feature pipelines enable integration of diverse data types while maintaining consistency and quality across all feature types

Chapter 9: Data Visualization and Insights

Data visualization bridges the gap between complex analytical results and actionable business decisions, transforming statistical patterns into compelling narratives that drive organizational change. The most sophisticated machine learning models provide little value if their insights remain locked in technical reports that business stakeholders cannot understand or act upon effectively.

AWS provides powerful visualization platforms that combine traditional dashboard capabilities with machine learning-enhanced insights, but using these tools effectively requires understanding both technical visualization principles and stakeholder communication strategies. The goal extends beyond creating attractive charts to building analytical experiences that enable better decision-making across the organization.

QuickSight ML Insights

Amazon QuickSight integrates machine learning capabilities directly into business intelligence workflows, enabling automated pattern detection, forecasting, and anomaly identification without requiring specialized data science expertise. These ML-enhanced features democratize advanced analytics while maintaining the accessibility and familiarity of traditional dashboard interfaces (18).

Automated Anomaly Detection:

QuickSight's anomaly detection algorithms continuously monitor business metrics to identify unusual patterns that merit investigation, learning normal behavior patterns automatically while adapting to changing business conditions. The service uses sophisticated statistical techniques including seasonal decomposition and robust outlier detection that handle complex time-series patterns.

Anomaly scoring provides quantitative assessments of unusual events while offering explanations that help business users understand why specific patterns triggered alerts. Natural language explanations translate statistical findings into business terms that enable effective investigation and response.

Interactive anomaly exploration enables drill-down analysis that investigates root causes while providing context about related metrics and external factors. Users can explore anomalies across different dimensions and time periods to understand broader patterns and implications.

Alert integration connects anomaly detection with notification systems that ensure critical issues receive immediate attention from appropriate stakeholders. Customizable alerting rules balance sensitivity with practicality while reducing alert fatigue through intelligent filtering.

Forecasting and Trend Analysis:

Built-in forecasting capabilities generate statistical predictions for key business metrics using algorithms that handle seasonality, trends, and external factors automatically. Forecasting models adapt to different data characteristics while providing confidence intervals that communicate prediction uncertainty.

What-if analysis enables exploration of different scenarios and their potential impacts on business outcomes. Users can adjust key parameters and assumptions to understand how changes affect forecasted results, supporting planning and decision-making processes.

Trend detection identifies significant changes in business patterns while distinguishing temporary fluctuations from meaningful shifts. Statistical trend analysis provides confidence levels and significance testing that guide appropriate business responses.

Seasonal pattern recognition automatically identifies recurring patterns in business data while accounting for holidays, business cycles, and other calendar effects. Seasonal insights support capacity planning, inventory management, and marketing campaign optimization.

Natural Language Insights:

Automated narrative generation creates natural language summaries of dashboard findings while highlighting key insights and notable patterns. Narratives translate complex visualizations into accessible explanations that support different audience needs and technical backgrounds.

Question-and-answer interfaces enable users to query data using everyday language rather than learning dashboard navigation or SQL syntax. Natural language processing interprets user questions while generating appropriate visualizations and analyses automatically.

Insight suggestions proactively identify interesting patterns and relationships in data while recommending additional analyses that might provide valuable insights. Suggestion algorithms learn from user behavior while adapting to different analytical workflows and business contexts.

Case Example 1: Supply Chain Performance Monitoring

A global manufacturing company implemented QuickSight ML insights to monitor supply chain performance across multiple regions, suppliers, and product lines. Traditional reporting systems provided historical views but lacked predictive capabilities and automated issue detection needed for proactive supply chain management.

Automated anomaly detection identified unusual patterns in supplier delivery times, inventory levels, and quality metrics that required immediate investigation. The system detected a 15% increase in delivery delays from a key supplier three weeks before manual reporting would have identified the issue, enabling proactive sourcing adjustments.

Forecasting capabilities predicted seasonal demand patterns and supply constraints while accounting for external factors like weather events and economic conditions. Forecast accuracy improved by 25% compared to traditional planning methods while reducing inventory carrying costs through better demand prediction.

Natural language insights automatically generated executive summaries of supply chain performance while highlighting critical issues and opportunities for improvement. Automated reporting reduced manual analysis time by 60% while improving communication between operations teams and executive leadership.

Custom Visualization with SageMaker

SageMaker notebooks provide flexible environments for creating custom visualizations that address specific analytical needs while integrating seamlessly with machine learning workflows. Custom visualization capabilities enable specialized analysis and presentation formats that standard dashboard tools cannot accommodate (19).

Advanced Plotting Libraries:

Matplotlib provides foundational plotting capabilities with extensive customization options for creating publication-quality visualizations. The library supports complex multi-panel layouts, statistical overlays, and precise formatting control needed for technical presentations.

Seaborn extends matplotlib with statistical visualization capabilities that simplify common analytical plots while maintaining customization flexibility. Statistical plotting functions automatically handle grouping, regression lines, and distribution comparisons that improve analytical efficiency.

Plotly enables interactive visualizations with zooming, hovering, and selection capabilities that support exploratory analysis. Interactive features improve user engagement while enabling deeper investigation of patterns and relationships in complex datasets.

Bokeh provides web-based interactive visualizations with server applications that support real-time data updates and user interactions. Server-based visualizations enable sharing of interactive analyses while maintaining performance for large datasets.

Machine Learning Specific Visualizations:

Model performance visualizations including ROC curves, precision-recall curves, and confusion matrices provide standardized assessments of classification model quality. Performance plots enable comparison between different models while identifying areas for improvement.

Feature importance plots help interpret model behavior while identifying most influential variables for predictions. Importance visualizations guide feature engineering decisions while providing explainability for business stakeholders.

Learning curves show model performance progression during training while identifying overfitting, underfitting, and convergence issues. Training visualizations guide hyperparameter tuning while ensuring optimal model performance.

Prediction distribution analysis compares model outputs with actual values while identifying systematic biases and performance issues across different data segments. Distribution analysis ensures model reliability across diverse scenarios and populations.

Integration with ML Workflows:

Automated visualization generation creates standard plots during model training and evaluation without manual intervention. Automated plotting ensures consistent visualization standards while reducing development time and improving reproducibility.

Template-based visualization systems enable standardized reporting formats while supporting customization for different models and analyses. Templates balance consistency with flexibility while improving collaboration across different teams and projects.

Export capabilities generate high-quality plots in multiple formats suitable for presentations, reports, and publication. Export functionality supports different resolution requirements while maintaining visual quality across different output media.

Case Example 2: Financial Risk Model Interpretation

A regional bank needed to visualize complex risk model outputs for regulatory reporting while ensuring model interpretability for business users and compliance officers. Standard risk reports provided numerical summaries but lacked visual insights needed for effective model validation and business communication.

Custom SageMaker visualizations created comprehensive model interpretation dashboards that combined technical performance metrics with business-relevant risk assessments. Visualizations included feature importance plots, partial dependence analyses, and scenario-based risk projections.

Interactive exploration tools enabled risk managers to investigate model behavior across different customer segments and economic scenarios. Drill-down capabilities supported detailed analysis while maintaining overview perspectives needed for portfolio-level risk management.

Regulatory reporting automation generated standardized visualization packages that met compliance requirements while reducing manual reporting overhead. Automated report generation ensured consistency while enabling rapid response to regulatory inquiries and model validation requests.

Stakeholder-Ready Dashboards

Effective dashboard design requires understanding audience needs, decision-making processes, and organizational communication patterns to create analytical experiences that drive action rather than just providing information. Stakeholder-focused design principles ensure dashboards serve their intended purpose while remaining accessible and actionable.

Audience-Specific Design Principles:

Executive dashboards prioritize high-level KPIs and trend summaries while minimizing technical complexity and information overload. Executive views focus on strategic metrics and exception reporting that support decision-making without overwhelming busy leaders with operational details.

Operational dashboards provide detailed monitoring capabilities and drill-down functionality that support day-to-day management activities. Operational views balance comprehensive information with usability while enabling rapid identification and response to emerging issues.

Analytical dashboards support exploratory investigation and hypothesis testing through interactive filtering, segmentation, and comparison capabilities. Analytical views provide tools and flexibility needed for detailed investigation while maintaining performance for large datasets.

Customer-facing dashboards present information in accessible formats that build trust and enable self-service while protecting sensitive operational information. Customer views balance transparency with privacy while providing value-added insights that strengthen business relationships.

Visual Design Best Practices:

Color strategy uses consistent schemes that support pattern recognition while accommodating accessibility requirements including color-blind users. Strategic color application highlights important information while avoiding visual confusion and maintaining professional appearance.

Layout organization follows established information hierarchy principles while supporting natural reading patterns and cognitive processing. Effective layouts guide attention to critical information while providing logical flow for different analytical workflows.

Typography selection ensures readability across different devices and viewing conditions while maintaining professional presentation standards. Font choices balance aesthetic appeal with functional requirements including mobile viewing and printed reports.

White space utilization improves information processing while reducing visual clutter that impedes comprehension. Strategic spacing creates visual breathing room while organizing related information into logical groupings.

Interactivity and User Experience:

Filter design enables intuitive data exploration while maintaining performance for large datasets and complex queries. Filter interfaces balance functionality with simplicity while providing clear feedback about current selections and their impacts.

Navigation structure supports different user workflows while maintaining orientation and context across dashboard sections. Navigation design enables efficient movement between related analyses while preventing users from becoming lost in complex interfaces.

Mobile responsiveness ensures dashboard accessibility across devices while maintaining functionality and visual appeal on smaller screens. Responsive design adapts layouts and interactions appropriately while preserving essential features and information.

Performance optimization ensures rapid loading and responsive interactions while managing large datasets efficiently. Performance considerations include query optimization, caching strategies, and progressive loading that maintain user experience standards.

Monitoring Data Drift

Data drift represents one of the most significant challenges for production ML systems, where changing data characteristics can silently degrade model performance without triggering traditional monitoring alerts. Visualization-based drift monitoring provides intuitive understanding of data changes while enabling proactive response to emerging issues.

Statistical Drift Detection:

Distribution comparison visualizations show how current data characteristics differ from training data distributions while highlighting specific features that exhibit significant changes. Statistical overlays provide quantitative assessments while visual comparisons enable intuitive understanding of drift magnitude and direction.

Population stability index (PSI) calculations provide standardized metrics for measuring drift magnitude while enabling comparison across different features and time periods. PSI visualization tracks drift trends over time while identifying periods of significant change that require investigation.

Kolmogorov-Smirnov test results provide statistical significance testing for distribution differences while controlling for multiple comparisons across numerous features. KS test visualization shows which features exhibit statistically significant drift while providing confidence levels for decision-making.

Jensen-Shannon divergence measurements provide symmetric measures of distribution differences that work well for both continuous and categorical features. Divergence visualization enables comparison of drift magnitude across different feature types while providing standardized metrics for alerting thresholds.

Feature-Level Analysis:

Individual feature monitoring tracks changes in mean, variance, percentiles, and other statistical properties over time while identifying patterns and trends in data evolution. Feature-level analysis enables targeted investigation of specific drift sources while prioritizing response efforts.

Correlation drift analysis identifies changes in relationships between features that can affect model performance even when individual feature distributions remain stable. Correlation monitoring detects subtle interaction changes that simple distribution monitoring might miss.

Missing value pattern analysis tracks changes in data completeness and missingness patterns that can indicate upstream system changes or data quality issues. Missingness monitoring provides early warning of potential data pipeline problems while enabling proactive response.

Categorical distribution monitoring tracks changes in category frequencies and rare category emergence that can affect categorical encoding stability. Category monitoring ensures encoding systems remain appropriate for current data characteristics while identifying retraining needs.

Business Impact Assessment:

Model performance correlation analysis relates drift metrics to actual model performance degradation while identifying which types of drift most significantly affect business outcomes. Performance correlation guides prioritization of drift response efforts while enabling predictive performance management.

Business metric impact visualization shows how data drift translates into changes in business-relevant outcomes including revenue, customer satisfaction, and operational efficiency. Business impact analysis enables cost-benefit evaluation of drift response investments while communicating urgency to stakeholders.

Threshold optimization balances drift detection sensitivity with alert frequency while minimizing false alarms that reduce response effectiveness. Threshold tuning considers both statistical significance and business impact while adapting to different feature characteristics and business requirements.

Case Example 3: E-commerce Recommendation System Monitoring

An online marketplace monitored data drift for recommendation systems that processed customer behavior, product catalogs, and market trends to provide personalized product suggestions. Seasonal changes, new product launches, and evolving customer preferences created continuous drift challenges that affected recommendation quality.

Statistical drift visualization provided real-time monitoring of customer behavior patterns, product feature distributions, and interaction rate changes while highlighting specific areas of concern. Drift dashboards enabled data science teams to identify emerging issues before they affected recommendation performance.

Feature importance drift analysis tracked how different behavioral signals changed in predictive value over time while identifying features that required reweighting or replacement. Importance monitoring guided feature engineering updates while maintaining recommendation system effectiveness.

Business impact correlation connected drift metrics with recommendation quality measures including click-through rates, conversion rates, and customer satisfaction scores. Impact analysis enabled prioritization of drift response efforts while demonstrating the business value of proactive monitoring investments.

Production Dashboard Architecture

Successful dashboard deployment requires robust architecture that handles varying user loads, data volumes, and performance requirements while maintaining reliability and security standards appropriate for business-critical applications.

Scalability and Performance:

Caching strategies balance data freshness with query performance while managing computational costs for complex analytical workloads. Multi-level caching including query result caching, data extract caching, and visualization caching optimizes performance for different usage patterns.

Query optimization techniques including materialized views, pre-aggregated summaries, and intelligent partitioning reduce dashboard loading times while managing database resource utilization. Optimization strategies adapt to different data sizes and complexity requirements while maintaining interactive responsiveness.

Auto-scaling configuration handles varying user loads while maintaining cost efficiency during low-demand periods. Scaling policies consider both user count and query complexity while ensuring adequate performance during peak usage periods.

Content delivery networks (CDNs) improve global dashboard performance while reducing bandwidth costs and server load. CDN integration provides consistent user experience across different geographic locations while handling static asset delivery efficiently.

Security and Access Control:

Row-level security ensures users see only data they're authorized to access while maintaining dashboard functionality and performance. Security implementation adapts to organizational hierarchies and data sensitivity requirements while providing seamless user experience.

Single sign-on integration provides convenient authentication while maintaining security standards and audit capabilities. SSO implementation reduces password management overhead while ensuring consistent access policies across organizational systems.

API security protects dashboard data sources while enabling authorized integrations and custom applications. API protection includes rate limiting, authentication, and authorization controls that prevent unauthorized access while supporting legitimate usage.

Audit logging captures user access patterns and dashboard usage while supporting compliance requirements and security analysis. Logging implementation balances comprehensive tracking with privacy considerations while providing actionable security insights.

The Path to Analytical Excellence

Effective data visualization requires combining technical capabilities with design principles and business understanding to create analytical experiences that drive better decisions. Investment in visualization infrastructure pays dividends through improved decision-making speed and quality across the organization.

The visualization capabilities established here support advanced model development and deployment activities covered in subsequent sections. Quality analytical insights enable more informed modeling decisions while improving stakeholder engagement and support for ML initiatives.

Essential Takeaways

- QuickSight ML insights provide automated pattern detection and forecasting that democratize advanced analytics for business users
- Custom SageMaker visualizations enable specialized analysis and interpretation that standard tools cannot accommodate
- Stakeholder-ready dashboards require audience-specific design that balances information content with usability and accessibility
- Data drift monitoring through visualization provides intuitive understanding of changing data characteristics and their business impacts
- Production dashboard architecture requires careful attention to scalability, performance, and security to support business-critical applications

Practice Questions: AWS ML Engineer Associate Exam Preparation

Question 46: A company wants to automatically detect unusual patterns in their daily sales data using QuickSight. Which feature provides this capability without requiring custom code development?

A) Custom SQL queries with statistical functions B) Built-in anomaly detection with ML insights C) Manual threshold alerting configuration D) Export to external analytics tools

Correct Answer: B - QuickSight's built-in anomaly detection uses machine learning algorithms to automatically identify unusual patterns in time-series data without requiring custom development.

Question 47: When creating visualizations for model performance analysis in SageMaker notebooks, which Python library combination provides the most comprehensive capabilities for ML-specific plots?

A) Matplotlib and NumPy for basic plotting B) Seaborn and Pandas for statistical visualization C) Plotly and Scikit-learn for interactive ML visualizations D) Bokeh and TensorFlow for deep learning plots

Correct Answer: C - Plotly provides interactive visualization capabilities while scikit-learn includes specialized functions for ML performance visualization like ROC curves and confusion matrices.

Question 48: A dashboard needs to serve both executive-level KPI summaries and detailed operational metrics for different user groups. What design approach best accommodates these different requirements?

A) Single dashboard with all information visible to all users B) Separate dashboards optimized for each audience type C) Complex dashboard with extensive filtering options D) Basic dashboard with external detailed reports

Correct Answer: B - Separate dashboards optimized for specific audiences provide the best user experience by focusing on relevant information and appropriate detail levels for each user group.

Question 49: For monitoring data drift in production ML models, which visualization approach provides the most intuitive understanding of distribution changes?

A) Statistical summary tables with drift metrics B) Distribution overlay plots comparing current vs. training data C) Time-series plots of individual feature means D) Correlation heatmaps between features

Correct Answer: B - Distribution overlay plots provide visual comparison between current and training data distributions, making drift magnitude and direction immediately apparent to users.

Question 50: When implementing QuickSight dashboards that need to handle sensitive customer data, what security feature ensures users only see data they're authorized to access?

A) Dashboard-level access controls only B) Row-level security with user-based filtering C) Data source encryption at rest D) VPC isolation for QuickSight instances

Correct Answer: B - Row-level security filters data based on user identity and permissions, ensuring users can only access data they're authorized to see while maintaining dashboard functionality.

Question 51: A SageMaker notebook needs to generate automated visualizations during model training experiments. What approach provides the most efficient implementation?

A) Manual plotting code in each experiment notebook B) Template-based visualization functions with standard formats C) External visualization tools with data exports D) Screenshots of notebook outputs

Correct Answer: B - Template-based visualization functions provide consistency, reduce development time, and ensure standardized formats while enabling automation during training workflows.

Question 52: For QuickSight dashboards that need real-time updates from streaming data sources, what data source configuration provides the best performance?

A) Direct connection to streaming APIs B) Scheduled refresh from data lakes with streaming ingestion C) Real-time refresh with in-memory caching D) Manual data uploads at regular intervals

Correct Answer: B - Scheduled refresh from data lakes with streaming ingestion balances real-time data availability with dashboard performance while managing computational costs effectively.

Question 53: When designing visualizations for model interpretability, which approach best communicates feature importance to business stakeholders?

A) Raw coefficient values from linear models B) Statistical significance tests for each feature C) Horizontal bar charts with business-relevant feature names D) Complex mathematical explanations of importance calculations

Correct Answer: C - Horizontal bar charts with business-relevant feature names provide intuitive visual communication of relative feature importance that stakeholders can easily understand and act upon.

Question 54: A company needs to monitor model drift across multiple features simultaneously. What visualization technique provides the most comprehensive overview?

A) Individual time-series plots for each feature B) Heatmap showing drift scores across features and time periods C) Statistical summary tables with numerical drift metrics D) Alert-only system without visualizations

Correct Answer: B - Heatmaps provide comprehensive overview of drift patterns across multiple features and time periods, enabling quick identification of problem areas and trends.

Question 55: For stakeholder presentations of ML model results, what visualization principle is most important for ensuring clear communication?

A) Include all available technical details and metrics B) Use consistent color schemes and clear labeling C) Maximize data density to show complete information D) Focus on statistical significance over practical significance

Correct Answer: B - Consistent color schemes and clear labeling improve comprehension and professional presentation while avoiding confusion that complex or inconsistent design can create.

Question 56: When implementing automated anomaly detection alerts in QuickSight, what configuration approach minimizes false alarms while ensuring important issues are detected?

A) Maximum sensitivity settings to catch all potential issues B) Minimum sensitivity settings to reduce noise C) Adaptive thresholds based on historical patterns and business impact D) Fixed thresholds based on statistical distributions only

Correct Answer: C - Adaptive thresholds that consider both statistical patterns and business impact provide the best balance between detection sensitivity and practical alert management.

Question 57: A dashboard displays customer segmentation results from ML models. What visualization approach best supports business decision-making about segment-specific strategies?

A) Complex multi-dimensional scatter plots with all variables B) Simple bar charts showing segment sizes and key characteristics C) Technical clustering algorithm output displays D) Raw data tables with customer lists by segment

Correct Answer: B - Simple bar charts showing segment sizes and key characteristics provide actionable insights for business strategy while remaining accessible to non-technical stakeholders.

Question 58: For monitoring feature drift in categorical variables, which visualization technique most effectively shows changes in category distributions?

A) Line plots of category counts over time B) Stacked bar charts comparing time periods C) Pie charts of current category distributions D) Statistical tables with percentage changes

Correct Answer: B - Stacked bar charts enable easy comparison of category distributions across time periods while showing both absolute and relative changes in category frequencies.

Question 59: When creating custom visualizations in SageMaker for model performance analysis, what consideration is most important for reproducibility?

A) Using the most advanced visualization libraries available B) Creating interactive plots with maximum functionality C) Standardizing plot styles and saving configuration code D) Generating plots in multiple formats simultaneously

Correct Answer: C - Standardized plot styles and saved configuration code ensure reproducible visualizations across different experiments and team members while maintaining consistency.

Question 60: A company needs to create dashboards that work effectively on both desktop and mobile devices. What design principle best supports this requirement?

A) Design primarily for desktop with mobile as secondary consideration B) Create separate mobile and desktop dashboard versions C) Use responsive design principles with adaptive layouts D) Focus on mobile design and scale up for desktop

Correct Answer: C - Responsive design principles with adaptive layouts provide optimal user experience across different devices while maintaining functionality and visual appeal.

Chapter 10: SageMaker Built-in Algorithms Mastery

Machine learning algorithms represent the mathematical engines that transform data into predictions, yet many practitioners select algorithms based on familiarity rather than problem characteristics. SageMaker provides seventeen built-in algorithms optimized for AWS infrastructure, each designed for specific data types and business scenarios. Understanding when and how to apply each algorithm determines the difference between models that barely function and those that deliver exceptional business value.

The temptation to reach for familiar algorithms like XGBoost or linear regression overlooks the specialized capabilities of purpose-built algorithms that often provide superior performance with less configuration effort. SageMaker's built-in algorithms handle common preprocessing tasks automatically while providing optimizations that can reduce training time and improve accuracy significantly compared to generic implementations.

Classification and Regression Algorithms

SageMaker's supervised learning algorithms address the most common machine learning tasks where historical examples guide model training for prediction on new data. These algorithms vary significantly in their assumptions about data characteristics, computational requirements, and interpretability trade-offs.

Linear Learner for Scalable Linear Models:

Linear Learner provides distributed implementations of linear and logistic regression that scale to massive datasets while maintaining mathematical rigor. The algorithm automatically handles feature normalization, regularization, and multiple solver options that adapt to different data characteristics and performance requirements (20).

Automatic hyperparameter tuning explores different regularization strengths, learning rates, and optimization methods to find optimal configurations without manual intervention. This automation reduces the expertise barrier while ensuring models achieve near-optimal performance across diverse scenarios.

Multi-class and multi-label classification capabilities enable complex prediction scenarios including document categorization, product classification, and customer segmentation tasks. Advanced classification options handle imbalanced classes and cost-sensitive learning automatically.

Incremental learning support enables model updates as new data arrives without complete retraining, making Linear Learner suitable for streaming applications and continuously evolving datasets. This capability reduces computational costs while maintaining model currency.

XGBoost for Gradient Boosting Excellence:

SageMaker's XGBoost implementation provides optimized gradient boosting with automatic distributed training across multiple instances. The algorithm consistently ranks among top performers in machine learning competitions while remaining relatively interpretable compared to deep learning approaches.

Feature importance analysis provides automatic ranking of input variables by their contribution to prediction accuracy, enabling feature selection and business interpretation. Importance scores guide data collection priorities while supporting model explanation requirements.

Cross-validation integration provides reliable performance estimates that prevent overfitting while optimizing hyperparameters systematically. Built-in validation reduces the complexity of experimental design while ensuring robust model evaluation.

Early stopping capabilities prevent overfitting by monitoring validation performance and terminating training when improvements cease. This automation balances model complexity with generalization while reducing training time and computational costs.

Factorization Machines for Sparse Data:

Factorization Machines excel with sparse, high-dimensional data common in recommendation systems, click prediction, and categorical feature scenarios. The algorithm captures feature interactions efficiently while handling missing values and new categories gracefully.

Automatic feature crossing discovers interaction patterns between categorical variables without manual feature engineering. This capability proves particularly useful for recommendation systems where user-item interactions follow complex patterns.

Scalable training handles datasets with millions of features and billions of examples using distributed computing. The algorithm's linear scaling characteristics enable application to enterprise-scale recommendation and advertising scenarios.

Cold start handling provides reasonable predictions for new users or items without historical data, addressing common challenges in recommendation systems and personalization applications.

Case Example 1: E-commerce Product Recommendation Engine

An online retailer needed to predict customer purchase likelihood across 50,000 products for 2 million active customers. Traditional collaborative filtering approaches failed due to extreme sparsity (less than 0.01% of user-product combinations had interactions) and cold start problems for new products and customers.

The Factorization Machines implementation automatically handled sparse interaction matrices while discovering latent factors that captured user preferences and product characteristics. Feature engineering included user demographics, browsing history, seasonal patterns, and product attributes without manual interaction term creation.

Model performance achieved 15% improvement in click-through rates compared to previous content-based filtering while reducing training time from 8 hours to 45 minutes through distributed optimization. Real-time inference provided sub-100ms response times for personalized product rankings.

A/B testing demonstrated 12% increase in conversion rates and 18% improvement in average order value compared to the previous recommendation system. The business impact translated to $2.3 million additional quarterly revenue while reducing infrastructure costs through more efficient training and serving.

Clustering and Dimensionality Reduction

Unsupervised learning algorithms discover hidden patterns in data without labeled examples, enabling customer segmentation, anomaly detection, and data exploration tasks that guide business strategy and operational decisions.

K-Means for Customer Segmentation:

SageMaker's K-Means implementation provides scalable clustering with automatic initialization and distributed training that handles large customer datasets efficiently. The algorithm identifies distinct customer groups based on behavior patterns, demographics, and transaction characteristics.

Automatic cluster initialization using K-Means++ improves convergence speed and result quality compared to random initialization. This enhancement reduces sensitivity to random seeds while providing more stable and interpretable clusters.

Distributed training scales to millions of customers and hundreds of features while maintaining mathematical accuracy. Parallel processing reduces training time significantly while enabling real-time segmentation updates as customer behavior evolves.

Cluster interpretation tools provide statistical summaries and visualizations that help business teams understand segment characteristics and develop targeted strategies. Automated profiling reduces analysis time while ensuring consistent segment definitions.

Principal Component Analysis for Dimensionality Reduction:

PCA implementation provides scalable dimensionality reduction that preserves maximum variance while reducing computational complexity for downstream algorithms. The service handles large feature sets automatically while providing variance explanation metrics.

Incremental PCA enables processing of datasets that exceed memory limitations by computing principal components incrementally. This capability extends PCA application to enterprise-scale datasets without infrastructure constraints.

Automatic scaling and centering preprocess features appropriately while maintaining mathematical correctness. Preprocessing automation reduces implementation errors while ensuring optimal algorithm performance.

Component interpretation helps identify which original features contribute most to each principal component, enabling business understanding of the underlying data structure and relationships.

Case Example 2: Financial Services Customer Segmentation

A credit union needed to develop targeted marketing campaigns based on customer financial behavior patterns across checking accounts, savings accounts, loans, and investment products. Manual segmentation based on demographic categories missed important behavioral patterns and failed to adapt to changing customer needs.

K-Means clustering analysis revealed seven distinct customer segments based on transaction patterns, product usage, and financial goals. Segments included young professionals focused on convenience, families prioritizing savings, and retirees emphasizing investment income.

Feature engineering incorporated transaction frequency, balance trends, product adoption patterns, and seasonal behavior to create rich customer profiles. Automated feature scaling ensured all characteristics contributed appropriately to clustering results.

Marketing campaign performance improved dramatically with targeted messaging for each segment. Email open rates increased 35%, loan application rates increased 28%, and cross-selling success rates improved 42% compared to previous demographic-based campaigns.

Time Series and Forecasting Algorithms

Time series algorithms address prediction scenarios where temporal patterns, seasonality, and trend information drive accurate forecasting for business planning and operational optimization.

DeepAR for Probabilistic Forecasting:

DeepAR combines recurrent neural networks with probabilistic modeling to generate forecasts with uncertainty quantification. The algorithm handles multiple related time series simultaneously while learning patterns that improve individual forecast accuracy.

Cold start capabilities provide reasonable forecasts for new time series with limited historical data by leveraging patterns learned from related series. This feature proves essential for new product launches, store openings, and market expansion scenarios.

Automatic feature engineering captures temporal patterns, seasonality, and external factors without manual preprocessing. Built-in time series transformations reduce implementation complexity while ensuring optimal algorithm performance.

Quantile forecasting provides prediction intervals that enable risk-aware planning and decision-making. Uncertainty estimates support inventory optimization, capacity planning, and financial budgeting with appropriate risk considerations.

Linear Time Series for Simple Trends:

Linear Time Series provides efficient forecasting for data with clear trends and seasonal patterns using traditional statistical methods. The algorithm works well for stable business metrics with predictable behavior patterns.

Automatic seasonality detection identifies weekly, monthly, and yearly patterns without manual specification. Pattern recognition adapts to different business cycles while providing interpretable forecast components.

Trend analysis separates underlying growth from seasonal fluctuations, enabling strategic planning that accounts for both short-term variations and long-term direction. Component decomposition supports business interpretation and planning processes.

Fast training and inference make Linear Time Series suitable for scenarios requiring frequent forecast updates or real-time predictions. Computational efficiency enables application to large numbers of time series simultaneously.

Case Example 3: Retail Demand Forecasting

A grocery chain needed accurate demand forecasts for 15,000 products across 200 stores to optimize inventory levels while minimizing stockouts and waste. Traditional statistical methods failed to capture complex interactions between products, stores, promotions, and external factors like weather and holidays.

DeepAR implementation learned cross-product relationships and store-specific patterns while handling new product introductions and seasonal variations. The model incorporated external features including weather forecasts, promotional calendars, and local events.

Forecast accuracy improved 23% compared to previous statistical methods while providing uncertainty estimates that enabled risk-based inventory decisions. Quantile forecasts supported different service level targets for different product categories.

Business impact included 15% reduction in inventory carrying costs, 8% decrease in stockout rates, and 12% reduction in food waste. The improved forecasting enabled better supplier negotiations and more efficient supply chain operations.

Algorithm Selection Decision Tree

Choosing appropriate algorithms requires systematic evaluation of problem characteristics, data properties, and business requirements rather than defaulting to familiar options. A structured decision framework ensures optimal algorithm selection while avoiding common selection biases.

Problem Type Classification:

Supervised learning problems require labeled training examples and fall into classification (predicting categories) or regression (predicting continuous values) scenarios. Problem type determines the appropriate algorithm family while business requirements guide specific algorithm selection.

Unsupervised learning scenarios lack labeled examples and include clustering (finding groups), dimensionality reduction (simplifying data), and anomaly detection (identifying outliers). Business objectives determine which unsupervised approach provides most value.

Time series forecasting requires temporal data with prediction horizons and accuracy requirements that guide algorithm selection. Business planning cycles and decision-making timelines influence appropriate forecasting approaches and model complexity trade-offs.

Data Characteristics Assessment:

Dataset size influences algorithm selection significantly, with some algorithms requiring large datasets for optimal performance while others work well with smaller samples. Training data volume, feature counts, and computational constraints guide appropriate choices.

Feature types including numerical, categorical, text, and image data require different algorithm capabilities and preprocessing approaches. Mixed data types may require ensemble methods or specialized algorithms designed for heterogeneous inputs.

Data quality considerations including missing values, outliers, and noise levels affect algorithm robustness requirements. Some algorithms handle imperfect data gracefully while others require extensive preprocessing for reliable performance.

Business Requirements Integration:

Interpretability requirements vary significantly across applications, with some scenarios demanding clear explanations while others prioritize predictive accuracy. Regulatory environments and stakeholder needs influence the interpretability-performance trade-off.

Latency constraints for real-time applications limit algorithm complexity and influence serving architecture decisions. Inference speed requirements must be balanced against model accuracy and computational costs.

Cost sensitivity analysis considers both training costs and ongoing serving expenses while evaluating algorithm alternatives. Total cost of ownership includes development time, infrastructure requirements, and maintenance overhead.

Performance Benchmarking Strategies

Systematic algorithm evaluation requires standardized benchmarking approaches that account for business objectives, data characteristics, and operational constraints. Proper benchmarking prevents algorithm selection based on insufficient or misleading performance assessments.

Cross-Validation Framework:

Time series cross-validation uses temporal splits that respect the chronological nature of data while providing realistic performance estimates. Forward-chaining validation prevents data leakage while simulating real-world prediction scenarios.

Stratified sampling ensures balanced representation across different data segments during validation, particularly important for imbalanced datasets or heterogeneous populations. Stratification improves performance estimate reliability while reducing variance.

Nested cross-validation provides unbiased hyperparameter optimization by separating model selection from performance estimation. This approach prevents overfitting to validation sets while providing realistic generalization estimates.

Business Metric Alignment:

Technical metrics like accuracy or RMSE may not reflect business value accurately, requiring custom evaluation metrics that align with actual business objectives. Revenue impact, customer satisfaction, and operational efficiency provide better algorithm comparison criteria.

Cost-weighted evaluation incorporates different costs for different types of errors while optimizing for business outcomes rather than technical performance. Asymmetric costs require specialized metrics that reflect real business consequences.

Multi-objective optimization balances competing objectives like accuracy and fairness, or performance and interpretability. Pareto frontier analysis helps identify optimal trade-offs while considering stakeholder priorities.

Statistical Significance Testing:

Hypothesis testing determines whether observed performance differences represent genuine algorithm superiority or random variation. Statistical rigor prevents incorrect algorithm selection based on noise rather than systematic improvement.

Effect size analysis quantifies the practical significance of performance differences while considering business relevance. Large statistical significance with small effect sizes may not justify algorithm changes or additional complexity.

Bootstrap confidence intervals provide robust performance estimates that account for sampling variation while supporting algorithm comparison decisions. Confidence intervals enable risk-aware algorithm selection based on performance uncertainty.

Cost-Performance Tradeoffs

Algorithm selection requires careful evaluation of the relationship between model performance and total cost of ownership, including development time, training costs, serving infrastructure, and maintenance overhead.

Training Cost Analysis:

Computational complexity varies dramatically across algorithms, with some requiring minutes of training while others need hours or days for optimal performance. Training costs must be evaluated against performance improvements and business value.

Distributed training capabilities enable handling of large datasets while reducing training time through parallel processing. Some algorithms scale efficiently across multiple instances while others show diminishing returns with additional resources.

Automated hyperparameter tuning reduces manual optimization effort but increases computational costs through systematic parameter exploration. Tuning costs must be balanced against performance improvements and development time savings.

Serving Infrastructure Requirements:

Inference latency requirements determine appropriate serving architectures and influence algorithm selection for real-time applications. Complex algorithms may require specialized hardware or caching strategies that increase serving costs.

Memory footprint considerations affect serving infrastructure costs, particularly for algorithms with large model sizes or those requiring significant preprocessing. Memory requirements scale with features and training data size.

Throughput capabilities determine how many predictions algorithms can generate per second while maintaining acceptable latency. High-throughput scenarios may require algorithm modifications or specialized serving architectures.

Project: Algorithm Shootout Framework

This project builds a systematic framework for comparing multiple algorithms across different performance dimensions while accounting for business requirements and operational constraints.

Experimental Design Framework:

Standardized data splitting ensures fair algorithm comparison through consistent train/validation/test partitions across all experiments. Reproducible splits enable reliable comparison while preventing data leakage that could bias results.

Hyperparameter optimization protocols provide each algorithm with appropriate tuning while maintaining computational budget constraints. Fair optimization ensures algorithms receive adequate tuning without overwhelming computational resources.

Performance measurement protocols capture both technical metrics and business-relevant measures while providing statistical significance testing. Standardized measurement enables objective algorithm comparison and selection.

Automation Infrastructure:

Pipeline orchestration manages multiple algorithm training and evaluation experiments while tracking results systematically. Automated workflows reduce manual effort while ensuring consistent experimental procedures.

Resource management optimizes computational resource allocation across multiple algorithm training jobs while managing costs effectively. Dynamic resource allocation balances experiment throughput with budget constraints.

Result aggregation and reporting provide comprehensive algorithm comparison dashboards that support decision-making. Automated reporting reduces analysis overhead while ensuring stakeholder communication.

Business Impact Assessment:

Cost modeling incorporates training costs, serving infrastructure requirements, and development time into algorithm comparison. Total cost of ownership analysis enables informed decisions about algorithm trade-offs.

Performance simulation estimates business impact of different algorithm choices using historical data and business models. Impact simulation translates technical performance into business value for stakeholder communication.

Risk analysis evaluates algorithm robustness and failure modes while considering business continuity requirements. Risk assessment ensures algorithm selection considers operational reliability alongside performance metrics.

Professional Algorithm Selection

Successful algorithm selection requires combining technical understanding with business judgment while avoiding common cognitive biases that lead to suboptimal choices. Systematic evaluation frameworks ensure optimal decisions while maintaining practical implementation constraints.

The investment in proper algorithm evaluation pays dividends through improved model performance, reduced development time, and more reliable production systems. Quality algorithm selection establishes foundations for successful model deployment and business impact.

Moving Forward with Confidence

The algorithm mastery developed here provides the foundation for custom model development and advanced optimization techniques covered in subsequent sections. Understanding built-in algorithm capabilities enables informed decisions about when custom development provides sufficient additional value to justify the complexity.

Essential Takeaways

- SageMaker's seventeen built-in algorithms provide optimized implementations for common ML tasks with automatic scaling and hyperparameter tuning
- Algorithm selection requires systematic evaluation of problem characteristics, data properties, and business requirements rather than defaulting to familiar options
- Performance benchmarking must align technical metrics with business objectives while providing statistical significance testing
- Cost-performance tradeoffs require evaluation of total ownership costs including training, serving infrastructure, and maintenance overhead
- Systematic algorithm comparison frameworks enable objective selection while accounting for business constraints and operational requirements

Chapter 11: Custom Model Development

Built-in algorithms provide excellent starting points for many machine learning scenarios, but business requirements often demand specialized approaches that require custom model development. The decision to build custom models should be driven by clear performance or capability gaps that justify the additional complexity, development time, and maintenance overhead compared to standard implementations.

SageMaker provides multiple pathways for custom model development, from simple script modifications to completely custom containers, each with different complexity levels and capability trade-offs. Understanding these options enables informed decisions about the appropriate level of customization while maintaining development efficiency and operational reliability.

Bring Your Own Container (BYOC) Fundamentals

The Bring Your Own Container approach provides maximum flexibility for custom model development while maintaining integration with SageMaker's training and serving infrastructure. BYOC enables use of specialized libraries, custom preprocessing logic, and proprietary algorithms that aren't available in standard implementations (21).

Container Architecture Requirements:

SageMaker containers must implement specific interfaces for training and inference that enable seamless integration with the platform's orchestration capabilities. Training containers receive data through mounted volumes while inference containers expose HTTP endpoints for prediction requests.

Environment variable handling provides configuration information including hyperparameters, data locations, and resource specifications without hardcoding values in container images. Proper environment handling enables flexible container reuse across different experiments and deployment scenarios.

Signal handling ensures containers respond appropriately to orchestration events including graceful shutdown requests and resource limit notifications. Correct signal implementation prevents data corruption and enables reliable container lifecycle management.

Health check endpoints enable SageMaker to monitor container status and respond to failures appropriately. Health checks should validate critical dependencies while responding quickly to avoid unnecessary container restarts.

Development Workflow Optimization:

Local development and testing reduces iteration time by enabling container debugging outside of SageMaker's managed environment. Local workflows identify issues early while reducing development costs through faster feedback cycles.

Image layering strategies optimize container build times and storage efficiency by separating stable dependencies from frequently changed code. Effective layering reduces development iteration time while minimizing container registry storage costs.

Multi-stage builds separate development dependencies from production runtime requirements while maintaining lean production images. Build optimization balances development convenience with production efficiency and security requirements.

Security scanning integration identifies vulnerabilities in container dependencies while ensuring compliance with organizational security policies. Automated scanning prevents deployment of vulnerable containers while maintaining development velocity.

Integration with SageMaker Services:

Training job integration enables custom containers to leverage SageMaker's distributed training capabilities while accessing managed data sources and experiment tracking. Integration maintains development simplicity while providing production-scale capabilities.

Model registry compatibility ensures custom models integrate with SageMaker's model management and deployment pipelines. Registry integration provides version control and approval workflows while maintaining deployment automation.

Endpoint serving integration enables custom inference containers to benefit from auto-scaling, monitoring, and blue-green deployment capabilities. Serving integration maintains operational excellence while supporting custom inference logic.

Case Example 1: Financial Time Series Risk Modeling

A hedge fund needed to implement proprietary time series models that incorporated alternative data sources including satellite imagery, social media sentiment, and economic indicators. Standard algorithms couldn't capture the complex multi-modal relationships that drove their investment strategy.

The BYOC implementation combined deep learning frameworks with custom mathematical libraries for options pricing and risk calculation. Container dependencies included specialized financial libraries, geospatial processing tools, and custom optimization algorithms not available in standard environments.

Training workflows processed terabytes of alternative data while maintaining compliance with financial regulations and data privacy requirements. Custom preprocessing logic handled data fusion from disparate sources while implementing proprietary feature engineering techniques.

Model performance achieved 18% improvement in risk-adjusted returns compared to previous approaches while reducing portfolio volatility by 12%. The custom implementation enabled competitive advantages that weren't possible with standard algorithms while maintaining operational reliability.

TensorFlow and PyTorch on SageMaker

SageMaker provides managed environments for TensorFlow and PyTorch that simplify custom deep learning model development while providing access to optimized infrastructure and distributed training capabilities. These frameworks enable sophisticated neural network architectures while maintaining development productivity.

Framework-Specific Optimizations:

TensorFlow integration includes XLA (Accelerated Linear Algebra) compilation that optimizes computational graphs for specific hardware configurations. XLA optimization can improve training speed by 20-40% while reducing memory usage for large models.

PyTorch distributed data parallel capabilities enable efficient multi-GPU training with automatic gradient synchronization and communication optimization. Distributed training scales model development to larger datasets while reducing training time significantly.

Mixed precision training support enables use of lower precision arithmetic that accelerates training while maintaining model accuracy. Mixed precision can reduce training time by 50% on modern GPUs while decreasing memory requirements.

Automatic model optimization converts trained models to optimized formats suitable for inference while maintaining compatibility with SageMaker serving infrastructure. Optimization includes graph simplification, operator fusion, and quantization techniques.

Custom Architecture Development:

Modular architecture design enables reusable components that can be combined for different model variations while maintaining code quality and testing coverage. Modular approaches accelerate development while reducing maintenance overhead.

Transfer learning integration enables leveraging pre-trained models as starting points for custom architectures while adapting to specific domain requirements. Transfer learning reduces training time and data requirements while improving model performance.

Custom loss function implementation enables optimization for business-specific objectives that aren't captured by standard loss functions. Custom losses align model training with actual business outcomes while maintaining mathematical correctness.

Regularization technique integration includes dropout, batch normalization, and custom regularization methods that prevent overfitting while improving generalization. Proper regularization ensures models perform well on unseen data while maintaining training efficiency.

Memory and Computational Optimization:

Gradient checkpointing reduces memory usage during training by recomputing intermediate values rather than storing them, enabling larger models or batch sizes with the same hardware. Checkpointing trades computation for memory while maintaining mathematical correctness.

Dynamic batching optimizes memory usage by adapting batch sizes to available hardware resources while maintaining training stability. Dynamic approaches maximize resource utilization while preventing out-of-memory errors.

Model parallelism enables training of models too large for single GPUs by distributing model components across multiple devices. Parallelism strategies balance computation and communication costs while scaling to larger model sizes.

Data loading optimization ensures training processes aren't bottlenecked by data access through efficient preprocessing pipelines and caching strategies. Optimized data loading maintains high GPU utilization while reducing training time.

Distributed Training Strategies

Large-scale model training requires distributed approaches that coordinate multiple compute resources while maintaining mathematical correctness and training efficiency. Understanding different distribution strategies enables optimal resource utilization while minimizing communication overhead.

Data Parallelism Implementation:

Synchronous data parallelism distributes training data across multiple workers while aggregating gradients before parameter updates. Synchronous approaches maintain mathematical equivalence to single-machine training while providing linear scaling for appropriate workloads.

Asynchronous parameter updates enable faster iteration by allowing workers to proceed independently, but introduce staleness that can affect convergence. Asynchronous training requires careful tuning to balance speed improvements with training stability.

Gradient compression reduces communication overhead in distributed training by compressing gradient information before aggregation. Compression techniques include quantization, sparsification, and error feedback that maintain training accuracy while reducing bandwidth requirements.

All-reduce optimization minimizes communication latency by using efficient gradient aggregation algorithms that scale logarithmically with worker count. Optimized communication enables scaling to hundreds of workers while maintaining training efficiency.

Model Parallelism Approaches:

Pipeline parallelism divides models into sequential stages that process different data batches concurrently while maintaining dependency relationships. Pipeline approaches enable training of models too large for single devices while maximizing hardware utilization.

Tensor parallelism distributes individual layers across multiple devices while maintaining mathematical correctness through carefully designed communication patterns. Tensor approaches enable scaling of extremely large models while minimizing communication overhead.

Hybrid parallelism combines data and model parallelism to optimize resource utilization for specific model architectures and hardware configurations. Hybrid strategies balance computational and communication requirements while maximizing training throughput.

Case Example 2: Large Language Model Training

A technology company needed to train domain-specific language models for legal document analysis using proprietary legal databases and specialized vocabulary. Standard pre-trained models lacked domain knowledge while generic fine-tuning approaches didn't capture complex legal reasoning patterns.

Distributed PyTorch implementation used pipeline parallelism to train 20-billion parameter models across multiple GPU instances while maintaining training stability. Pipeline optimization balanced compute utilization with communication efficiency while scaling to 64 GPUs.

Custom tokenization and vocabulary handling incorporated legal terminology and document structure while maintaining compatibility with transformer architectures. Domain-specific preprocessing improved model understanding of legal concepts while reducing training data requirements.

Model performance achieved 35% improvement in legal document classification accuracy compared to general-purpose models while reducing annotation requirements by 60%. The domain-specific approach enabled automated legal research capabilities that provided significant competitive advantages.

GPU Optimization Techniques

Graphics Processing Units provide the computational power needed for large-scale machine learning training, but achieving optimal performance requires understanding GPU architecture and optimization techniques that maximize utilization while minimizing costs.

Memory Management Strategies:

GPU memory optimization requires careful management of tensors, gradients, and intermediate values to maximize batch sizes while preventing out-of-memory errors. Memory profiling identifies bottlenecks while guiding optimization efforts.

Gradient accumulation enables training with larger effective batch sizes by accumulating gradients across multiple forward passes before parameter updates. Accumulation techniques overcome memory limitations while maintaining training stability.

Memory pooling reduces allocation overhead by reusing memory buffers across training iterations while preventing memory fragmentation. Pooling strategies improve training throughput while reducing memory management overhead.

Activation recomputation trades computation for memory by recomputing intermediate values during backpropagation rather than storing them. Recomputation enables larger models or batch sizes while maintaining mathematical correctness.

Computational Optimization:

Kernel fusion combines multiple operations into single GPU kernels that reduce memory bandwidth requirements while improving computational efficiency. Fusion optimization requires deep understanding of operation patterns and GPU architecture.

Quantization reduces numerical precision to accelerate computation while maintaining model accuracy through careful calibration. Quantization techniques include 8-bit integers, mixed precision, and dynamic scaling that balance speed with quality.

Sparsity exploitation leverages sparse tensor operations that skip zero computations while maintaining mathematical correctness. Sparsity optimizations become particularly important for large models with natural sparsity patterns.

Multi-GPU Coordination:

NUMA topology awareness optimizes data placement and communication patterns based on hardware architecture while minimizing transfer latencies. Topology optimization ensures efficient scaling across multiple GPUs and compute nodes.

Communication overlap hides gradient synchronization latency by overlapping computation with communication while maintaining training correctness. Overlap techniques improve training throughput while scaling to larger distributed systems.

Load balancing ensures even work distribution across GPUs while adapting to different model architectures and data characteristics. Balanced loading maximizes resource utilization while preventing training bottlenecks.

Project: Custom Model with Automatic Scaling

This project develops a custom model training and serving system that automatically scales based on demand while maintaining cost efficiency and performance standards.

Model Architecture Design:

Modular neural network architecture enables flexible model scaling and configuration while maintaining reusable components across different problem scenarios. Architecture modularity accelerates development while ensuring consistent implementation quality.

Transfer learning integration provides pre-trained foundation models that can be adapted for specific domains while reducing training time and data requirements. Transfer learning strategies balance customization with development efficiency.

Multi-objective optimization balances model accuracy, inference latency, and resource utilization while adapting to different deployment scenarios. Optimization techniques enable automatic trade-off management based on business requirements.

Training Infrastructure:

Distributed training orchestration manages multi-GPU training jobs while optimizing resource allocation and cost efficiency. Orchestration systems handle resource procurement, job scheduling, and failure recovery automatically.

Experiment tracking integration maintains comprehensive records of training configurations, performance metrics, and resource utilization while supporting reproducibility and comparison. Tracking systems enable systematic model improvement and optimization.

Automatic hyperparameter optimization explores model configurations systematically while balancing exploration with computational budget constraints. Optimization strategies adapt to model characteristics while maintaining development velocity.

Serving Architecture:

Auto-scaling inference endpoints adjust capacity based on request patterns while maintaining latency requirements and cost efficiency. Scaling policies balance responsiveness with resource utilization while adapting to traffic variations.

Model version management enables blue-green deployments and gradual rollouts while maintaining serving availability during updates. Version management supports safe model deployment while enabling rapid rollback if issues arise.

Performance monitoring tracks inference latency, throughput, and resource utilization while providing alerts for performance degradation. Monitoring systems enable proactive performance management while supporting capacity planning.

Cost Optimization:

Spot instance utilization reduces training costs while implementing fault tolerance mechanisms that handle instance interruptions gracefully. Spot strategies balance cost savings with training reliability while maintaining development velocity.

Resource scheduling optimizes training job timing to take advantage of lower-cost periods while meeting deadline requirements. Scheduling optimization reduces costs while maintaining development productivity and business requirements.

Model compression techniques reduce serving infrastructure requirements while maintaining prediction accuracy through quantization, pruning, and knowledge distillation. Compression strategies balance performance with cost efficiency while meeting latency requirements.

Building Production-Ready Custom Models

Custom model development requires balancing innovation with operational reliability while ensuring models meet production requirements for performance, scalability, and maintainability. Production readiness involves more than model accuracy and requires comprehensive system design.

Testing strategies must cover model behavior, infrastructure reliability, and business logic while ensuring comprehensive coverage of edge cases and failure modes. Quality assurance prevents production issues while maintaining development velocity.

Documentation and knowledge transfer ensure custom models can be maintained and improved by different team members while preserving institutional knowledge and implementation details.

Advancing to Sophisticated Solutions

Custom model development provides the foundation for advanced optimization and automation techniques that further improve model performance while reducing operational overhead. The capabilities established here enable more sophisticated MLOps practices and business applications.

Essential Takeaways

- BYOC provides maximum flexibility for custom models while requiring careful attention to container interfaces and SageMaker integration requirements
- TensorFlow and PyTorch on SageMaker offer framework-specific optimizations while maintaining managed infrastructure benefits
- Distributed training strategies enable scaling to larger models and datasets while requiring optimization of communication and coordination overhead
- GPU optimization techniques maximize computational efficiency while managing memory constraints and cost considerations
- Custom model projects require comprehensive architecture that balances performance, scalability, and operational requirements

Chapter 12: Hyperparameter Optimization and AutoML

Hyperparameter optimization represents one of the most time-consuming and expertise-dependent aspects of machine learning model development, yet it often determines the difference between mediocre and exceptional model performance. Traditional manual tuning approaches consume weeks of expert time while exploring only tiny fractions of possible parameter combinations, leaving significant performance improvements undiscovered.

AWS SageMaker provides automated hyperparameter optimization and AutoML capabilities that democratize advanced optimization techniques while achieving better results than manual approaches in fraction of the time. These automation capabilities enable both novice practitioners and expert data scientists to achieve superior model performance while focusing their expertise on higher-value activities like problem formulation and business impact analysis.

SageMaker Automatic Model Tuning

SageMaker's automatic model tuning service uses sophisticated optimization algorithms to explore hyperparameter spaces intelligently while minimizing the number of training jobs required to find optimal configurations. This approach dramatically reduces the time and computational resources needed for effective hyperparameter optimization (22).

Bayesian Optimization Foundations:

Bayesian optimization treats hyperparameter tuning as a sequential decision problem where each training job provides information that guides selection of the next parameter combination to evaluate. This intelligent exploration focuses computational resources on promising regions of parameter space rather than random or grid-based exploration.

Gaussian process modeling builds probabilistic models of the relationship between hyperparameters and model performance, enabling prediction of performance for untested parameter combinations. These predictive models guide optimization toward areas likely to yield improvements while balancing exploration of uncertain regions.

Acquisition functions determine which parameter combinations to evaluate next by balancing exploitation of known good regions with exploration of uncertain areas. Different acquisition functions like Expected Improvement and Upper Confidence Bound provide different exploration strategies for various optimization scenarios.

Early stopping integration prevents wasting computational resources on obviously poor parameter combinations by terminating training jobs that show no promise of achieving competitive performance. Early stopping can reduce optimization time by 60-80% while maintaining solution quality.

Search Strategy Configuration:

Random search provides baseline optimization performance while serving as a robust fallback when more sophisticated strategies encounter difficulties. Random search often outperforms grid search while requiring no domain knowledge about parameter relationships.

Hyperband optimization combines random search with early stopping to efficiently explore parameter spaces while adaptively allocating resources to promising configurations. Hyperband provides strong performance guarantees while scaling to large parameter spaces efficiently.

Multi-fidelity optimization uses faster approximate evaluations (smaller datasets, fewer epochs) to guide selection of candidates for full evaluation. Multi-fidelity approaches can reduce optimization time by 90% while maintaining solution quality for appropriate problem types.

Parallel optimization coordinates multiple training jobs to explore parameter space efficiently while managing computational budgets. Parallel strategies balance exploration breadth with computational efficiency while adapting to available resources.

Performance Metric Optimization:

Objective metric selection determines what the optimization process maximizes, requiring careful alignment with business goals rather than defaulting to accuracy or loss functions. Business-relevant metrics like F1-score, AUC, or custom business metrics often provide better optimization targets.

Multi-metric optimization handles scenarios where multiple objectives matter simultaneously, such as balancing accuracy with inference latency or model size. Multi-objective approaches identify Pareto-optimal solutions that represent different trade-offs between competing objectives.

Constraints handling enables optimization subject to requirements like maximum inference time, minimum precision, or resource utilization limits. Constrained optimization ensures solutions meet operational requirements while maximizing performance within feasible regions.

Case Example 1: Fraud Detection Model Optimization

A payment processing company needed to optimize fraud detection models that balanced fraud catch rates with false positive impacts on customer experience. Manual tuning required weeks of expert time while achieving suboptimal trade-offs between competing objectives.

Automatic model tuning explored 200 hyperparameter combinations across multiple algorithms while optimizing for a custom business metric that weighted false negatives ten times more heavily than false positives. The optimization incorporated operational constraints including maximum inference latency and minimum daily processing capacity.

Results achieved 23% improvement in fraud detection rates while reducing false positives by 15% compared to manually tuned baselines. Optimization completed in 3 days rather than the 2-3 weeks typically required for manual approaches while exploring parameter combinations no human expert would have considered.

Business impact included preventing an additional $1.2M in fraudulent transactions annually while reducing customer service calls about declined legitimate transactions by 18%. The automated approach enabled rapid adaptation to new fraud patterns while maintaining operational efficiency.

Bayesian Optimization Strategies

Bayesian optimization provides principled approaches to hyperparameter tuning that leverage probabilistic models to guide search efficiently. Understanding Bayesian optimization principles enables effective application while avoiding common pitfalls that reduce optimization effectiveness.

Surrogate Model Selection:

Gaussian processes provide flexible surrogate models that capture uncertainty about parameter relationships while scaling to moderate-dimensional parameter spaces. GP models adapt to parameter space structure automatically while providing calibrated uncertainty estimates.

Random forests offer alternative surrogate models that handle categorical parameters and high-dimensional spaces more naturally than Gaussian processes. Tree-based surrogates scale better to large parameter spaces while maintaining reasonable computational efficiency.

Neural network surrogates enable modeling of complex parameter relationships in high-dimensional spaces while providing fast evaluation for acquisition function optimization. Neural surrogates trade training overhead for evaluation speed while handling complex parameter interactions.

Ensemble surrogates combine multiple surrogate model types to improve robustness and capture different aspects of parameter space structure. Ensemble approaches provide better uncertainty calibration while reducing sensitivity to surrogate model selection.

Acquisition Function Design:

Expected Improvement balances exploitation of known good regions with exploration of uncertain areas while providing intuitive trade-off control through exploration parameters. EI provides robust performance across diverse optimization scenarios while maintaining computational efficiency.

Probability of Improvement focuses optimization on parameter combinations likely to exceed current best performance while providing conservative exploration behavior. PI works well for scenarios where finding any improvement matters more than finding large improvements.

Upper Confidence Bound uses uncertainty estimates to guide exploration while providing theoretical convergence guarantees for appropriate problem classes. UCB provides principled exploration control while adapting to optimization progress automatically.

Knowledge gradient acquisition functions optimize for maximum information gain rather than immediate performance improvement while considering finite optimization budgets. KG approaches work particularly well for expensive evaluation scenarios with limited computational resources.

Multi-Objective Optimization:

Pareto frontier estimation identifies trade-offs between competing objectives while providing decision-makers with multiple optimal solutions representing different priorities.

Pareto approaches enable informed trade-off decisions while considering stakeholder preferences.

Scalarization techniques combine multiple objectives into single optimization targets while preserving solution diversity through different weighting schemes. Scalarization simplifies optimization while requiring careful weight selection to capture desired trade-offs.

Hypervolume improvement measures solution set quality by considering dominated volume in objective space while providing robust progress indicators for multi-objective optimization. Hypervolume metrics guide optimization toward well-distributed Pareto frontiers.

SageMaker Autopilot for Rapid Prototyping

SageMaker Autopilot provides end-to-end automated machine learning that handles data preprocessing, algorithm selection, hyperparameter optimization, and model interpretation without requiring deep ML expertise. Autopilot enables rapid prototyping while providing transparency about modeling decisions (23).

Automated Feature Engineering:

Data type detection automatically identifies numerical, categorical, and text features while applying appropriate preprocessing transformations. Automatic detection reduces manual preprocessing effort while ensuring appropriate handling of different data types.

Missing value imputation uses sophisticated strategies that consider feature relationships and missing patterns while maintaining statistical validity. Intelligent imputation preserves data relationships while enabling complete case analysis for downstream algorithms.

Feature transformation includes scaling, encoding, and mathematical transformations that improve algorithm performance while maintaining interpretability. Automated transformations apply best practices while adapting to specific data characteristics and algorithm requirements.

Feature selection identifies most informative variables while removing redundant or noisy features that could degrade model performance. Selection algorithms balance predictive value with model complexity while maintaining adequate feature diversity.

Algorithm Selection and Evaluation:

Automated algorithm screening evaluates multiple algorithm families including linear models, tree-based methods, and neural networks while identifying most promising approaches for specific datasets. Screening saves development time while ensuring consideration of diverse algorithmic approaches.

Cross-validation strategies provide reliable performance estimates while accounting for data characteristics and evaluation requirements. Automated validation prevents overfitting while providing realistic performance expectations for production deployment.

Ensemble methods combine multiple algorithms to achieve better performance than individual models while maintaining reliability and robustness. Ensemble approaches balance performance improvement with model complexity while providing automatic algorithm combination.

Model interpretation includes feature importance analysis, partial dependence plots, and explanation summaries that help understand model behavior and build stakeholder confidence. Interpretation capabilities make automated models accessible to business users while supporting regulatory requirements.

Deployment and Monitoring Integration:

One-click deployment enables immediate transition from development to production serving while maintaining performance and reliability standards. Automated deployment reduces time-to-value while ensuring proper configuration and monitoring setup.

Model monitoring integration provides automatic drift detection and performance tracking that alerts when models require attention or retraining. Monitoring automation maintains model reliability while reducing operational overhead.

Cost optimization provides recommendations for serving infrastructure that balance performance requirements with operational expenses. Cost guidance helps organizations deploy models efficiently while meeting business requirements.

Case Example 2: Small Business Loan Approval Automation

A community bank needed to automate small business loan approval decisions while maintaining regulatory compliance and fair lending practices. Traditional manual underwriting required 2-3 weeks per application while creating consistency issues across different loan officers.

Autopilot analysis processed five years of loan performance data including financial statements, credit scores, business characteristics, and economic indicators. The automated feature engineering identified 47 predictive features from 200+ original variables while handling missing data appropriately.

Model performance achieved 92% accuracy in predicting loan default risk while providing interpretable explanations for each decision. The automated approach identified previously unknown risk factors while maintaining compliance with fair lending regulations through bias detection and mitigation.

Implementation reduced loan approval time from 3 weeks to 2 days while improving prediction accuracy by 15% compared to manual underwriting. The automated system processed 3x more loan applications while maintaining consistent decision quality across all applications.

Multi-Objective Optimization

Real-world machine learning applications often require balancing multiple competing objectives like accuracy versus latency, performance versus fairness, or predictive power versus interpretability. Multi-objective optimization provides principled approaches to these trade-offs while identifying optimal solutions.

Pareto Optimality Concepts:

Pareto optimal solutions represent configurations where improving one objective requires sacrificing performance on other objectives. Understanding Pareto optimality enables identification of fundamental trade-offs while avoiding suboptimal compromises.

Dominated solution identification eliminates configurations that are strictly worse on all objectives while focusing optimization effort on non-dominated alternatives. Dominance analysis reduces solution complexity while maintaining optimal choices.

Solution diversity ensures Pareto frontiers represent different trade-off preferences while providing decision-makers with meaningful alternatives. Diversity preservation prevents convergence to narrow solution clusters while maintaining choice flexibility.

Trade-off Analysis:

Sensitivity analysis quantifies how changes in one objective affect others while providing guidance about acceptable trade-off ranges. Sensitivity insights help stakeholders understand costs of different priority decisions while informing requirement negotiations.

Knee point identification finds solutions that provide good balance across objectives while avoiding extreme trade-offs that heavily sacrifice any single objective. Knee solutions often provide practical starting points for stakeholder discussions about acceptable trade-offs.

Business impact modeling translates technical trade-offs into business terms while enabling stakeholder evaluation of different solution alternatives. Impact modeling bridges technical optimization with business decision-making while ensuring alignment with organizational priorities.

Implementation Strategies:

Weighted sum approaches combine multiple objectives into single optimization targets while exploring different trade-offs through systematic weight variation. Weighted approaches require careful calibration while providing computational efficiency for large-scale optimization.

Epsilon-constraint methods optimize primary objectives subject to constraints on secondary objectives while systematically varying constraint levels. Constraint approaches provide explicit control over trade-offs while ensuring minimum performance levels on all objectives.

Evolutionary multi-objective algorithms maintain populations of diverse solutions while evolving toward Pareto optimal frontiers through selection and variation operators. Evolutionary approaches handle complex objective landscapes while providing robust optimization performance.

Project: Automated Model Selection Pipeline

This project builds a production system that automatically evaluates multiple algorithms and optimization strategies while selecting optimal models based on comprehensive performance assessment.

Pipeline Architecture Design:

Modular optimization framework supports pluggable algorithms, hyperparameter strategies, and evaluation metrics while maintaining consistent experimental protocols. Modular design enables systematic comparison while adapting to different problem requirements.

Resource management optimizes computational allocation across multiple optimization experiments while managing costs and completion times. Management systems balance exploration breadth with resource constraints while ensuring fair algorithm evaluation.

Result tracking and comparison maintains comprehensive experiment records while enabling systematic performance analysis and model selection. Tracking systems support reproducibility while providing audit trails for model approval processes.

Algorithm Evaluation Framework:

Standardized preprocessing ensures fair algorithm comparison while maintaining appropriate data handling for different algorithm requirements. Standardization prevents preprocessing bias while enabling meaningful performance comparison across diverse algorithmic approaches.

Performance metric calculation includes technical metrics, business objectives, and operational requirements while providing comprehensive model assessment. Metric frameworks adapt to different problem types while maintaining evaluation consistency.

Statistical significance testing determines whether performance differences represent genuine algorithm superiority while controlling for multiple comparisons. Statistical rigor prevents false conclusions while providing confidence in model selection decisions.

Optimization Strategy Integration:

Hyperparameter optimization coordination manages multiple optimization strategies while adapting approaches to algorithm characteristics and computational budgets. Coordination systems balance optimization thoroughness with practical constraints while ensuring adequate exploration.

Multi-objective handling balances competing performance requirements while identifying Pareto optimal solutions for stakeholder evaluation. Multi-objective frameworks support complex decision-making while maintaining mathematical rigor.

Early stopping coordination prevents computational waste while ensuring adequate optimization exploration for reliable model selection. Stopping strategies balance resource efficiency with solution quality while adapting to optimization progress.

Model Selection and Deployment:

Automated model ranking combines multiple performance dimensions while accounting for stakeholder priorities and operational requirements. Ranking systems provide objective model selection while supporting business decision-making processes.

A/B testing integration enables validation of automated model selection through controlled experiments that measure real-world performance impact. Testing frameworks provide empirical validation while supporting confidence in automated decisions.

Deployment automation enables seamless transition from model selection to production serving while maintaining performance monitoring and rollback capabilities. Automation reduces deployment friction while ensuring operational reliability.

Professional Optimization Practices

Successful hyperparameter optimization requires combining automated tools with domain expertise while understanding business constraints and operational requirements. Automation enhances rather than replaces human expertise while improving optimization efficiency and reliability.

Experimental design principles ensure optimization experiments provide reliable and actionable results while managing computational resources effectively. Good experimental practices prevent bias while supporting confident decision-making about model selection and deployment.

Stakeholder communication about optimization results requires translating technical performance into business impact while ensuring understanding of trade-offs and limitations. Effective communication builds confidence in automated approaches while supporting informed business decisions.

The Optimization Advantage

Advanced optimization capabilities provide competitive advantages through better model performance, faster development cycles, and more reliable production systems.

Organizations that master optimization techniques achieve superior results while reducing development costs and time-to-market.

The optimization foundations established here enable advanced model evaluation and validation techniques that further improve model reliability and business impact. Quality optimization practices support confident model deployment while reducing operational risks.

Essential Takeaways

- SageMaker automatic model tuning uses Bayesian optimization to efficiently explore hyperparameter spaces while achieving better results than manual approaches
- Bayesian optimization strategies balance exploration and exploitation while adapting to parameter space characteristics and computational constraints
- SageMaker Autopilot provides end-to-end AutoML capabilities that democratize advanced machine learning while maintaining transparency and interpretability
- Multi-objective optimization addresses real-world trade-offs between competing requirements while identifying Pareto optimal solutions
- Automated model selection pipelines enable systematic algorithm evaluation while supporting objective model selection based on comprehensive performance assessment

Chapter 13: Model Evaluation and Validation

Model evaluation represents the critical bridge between development experimentation and production deployment, yet many organizations approach validation with insufficient rigor that leads to models failing catastrophically when confronted with real-world conditions. The difference between models that succeed in production and those that create business problems often lies not in algorithmic sophistication but in the thoroughness and appropriateness of evaluation procedures.

Effective model validation requires understanding the relationship between technical performance metrics and business outcomes while accounting for operational constraints and stakeholder requirements. AWS SageMaker provides tools for comprehensive model evaluation, but using them effectively requires systematic approaches that align technical assessment with business value creation.

Cross-Validation Strategies

Cross-validation provides the foundation for reliable model performance estimation by testing models on data not used during training. However, naive application of cross-validation can lead to overly optimistic performance estimates that don't reflect production reality, particularly for time-series data or scenarios with distribution shifts.

Time Series Validation Approaches:

Forward-chaining validation respects the temporal nature of time-series data by training on historical periods and testing on subsequent periods, mimicking the actual prediction scenario where models must forecast future events based on past data. This approach prevents data leakage that can artificially inflate performance estimates.

Rolling window validation provides multiple evaluation points by systematically moving training and testing windows through time while maintaining temporal ordering. Rolling approaches offer more robust performance estimates while revealing how model performance varies across different time periods and market conditions.

Expanding window strategies incrementally add new data to training sets while testing on fixed future periods, reflecting scenarios where models can be retrained with additional historical data. Expanding windows show how performance improves with more training data while maintaining realistic evaluation conditions.

Gap-based validation introduces intentional delays between training and testing periods to account for practical deployment constraints like data availability delays and model retraining cycles. Gap inclusion provides more realistic performance estimates while accounting for operational realities.

Stratified Sampling Techniques:

Balanced stratification ensures evaluation sets contain representative proportions of different classes or categories while maintaining statistical validity. Proper stratification prevents biased performance estimates while ensuring adequate representation of minority classes or rare events.

Geographic stratification accounts for regional variations in data characteristics while ensuring models perform reliably across different markets or operational areas. Geographic considerations become particularly important for models deployed across diverse markets with different characteristics.

Temporal stratification samples evaluation data across different time periods while accounting for seasonal patterns and long-term trends. Temporal sampling ensures performance estimates reflect different operating conditions while identifying potential seasonal performance variations.

Feature-based stratification groups similar examples based on key characteristics while ensuring evaluation sets span the full range of expected input conditions. Feature stratification identifies potential performance gaps while ensuring comprehensive evaluation coverage.

Cross-Validation for Different Data Types:

Grouped cross-validation handles scenarios where multiple examples come from the same entity (customer, transaction, location) by ensuring all examples from each group appear in either training or testing sets, never both. Grouping prevents leakage while providing realistic performance estimates.

Nested cross-validation separates hyperparameter optimization from performance estimation by using inner loops for model selection and outer loops for unbiased performance assessment. Nested approaches prevent overfitting to validation sets while providing realistic generalization estimates.

Leave-one-group-out validation provides conservative performance estimates by testing models on completely unseen groups while training on all others. This approach works well for scenarios where generalization to new entities or contexts represents the primary modeling challenge.

Case Example 1: Credit Risk Model Validation

A regional bank developed credit risk models for small business loans where default prediction accuracy directly affected loan portfolio performance and regulatory compliance. Traditional random sampling approaches provided overly optimistic performance estimates that didn't reflect actual loan performance in practice.

Time-aware validation used forward-chaining approaches that trained models on historical loan data and tested prediction accuracy on subsequent loan cohorts. The validation framework accounted for economic cycle variations and seasonal business patterns that affected default rates significantly.

Customer-level grouping ensured no borrower appeared in both training and testing sets while accounting for the reality that some customers had multiple loans over time. Customer grouping provided more conservative performance estimates while reflecting actual deployment scenarios.

Validation results showed 15% lower performance than traditional random sampling approaches, but the time-aware estimates accurately predicted actual model performance in production. The realistic evaluation enabled appropriate risk management decisions while preventing overconfident model deployment.

Business Metric Alignment

Technical metrics like accuracy and RMSE often provide poor proxies for actual business value, requiring custom evaluation approaches that align with organizational objectives and decision-making processes. Business-aligned evaluation ensures model selection optimizes real value creation rather than statistical abstractions.

Revenue Impact Assessment:

Customer lifetime value modeling connects prediction accuracy to long-term revenue impact while accounting for customer acquisition costs and retention rates. CLV-based evaluation ensures models optimize for profitable customer relationships rather than just prediction accuracy.

Conversion rate optimization focuses evaluation on metrics that directly affect sales and marketing efficiency while considering the full customer journey from awareness to purchase. Conversion-focused metrics ensure marketing models drive actual business results rather than just engagement metrics.

Cost reduction quantification measures model impact on operational efficiency, customer service expenses, and manual processing costs while accounting for implementation overhead. Cost-focused evaluation ensures automation models provide net positive business impact.

Risk-adjusted returns incorporate uncertainty and potential losses into model evaluation while balancing return opportunities with downside protection. Risk-adjusted metrics prove particularly important for financial and insurance applications where model failures can have severe consequences.

Operational Efficiency Metrics:

Processing time reduction measures how models improve operational workflows while considering implementation costs and change management challenges. Efficiency metrics ensure automation models provide practical operational improvements rather than just theoretical capabilities.

Resource utilization optimization evaluates model impact on infrastructure costs, staff productivity, and system capacity while accounting for scaling requirements. Utilization metrics guide deployment decisions while ensuring sustainable operational improvements.

Quality consistency assessment measures how models improve standardization and reduce variability in business processes while maintaining flexibility for exceptional cases. Consistency metrics ensure automation models enhance rather than constrain business capabilities.

Error cost analysis quantifies the business impact of different types of model errors while optimizing for minimal total cost rather than maximum accuracy. Cost-aware evaluation ensures models optimize for business outcomes rather than technical performance measures.

Customer Experience Integration:

Satisfaction score correlation connects model performance with customer feedback while accounting for factors beyond model predictions that affect customer experience.

Experience-based evaluation ensures models enhance rather than degrade customer relationships.

Response time optimization balances prediction accuracy with system responsiveness while considering customer expectations and competitive requirements. Latency-aware evaluation ensures models meet practical performance requirements for user-facing applications.

Personalization effectiveness measures how well models adapt to individual preferences while maintaining fairness and avoiding filter bubbles. Personalization metrics ensure recommendation and targeting models enhance rather than limit customer experiences.

Trust and transparency assessment evaluates model explainability and decision transparency while ensuring compliance with regulatory and organizational requirements. Trust metrics become increasingly important as models affect high-stakes decisions.

A/B Testing Frameworks

A/B testing provides gold-standard validation for model performance by comparing model-driven decisions against control groups in real business environments. However, effective A/B testing for machine learning requires specialized considerations that account for model complexity and business constraints.

Experimental Design Principles:

Statistical power analysis determines required sample sizes and test durations to detect meaningful performance differences while controlling for Type I and Type II errors. Power analysis prevents underpowered tests that waste resources while ensuring adequate sensitivity to detect important effects.

Randomization strategies ensure unbiased group assignment while accounting for potential confounding factors like seasonality, marketing campaigns, or operational changes. Proper randomization isolates model effects while controlling for external influences that could bias results.

Stratification techniques ensure balanced representation across important customer segments while maintaining statistical validity. Stratified designs provide more precise effect estimates while enabling analysis of model performance across different populations.

Sequential testing enables early stopping when sufficient evidence accumulates while controlling overall error rates through appropriate statistical procedures. Sequential approaches reduce opportunity costs while maintaining statistical rigor for business decision-making.

Model-Specific Testing Considerations:

Champion-challenger frameworks compare new models against existing production systems while gradually scaling successful challengers. Champion-challenger approaches minimize business risk while enabling systematic model improvement and replacement.

Multi-armed bandit optimization dynamically allocates traffic between model variants while optimizing for business outcomes during the testing period. Bandit approaches balance exploration with exploitation while maximizing business value during experimentation.

Interaction effect analysis identifies how models perform differently across customer segments, time periods, or operational conditions while accounting for complex interaction patterns. Interaction analysis ensures models work reliably across diverse operating scenarios.

Business continuity planning addresses potential negative effects of model testing while ensuring rapid response capabilities when tests reveal problems. Continuity planning protects business operations while enabling aggressive model innovation and testing.

Implementation Infrastructure:

Traffic allocation systems randomly assign customers or transactions to test groups while maintaining consistent experiences and reliable data collection. Allocation systems must handle high volumes while maintaining statistical validity and operational reliability.

Metric collection frameworks capture both technical performance measures and business outcomes while enabling real-time monitoring and analysis. Collection systems balance comprehensive measurement with system performance while supporting rapid decision-making.

Statistical analysis automation provides real-time test results and significance testing while controlling for multiple comparisons and sequential testing considerations. Analysis automation enables responsive test management while maintaining statistical rigor.

Case Example 2: E-commerce Recommendation System Testing

An online marketplace needed to validate new recommendation algorithms that promised improved customer engagement and sales conversion. Traditional offline evaluation showed promising results, but business stakeholders required proof of real-world impact before full deployment.

A/B testing framework randomly assigned 20% of website traffic to the new recommendation system while maintaining 80% on the existing system for comparison. The test measured click-through rates, conversion rates, average order values, and customer satisfaction scores over a six-week period.

Stratification ensured balanced representation across customer segments including new customers, returning customers, and high-value customers. Segment analysis revealed that new recommendations performed particularly well for returning customers but showed limited improvement for first-time visitors.

Results demonstrated 12% improvement in overall conversion rates and 8% increase in average order values with strong statistical significance. The business impact translated to projected annual revenue increase of $3.2 million, easily justifying the development and deployment costs.

Model Interpretability with Clarify

Amazon SageMaker Clarify provides automated model interpretation and bias detection capabilities that help stakeholders understand model behavior while ensuring fair and responsible AI deployment. Model interpretability becomes increasingly important as ML systems affect high-stakes decisions requiring transparency and accountability (24).

Feature Importance Analysis:

SHAP (SHapley Additive exPlanations) values provide unified measure of feature contributions that satisfy mathematical properties ensuring consistent and fair attribution. SHAP analysis works across different algorithm types while providing both global and local explanations of model behavior.

Permutation importance measures feature impact by randomly shuffling feature values and measuring performance degradation while providing model-agnostic importance assessment. Permutation approaches work with any model type while providing intuitive importance interpretations.

Partial dependence plots show how individual features affect model predictions while holding other features constant, revealing non-linear relationships and interaction effects. Partial dependence analysis helps identify unexpected model behavior while supporting feature engineering decisions.

Global feature ranking identifies most influential variables across the entire dataset while providing overall model interpretation and feature selection guidance. Global analysis supports strategic decisions about data collection and feature engineering investments.

Local Explanation Capabilities:

Individual prediction explanations break down specific model decisions into feature contributions while providing stakeholder-friendly interpretations. Local explanations support customer service, regulatory compliance, and trust-building initiatives.

Counterfactual analysis identifies minimal changes needed to alter model predictions while revealing decision boundaries and sensitivity patterns. Counterfactual insights help understand model robustness while supporting actionable recommendations for improvement.

Example-based explanations identify similar historical cases that support current predictions while providing intuitive reasoning that stakeholders can understand and validate. Example-based approaches bridge statistical models with human reasoning patterns.

Bias Detection and Mitigation:

Demographic parity analysis measures whether model predictions show systematic differences across protected groups while identifying potential discrimination patterns. Parity analysis ensures fair treatment while supporting regulatory compliance and ethical AI practices.

Equalized odds assessment evaluates whether model accuracy remains consistent across different demographic groups while identifying performance disparities that could indicate bias. Equalized odds analysis ensures reliable performance for all populations.

Calibration analysis measures whether prediction confidence aligns with actual accuracy across different groups while identifying overconfidence or underconfidence patterns. Calibration analysis ensures reliable uncertainty estimates for all populations.

Bias mitigation techniques include preprocessing adjustments, algorithmic constraints, and post-processing corrections that reduce discriminatory patterns while maintaining model performance. Mitigation approaches balance fairness with predictive accuracy while meeting regulatory requirements.

Case Example 3: Healthcare Risk Prediction Interpretation

A health insurance company developed models to predict patient hospitalization risk for care management programs. Regulatory requirements demanded transparent explanations for coverage decisions while clinical teams needed interpretable risk factors to guide patient interventions.

Clarify analysis revealed that the model relied heavily on previous hospitalization history, comorbidity patterns, and medication compliance while identifying unexpected influences from geographic factors and insurance claim patterns. Feature importance analysis guided clinical teams toward most impactful intervention strategies.

Individual patient explanations helped case managers understand specific risk factors while providing actionable guidance for care planning. Local explanations improved care manager confidence while supporting patient communication about risk reduction opportunities.

Bias analysis identified systematic differences in risk predictions across racial and economic groups that reflected historical healthcare disparities rather than actual risk differences. Bias detection enabled model adjustments that improved fairness while maintaining predictive accuracy for legitimate medical risk factors.

Statistical Validation Rigor

Comprehensive model validation requires statistical approaches that provide confidence in model performance while accounting for uncertainty and potential failure modes. Statistical rigor prevents overconfident deployment while supporting informed risk management decisions.

Confidence Interval Estimation:

Bootstrap sampling provides non-parametric confidence intervals for performance metrics while accounting for data uncertainty and sampling variation. Bootstrap approaches work with any performance metric while providing reliable uncertainty quantification.

Bayesian performance estimation incorporates prior knowledge about model performance while updating beliefs based on validation results. Bayesian approaches provide natural uncertainty quantification while enabling incorporation of domain expertise.

Cross-validation confidence intervals account for both sampling variation and model selection uncertainty while providing realistic performance ranges. Cross-validation intervals support conservative performance estimates while enabling risk-aware deployment decisions.

Hypothesis Testing Frameworks:

Model comparison testing determines whether performance differences between models represent genuine improvements rather than random variation. Comparison testing prevents unnecessary model complexity while ensuring meaningful performance improvements.

Baseline significance testing validates whether models provide meaningful improvement over simple heuristics or business rules while establishing minimum performance thresholds. Baseline testing ensures models justify their complexity and implementation costs.

Performance degradation testing identifies conditions under which model performance degrades significantly while establishing monitoring thresholds and failure detection criteria. Degradation testing supports proactive model maintenance while preventing silent failures.

Production Readiness Assessment

Model validation must extend beyond performance metrics to include operational considerations that affect production deployment success. Production readiness requires comprehensive assessment of technical, business, and organizational factors that influence model success.

Infrastructure requirements assessment ensures models can meet production performance and reliability standards while operating within computational and budget constraints. Infrastructure analysis prevents deployment failures while optimizing resource utilization.

Monitoring and alerting capabilities ensure models can be managed effectively in production while providing early warning of performance degradation or failure conditions. Monitoring assessment supports reliable operations while enabling proactive maintenance.

Change management planning ensures organizations can adopt new models successfully while minimizing disruption to existing processes and stakeholder workflows. Change planning supports successful model adoption while maintaining business continuity.

Validation Excellence in Practice

Successful model validation requires combining technical rigor with business understanding while maintaining focus on real-world value creation. Excellence in validation practices provides competitive advantages through more reliable models and faster deployment cycles.

The validation frameworks established here support confident model deployment while minimizing production risks and maximizing business impact. Quality validation practices enable organizations to realize the full potential of machine learning investments while maintaining operational excellence.

Summary Reflection

Model evaluation and validation represent perhaps the most critical phase of the machine learning lifecycle, determining whether months of development effort translate into business value or costly failures. The systematic approaches outlined here provide the foundation for confident model deployment while supporting continuous improvement and optimization.

Essential Takeaways

- Cross-validation strategies must account for data characteristics and temporal dependencies while providing realistic performance estimates for production scenarios
- Business metric alignment ensures model optimization focuses on actual value creation rather than technical performance abstractions
- A/B testing frameworks provide gold-standard validation while requiring specialized considerations for machine learning applications
- SageMaker Clarify enables model interpretability and bias detection that support responsible AI deployment and stakeholder confidence
- Statistical validation rigor provides confidence in model performance while accounting for uncertainty and supporting risk-aware deployment decisions

Practice Questions: AWS ML Engineer Associate Exam Preparation

Question 61: A time-series forecasting model needs validation that reflects real-world deployment conditions. Which cross-validation approach is most appropriate?

A) Random k-fold cross-validation with shuffled data B) Forward-chaining validation with temporal ordering preserved C) Stratified sampling across all time periods D) Leave-one-out cross-validation for maximum data usage

Correct Answer: B - Forward-chaining validation preserves temporal ordering and mimics real deployment conditions where models predict future events based on historical data.

Question 62: A company wants to evaluate models based on business impact rather than technical metrics. Which approach best aligns with this requirement?

A) Focus on accuracy and precision across all models B) Use custom evaluation metrics that incorporate revenue impact and operational costs C) Apply standard statistical measures like RMSE and AUC D) Evaluate models using only computational efficiency metrics

Correct Answer: B - Custom evaluation metrics incorporating revenue impact and operational costs align model selection with actual business value creation.

Question 63: When conducting A/B testing for a recommendation system, what consideration is most important for valid results?

A) Equal computational resources for all model variants B) Identical training data for control and treatment groups
C) Random assignment of users with proper stratification D) Maximum possible sample size regardless of cost

Correct Answer: C - Random assignment with proper stratification ensures unbiased comparison while controlling for potential confounding factors.

Question 64: SageMaker Clarify is being used to explain model predictions for a loan approval system. Which explanation type best supports individual loan decisions?

A) Global feature importance rankings across all applications B) SHAP values showing feature contributions for specific applications C) Partial dependence plots for key demographic variables D) Aggregate bias metrics across different customer segments

Correct Answer: B - SHAP values provide local explanations that break down specific predictions into individual feature contributions, supporting transparent loan decisions.

Question 65: A model shows different performance across geographic regions during validation. Which analysis approach best addresses this finding?

A) Increase overall training data volume equally across regions B) Use stratified validation that ensures representative sampling from each region C) Apply the same model configuration to all regions uniformly D) Focus optimization only on the best-performing regions

Correct Answer: B - Stratified validation ensures each region is adequately represented in evaluation while revealing performance variations that may require region-specific adjustments.

Question 66: For nested cross-validation, what is the primary purpose of the inner cross-validation loop?

A) Final model performance estimation B) Hyperparameter optimization and model selection C) Feature importance calculation D) Bias detection across different groups

Correct Answer: B - Inner cross-validation loops handle hyperparameter optimization and model selection, while outer loops provide unbiased performance estimates.

Question 67: A healthcare model requires validation that accounts for patient privacy while ensuring robust performance assessment. Which approach is most appropriate?

A) Use all available patient data without restrictions B) Implement patient-level grouping to prevent data leakage between folds C) Focus on aggregate statistics without individual patient analysis D) Use only anonymized data without performance tracking

Correct Answer: B - Patient-level grouping ensures no individual patient appears in both training and testing sets, preventing leakage while maintaining privacy.

Question 68: When using Clarify for bias detection, which metric best evaluates whether a model treats different demographic groups fairly?

A) Overall model accuracy across the entire dataset B) Feature importance rankings for demographic variables C) Equalized odds comparing accuracy across protected groups D) Prediction confidence scores for individual cases

Correct Answer: C - Equalized odds measures whether model accuracy remains consistent across different demographic groups, indicating fair treatment.

Question 69: A model validation framework needs to determine statistical significance of performance improvements. Which approach provides the most reliable results?

A) Single validation run with large test set B) Multiple validation runs with confidence interval estimation C) Comparison of training and validation loss curves D) Analysis of prediction distribution patterns

Correct Answer: B - Multiple validation runs with confidence intervals account for sampling variation and provide reliable statistical assessment of performance differences.

Question 70: For champion-challenger A/B testing of ML models, what traffic allocation strategy minimizes business risk?

A) Equal 50/50 split between champion and challenger B) Small challenger allocation (10-20%) with gradual increase based on performance C) Random allocation that changes daily D) Complete replacement of champion with challenger

Correct Answer: B - Small initial challenger allocation minimizes business risk while allowing performance assessment and gradual scaling of successful models.

Question 71: When validating models with grouped data (multiple records per customer), which cross-validation approach prevents data leakage?

A) Random sampling across all records B) Temporal splitting based on record timestamps C) Group-based splitting ensuring customers appear in only one fold D) Stratified sampling based on customer demographics

Correct Answer: C - Group-based splitting ensures all records from each customer appear in either training or testing, never both, preventing leakage.

Question 72: A model's SHAP analysis reveals unexpected feature importance patterns. What action should be taken?

A) Ignore the patterns and proceed with deployment B) Investigate the patterns to understand model behavior and potential issues C) Remove the important features from the model D) Increase model complexity to change the patterns

Correct Answer: B - Unexpected patterns require investigation to understand model behavior, identify potential biases, or discover genuine insights about the problem.

Question 73: For time-series validation with seasonal patterns, which approach best accounts for seasonality?

A) Random sampling across all time periods B) Validation periods that include complete seasonal cycles C) Focus on recent data only to capture current patterns D) Equal weighting of all time periods regardless of patterns

Correct Answer: B - Including complete seasonal cycles in validation periods ensures performance estimates account for seasonal variations that affect real-world deployment.

Question 74: When conducting multi-objective model evaluation (accuracy vs. latency), which approach best supports decision-making?

A) Optimize only for accuracy as the primary objective B) Find solutions that optimize the weighted sum of all objectives C) Identify Pareto optimal solutions representing different trade-offs D) Choose the fastest model regardless of accuracy

Correct Answer: C - Pareto optimal solutions provide decision-makers with alternatives representing different trade-offs between competing objectives.

Question 75: A validation framework needs to assess model calibration (prediction confidence accuracy). Which metric is most appropriate?

A) Overall prediction accuracy B) Calibration plots comparing predicted probabilities with actual outcomes C) Feature importance rankings D) Model training convergence curves

Correct Answer: B - Calibration plots directly compare predicted confidence levels with actual outcome frequencies, revealing whether confidence estimates are reliable.

Question 76: For validating recommendation systems, which business metric best captures long-term value?

A) Click-through rates on recommended items B) Customer lifetime value and retention rates C) Number of recommendations served per day D) Model inference latency and throughput

Correct Answer: B - Customer lifetime value and retention capture long-term business impact of recommendations beyond immediate engagement metrics.

Question 77: When using bootstrap sampling for confidence intervals, what sample size consideration is most important?

A) Use exactly the same size as the original dataset B) Use the largest possible sample size available C) Use sample sizes appropriate for the confidence level desired D) Use the minimum sample size to reduce computation

Correct Answer: C - Bootstrap sample sizes should be chosen based on desired confidence levels and the precision needed for business decisions.

Question 78: A model shows high accuracy but low precision for minority classes. Which validation approach best addresses this imbalance?

A) Focus on overall accuracy metrics only B) Use class-weighted evaluation metrics and stratified sampling C) Increase the size of the majority class in training D) Remove minority class examples from evaluation

Correct Answer: B - Class-weighted metrics and stratified sampling ensure minority class performance receives appropriate attention during evaluation.

Question 79: For regulatory compliance, model explanations must be auditable and reproducible. Which Clarify feature best supports this requirement?

A) Real-time explanation generation during inference B) Batch explanation jobs with persistent result storage C) Interactive explanation exploration tools D) Automated explanation summaries

Correct Answer: B - Batch explanation jobs with persistent storage provide auditable records of model explanations that support regulatory compliance.

Question 80: When validating models across different customer segments, which approach ensures representative evaluation?

A) Use the largest customer segment for all validation B) Combine all segments into a single validation set C) Perform separate validation for each segment with segment-specific metrics D) Use only average performance across all segments

Correct Answer: C - Separate validation for each segment reveals performance variations and ensures models work reliably across all customer populations.

Question 81: A production model validation framework needs early warning of performance degradation. Which monitoring approach is most effective?

A) Monthly performance reports B) Real-time statistical process control with adaptive thresholds C) Annual model retraining and evaluation D) User feedback collection and analysis

Correct Answer: B - Real-time statistical process control provides immediate detection of performance changes while adaptive thresholds reduce false alarms.

Question 82: For models with external data dependencies, which validation consideration is most critical?

A) Training data volume and quality B) Model complexity and parameter count C) Data availability and latency in production environment D) Algorithm selection and optimization

Correct Answer: C - External data dependencies require validation of data availability and latency characteristics that will affect production performance.

Question 83: When comparing multiple model architectures, which statistical approach best controls for multiple comparison bias?

A) Use the model with highest single performance metric B) Apply Bonferroni correction or similar multiple testing procedures C) Compare only the top two performing models D) Use different datasets for each model comparison

Correct Answer: B - Multiple testing corrections like Bonferroni control the increased probability of false positives when making many statistical comparisons simultaneously.

Question 84: A model validation process reveals inconsistent performance across different data collection periods. Which analysis approach best identifies the root cause?

A) Increase overall training data volume B) Perform temporal analysis of data characteristics and feature distributions C) Apply the same preprocessing to all time periods D) Use only the most recent data for validation

Correct Answer: B - Temporal analysis of data characteristics helps identify distribution shifts, seasonal patterns, or data collection changes that cause performance inconsistencies.

Question 85: For interpretable model validation in regulated industries, which combination of techniques provides the most comprehensive assessment?

A) Technical performance metrics only B) SHAP analysis, bias detection, and business metric alignment C) Feature importance rankings and accuracy measures D) Statistical significance testing and computational efficiency

Correct Answer: B - SHAP analysis provides explainability, bias detection ensures fairness, and business metric alignment confirms value creation - all critical for regulated industries.

Question 86: When validating ensemble models, which approach best evaluates both individual component performance and ensemble effectiveness?

A) Evaluate only the final ensemble predictions B) Test individual models separately and ignore ensemble effects C) Assess both component model contributions and overall ensemble performance D) Focus on the best-performing individual model only

Correct Answer: C - Comprehensive ensemble validation requires understanding both how individual components perform and how they combine to create overall ensemble effectiveness.

Question 87: A validation framework needs to handle missing data during evaluation. Which approach maintains the most realistic performance assessment?

A) Remove all samples with any missing values B) Impute missing values using the same methods planned for production C) Use only features without missing values D) Replace missing values with dataset averages

Correct Answer: B - Using the same imputation methods planned for production ensures validation reflects actual deployment conditions and data handling procedures.

Question 88: For models with real-time latency requirements, which validation metric combination is most important?

A) Accuracy and computational complexity only B) Precision, recall, and statistical significance C) Prediction accuracy, inference latency, and throughput under load D) Feature importance and model interpretability

Correct Answer: C - Real-time applications require validation of both predictive performance and operational characteristics like latency and throughput under realistic load conditions.

Question 89: When using cross-validation for hyperparameter optimization, which practice prevents overfitting to validation performance?

A) Use the same validation set for all hyperparameter combinations B) Implement nested cross-validation with separate optimization and evaluation loops C) Maximize validation performance regardless of training performance D) Use validation performance as the only model selection criterion

Correct Answer: B - Nested cross-validation separates hyperparameter optimization from final performance evaluation, preventing overfitting to validation sets.

Question 90: A model validation reveals different optimal decision thresholds for different customer segments. Which deployment strategy best addresses this finding?

A) Use a single threshold optimized for overall performance B) Implement segment-specific thresholds with appropriate routing logic C) Choose the threshold that works best for the largest segment D) Avoid using decision thresholds entirely

Correct Answer: B - Segment-specific thresholds optimize performance for each group while requiring routing logic to apply appropriate thresholds during inference.

Question 91: For continuous model validation in production, which approach provides the most comprehensive monitoring?

A) Daily accuracy calculations on recent predictions B) Multi-dimensional monitoring including accuracy, bias, drift, and business metrics C) Weekly comparison with development performance D) Monthly model retraining and evaluation

Correct Answer: B - Comprehensive monitoring across multiple dimensions provides early warning of various failure modes while supporting proactive model maintenance.

Question 92: When validating models with privacy constraints, which technique best balances evaluation rigor with privacy protection?

A) Use only aggregated statistics without individual-level analysis B) Implement differential privacy with appropriate noise calibration C) Avoid validation entirely to protect privacy D) Use publicly available datasets only

Correct Answer: B - Differential privacy enables rigorous validation while providing mathematical guarantees about privacy protection through carefully calibrated noise addition.

Question 93: A model shows excellent offline validation performance but poor online A/B test results. Which factor most likely explains this discrepancy?

A) Insufficient training data volume B) Distribution differences between offline evaluation and online deployment C) Incorrect algorithm selection D) Poor hyperparameter optimization

Correct Answer: B - Distribution differences between offline evaluation data and real-world deployment conditions often cause performance gaps between offline and online results.

Question 94: For models affecting high-stakes decisions, which validation approach provides the strongest confidence in performance estimates?

A) Single large holdout test set B) Multiple validation approaches including cross-validation, holdout testing, and temporal validation C) Expert review of model predictions D) Comparison with simple baseline models only

Correct Answer: B - Multiple validation approaches provide convergent evidence about model performance while reducing reliance on any single evaluation method.

Question 95: When model validation reveals bias against protected groups, which remediation approach best balances fairness with performance?

A) Remove all demographic features from the model B) Apply post-processing corrections that equalize outcomes across groups C) Implement algorithmic constraints during training to ensure fair treatment D) Use separate models for each demographic group

Correct Answer: C - Algorithmic fairness constraints during training integrate fairness considerations into the optimization process while maintaining model coherence and performance.

Question 96: A validation framework needs to assess model robustness to input perturbations. Which testing approach is most comprehensive?

A) Add random noise to all input features B) Apply systematic perturbations based on expected real-world variations C) Test only with perfect, clean input data D) Use adversarial examples designed to break the model

Correct Answer: B - Systematic perturbations based on expected real-world variations provide realistic robustness assessment while covering likely deployment scenarios.

Question 97: For model validation with limited labeled data, which approach maximizes the reliability of performance estimates?

A) Use all data for training and rely on training metrics B) Apply cross-validation with careful attention to sampling strategies C) Create synthetic test data to supplement real data D) Use unsupervised metrics instead of supervised evaluation

Correct Answer: B - Cross-validation with appropriate sampling maximizes use of limited labeled data while providing robust performance estimates through multiple evaluation folds.

Question 98: When validating recommendation systems, which combination of metrics best captures both immediate and long-term success?

A) Click-through rates and immediate conversion rates only B) Engagement metrics, diversity measures, and long-term user satisfaction C) Technical performance metrics like latency and throughput D) Model complexity and computational efficiency measures

Correct Answer: B - Comprehensive recommendation evaluation requires immediate engagement metrics, diversity to prevent filter bubbles, and long-term satisfaction measures.

Question 99: A model validation process needs to handle concept drift over time. Which monitoring strategy provides the earliest detection?

A) Monthly model retraining and performance comparison B) Continuous monitoring of prediction distributions and feature statistics C) Annual comprehensive model evaluation D) User feedback collection and analysis

Correct Answer: B - Continuous monitoring of predictions and features provides immediate detection of distribution changes that indicate concept drift before performance degradation becomes severe.

Question 100: For regulatory model validation, which documentation approach best supports compliance requirements?

A) Technical performance metrics in spreadsheets B) Comprehensive validation reports with methodology, results, and business justification C) Code comments explaining model implementation D) Informal notes about model development decisions

Correct Answer: B - Regulatory compliance requires comprehensive documentation that explains validation methodology, presents results clearly, and justifies business decisions based on evidence.

Chapter 14: Production Deployment Architectures

Production deployment separates successful machine learning initiatives from expensive experiments that never deliver business value. The transition from development notebooks to production systems requires architectural decisions that affect performance, cost, reliability, and maintainability for years to come. Making these decisions correctly the first time prevents costly rework and enables sustainable scaling as business requirements grow.

AWS SageMaker provides multiple deployment patterns, each optimized for different performance requirements, cost constraints, and operational scenarios. Understanding the trade-offs between these approaches enables informed architectural decisions that balance technical requirements with business objectives while maintaining operational excellence.

Real-time Endpoints vs Batch Transform

The choice between real-time inference endpoints and batch transform jobs represents one of the most fundamental architectural decisions for ML deployment. This decision affects infrastructure costs, development complexity, and system performance characteristics in ways that become increasingly difficult to change as systems mature.

Real-time Endpoint Characteristics:

Real-time endpoints provide synchronous inference through REST APIs that respond to individual prediction requests with sub-second latency. These endpoints maintain persistent infrastructure that remains ready to serve predictions immediately, making them suitable for user-facing applications and time-sensitive decision-making scenarios (25).

Auto-scaling capabilities adjust endpoint capacity based on traffic patterns while maintaining response time requirements. SageMaker endpoints can scale from zero to hundreds of instances automatically, though scaling events introduce brief latency spikes that may affect user experience during rapid traffic increases.

Load balancing distributes requests across multiple instances while providing fault tolerance and consistent performance during instance failures. Built-in health checks ensure traffic routes only to healthy instances while automatic recovery procedures replace failed instances without manual intervention.

Multi-model endpoints enable hosting multiple models on shared infrastructure while reducing costs for scenarios with many small models or infrequently accessed models. This approach provides cost efficiency while maintaining the flexibility to serve different models based on request parameters.

Batch Transform Capabilities:

Batch transform jobs process large datasets efficiently by distributing inference workloads across multiple instances that scale automatically based on data volume. This approach provides optimal cost efficiency for scenarios where immediate responses aren't required and data can be processed in groups.

Input data handling supports various formats including CSV, JSON, and custom formats while providing automatic data distribution across processing instances. Flexible input handling enables batch processing of complex data types without custom preprocessing infrastructure.

Output aggregation collects results from distributed processing while maintaining data order and enabling custom output formatting. Result handling includes error management and partial failure recovery that ensures reliable processing of large datasets.

Cost optimization through spot instances can reduce batch processing costs by 70-90% for workloads that tolerate instance interruptions. Spot usage requires fault-tolerant job design but provides significant cost savings for appropriate scenarios.

Decision Framework Application:

Latency requirements represent the primary factor distinguishing real-time from batch scenarios. Applications requiring responses within seconds need real-time endpoints, while scenarios accepting delays from minutes to hours can utilize batch processing for better cost efficiency.

Traffic patterns influence infrastructure costs significantly between the two approaches. Steady, predictable traffic favors real-time endpoints with reserved capacity, while sporadic or highly variable demand often works better with batch processing that scales to zero between jobs.

Data volume considerations affect processing efficiency and cost optimization opportunities. Large datasets with complex preprocessing requirements often achieve better resource utilization through batch processing, while small, frequent requests work better with persistent endpoints.

Integration requirements with existing systems may dictate deployment architecture choices. Real-time applications need synchronous API responses, while analytical pipelines often integrate better with batch processing workflows and scheduling systems.

Case Example 1: Financial Risk Assessment Platform

A commercial bank needed to deploy credit risk models for both real-time loan approvals and batch portfolio risk analysis. The same underlying models required different deployment architectures to serve distinct business requirements efficiently.

Real-time deployment served loan origination systems that required approval decisions within 30 seconds to maintain customer experience standards. Multi-model endpoints hosted different risk models for various loan types while auto-scaling handled traffic variations during business hours and seasonal lending periods.

Batch deployment processed entire loan portfolios monthly for regulatory reporting and risk management analysis. Batch transform jobs scaled to process 500,000 loan records in 2 hours using spot instances, reducing processing costs by 80% compared to equivalent real-time infrastructure.

The hybrid architecture enabled optimal cost-performance balance while serving both operational and analytical requirements. Real-time endpoints cost $1,200 monthly for persistent availability, while batch processing cost $150 monthly for actual usage, demonstrating significant cost differences between deployment patterns.

Multi-model Endpoints

Multi-model endpoints provide cost-efficient hosting for scenarios involving multiple models with different traffic patterns or resource requirements. This approach reduces infrastructure costs while maintaining deployment flexibility and enabling efficient resource utilization across model portfolios.

Architecture and Resource Sharing:

Shared infrastructure enables multiple models to utilize the same computational resources while maintaining isolation and performance guarantees. Resource sharing reduces fixed costs while providing automatic load balancing across different models based on actual usage patterns.

Model caching strategies keep frequently accessed models in memory while loading less popular models on-demand. Intelligent caching reduces response latency for popular models while managing memory usage efficiently across large model collections.

Dynamic model loading enables adding new models without endpoint downtime while supporting A/B testing and gradual rollouts. Model management APIs provide programmatic control over model availability and traffic routing without infrastructure changes.

Resource allocation algorithms distribute computational capacity across models based on traffic patterns, model complexity, and business priorities. Allocation strategies balance fairness with efficiency while ensuring adequate performance for critical models.

Cost Optimization Strategies:

Instance utilization improvements through model sharing can reduce hosting costs by 60-90% compared to dedicated endpoints for each model. Shared hosting becomes particularly effective for scenarios with many small models or models with complementary traffic patterns.

Reserved capacity planning balances cost savings with performance requirements by analyzing traffic patterns across all hosted models. Strategic capacity planning captures discounts while ensuring adequate performance during peak usage periods.

Auto-scaling coordination manages capacity changes across all hosted models while maintaining individual model performance requirements. Coordinated scaling prevents resource conflicts while optimizing costs through shared infrastructure efficiency.

Model Management and Operations:

Version control enables independent model updates without affecting other hosted models while maintaining deployment consistency and rollback capabilities. Isolated versioning reduces deployment risks while enabling rapid iteration on individual models.

Monitoring and alerting provide model-specific performance tracking while maintaining overall endpoint health visibility. Granular monitoring enables rapid issue identification and resolution without affecting unrelated models.

Traffic routing capabilities enable sophisticated request handling including model selection based on request parameters, A/B testing configurations, and canary deployments. Flexible routing supports complex deployment scenarios while maintaining operational simplicity.

Case Example 2: E-commerce Personalization Service

An online marketplace deployed 50+ personalization models serving different customer segments, product categories, and recommendation scenarios. Traditional deployment approaches would have required dedicated infrastructure for each model, creating prohibitive costs and operational complexity.

Multi-model endpoint implementation hosted all personalization models on shared infrastructure while maintaining sub-100ms response times for 95% of requests. Intelligent model caching kept the 10 most frequently used models in memory while loading specialized models on-demand.

Cost analysis showed 85% reduction in infrastructure expenses compared to dedicated endpoints while maintaining performance requirements. The shared approach enabled experimentation with new models without infrastructure provisioning delays or additional fixed costs.

Traffic routing enabled sophisticated A/B testing where different customer segments received predictions from different models simultaneously. This capability accelerated model improvement cycles while providing detailed performance comparison data for optimization decisions.

Edge Deployment with Neo

SageMaker Neo enables deployment of optimized models to edge devices and embedded systems while maintaining prediction accuracy and reducing inference latency through hardware-specific optimizations. Edge deployment becomes increasingly important for applications requiring offline operation, data privacy, or ultra-low latency responses.

Model Optimization Process:

Compilation transforms trained models into optimized representations that leverage specific hardware capabilities including CPUs, GPUs, and specialized inference accelerators. Optimization includes operator fusion, memory layout optimization, and precision reduction that improve performance without affecting accuracy.

Hardware target selection enables optimization for specific device types including mobile phones, embedded systems, IoT devices, and edge servers. Target-specific optimization ensures models utilize available hardware efficiently while meeting device constraints.

Accuracy preservation validates that optimized models maintain prediction quality comparable to original implementations while achieving performance improvements. Validation procedures ensure optimization benefits don't compromise model reliability or business value.

Deployment Infrastructure:

Device management enables large-scale deployment of optimized models across distributed edge infrastructure while providing centralized monitoring and update capabilities. Management systems handle device diversity, connectivity constraints, and security requirements.

Update mechanisms support over-the-air model updates that enable continuous improvement without manual device access. Update systems balance freshness with bandwidth constraints while ensuring reliable deployment across diverse network conditions.

Offline operation capabilities ensure edge devices continue functioning during network connectivity loss while maintaining prediction accuracy and data security. Offline design prevents service degradation while supporting applications in challenging connectivity environments.

Performance and Cost Benefits:

Latency reduction through edge processing eliminates network round-trips while providing consistent response times regardless of connectivity quality. Edge processing particularly benefits real-time applications requiring immediate responses to local conditions.

Bandwidth optimization reduces data transmission requirements by processing data locally rather than sending raw inputs to cloud services. Local processing provides cost savings while supporting applications with high-frequency data collection requirements.

Privacy protection keeps sensitive data on local devices while maintaining model functionality and prediction accuracy. Local processing addresses privacy concerns while enabling ML applications in regulated industries with strict data handling requirements.

Case Example 3: Manufacturing Quality Control System

A automotive manufacturer needed real-time defect detection for production lines where network connectivity was unreliable and latency requirements demanded immediate responses to prevent defective products from proceeding through assembly.

Neo compilation optimized computer vision models for edge computing devices installed at each inspection station. Optimized models achieved 40% faster inference times while maintaining 99.2% accuracy in defect detection compared to cloud-based processing.

Edge deployment eliminated network dependencies that previously caused production delays during connectivity issues. Local processing provided consistent 15ms response times regardless of network conditions while supporting 24/7 operation requirements.

Cost analysis showed 60% reduction in cloud inference costs while improving system reliability and reducing quality escape rates. Edge deployment enabled expansion to additional production lines without proportional increases in cloud infrastructure costs.

Serverless Inference Patterns

Serverless inference provides automatic scaling and pay-per-use pricing that eliminates infrastructure management overhead while optimizing costs for variable or unpredictable workloads. This approach particularly benefits applications with sporadic usage patterns or experimental deployments.

AWS Lambda Integration:

Function-based deployment enables hosting lightweight models within Lambda functions that scale automatically from zero to thousands of concurrent executions. Lambda deployment works well for simple models with small memory footprints and moderate computational requirements.

Event-driven triggers enable inference execution in response to various AWS events including S3 uploads, API Gateway requests, and scheduled events. Event integration provides flexible automation while maintaining cost efficiency through pay-per-execution pricing.

Memory and timeout optimization balances function performance with costs while ensuring adequate resources for model inference. Optimization requires understanding model requirements and usage patterns to configure appropriate resource allocations.

Cold start mitigation strategies reduce initial response latency through provisioned concurrency, deployment optimization, and architectural patterns that minimize initialization overhead. Mitigation techniques balance latency requirements with cost implications.

SageMaker Serverless Endpoints:

Managed serverless inference provides automatic scaling without function size limitations while maintaining SageMaker's model management and monitoring capabilities. Serverless endpoints combine Lambda's scaling benefits with SageMaker's ML-optimized infrastructure.

Automatic capacity management scales inference capacity based on request volume while maintaining target response times. Capacity management eliminates manual scaling decisions while providing predictable performance characteristics.

Pay-per-inference pricing charges only for actual usage without fixed infrastructure costs, making serverless endpoints cost-effective for variable or experimental workloads. Usage-based pricing particularly benefits development and testing scenarios.

Hybrid Deployment Strategies:

Traffic routing enables intelligent request distribution between serverless and traditional endpoints based on request characteristics, urgency, or cost optimization goals. Hybrid approaches balance cost efficiency with performance requirements across diverse usage patterns.

Failover mechanisms provide reliability through automatic switching between deployment types during capacity limitations or performance issues. Failover capabilities ensure service availability while maintaining cost optimization during normal operations.

Cost optimization algorithms dynamically select deployment types based on traffic patterns, cost targets, and performance requirements. Intelligent selection maximizes cost efficiency while meeting service level objectives across changing conditions.

Project: Multi-environment Deployment Pipeline

This project builds a production deployment system that manages model deployment across development, staging, and production environments while ensuring consistency, reliability, and automated promotion workflows.

Environment Configuration Management:

Infrastructure as code defines consistent environment configurations while enabling customization for different stages of the deployment pipeline. IaC approaches ensure reproducible deployments while supporting environment-specific requirements and constraints.

Configuration management separates environment-specific parameters from model artifacts while maintaining deployment consistency across all stages. Parameter management enables testing realistic production configurations in staging environments while maintaining security boundaries.

Resource allocation strategies optimize costs and performance for different environment purposes while ensuring adequate capacity for testing and production workloads. Strategic allocation balances resource availability with budget constraints across all environments.

Automated Deployment Workflows:

Continuous integration triggers automated deployment processes when new models pass validation criteria while maintaining quality gates and approval workflows. CI integration ensures reliable deployment processes while preventing manual errors and delays.

Progressive deployment enables gradual rollout of new models through development, staging, and production environments while maintaining rollback capabilities at each stage. Progressive approaches reduce deployment risks while enabling rapid iteration and improvement.

Quality assurance integration validates model performance, infrastructure configuration, and business logic at each deployment stage while preventing problematic deployments from reaching production. QA automation ensures consistent validation while reducing manual testing overhead.

Monitoring and Alerting Integration:

Environment-specific monitoring adapts alerting thresholds and metrics collection to different environment purposes while providing comprehensive visibility into system health and performance. Adaptive monitoring ensures appropriate oversight without unnecessary noise.

Cross-environment correlation identifies issues that affect multiple environments while enabling efficient troubleshooting and root cause analysis. Correlation capabilities support rapid issue resolution while maintaining system reliability.

Automated rollback procedures respond to performance degradation or failure conditions while minimizing service disruption and enabling rapid recovery. Rollback automation provides safety nets while supporting aggressive deployment schedules.

Security and Compliance Framework:

Access control implementation ensures appropriate permissions for different environments while maintaining security boundaries and audit capabilities. Access management balances operational efficiency with security requirements across all deployment stages.

Secrets management provides secure handling of sensitive configuration data while enabling automated deployment processes. Secret handling ensures security compliance while supporting operational automation requirements.

Audit logging captures all deployment activities while providing compliance documentation and change tracking capabilities. Audit systems support regulatory requirements while enabling operational analysis and improvement.

Building Production Excellence

Successful production deployment requires balancing multiple competing objectives including performance, cost, reliability, and maintainability. Excellence in deployment architecture provides competitive advantages through faster time-to-market, better resource utilization, and more reliable service delivery.

Understanding the trade-offs between different deployment patterns enables informed decisions that align technical implementation with business objectives. Strategic deployment decisions provide foundations for sustainable scaling and long-term operational success.

The deployment architecture established here supports advanced CI/CD and monitoring capabilities that further improve system reliability and operational efficiency. Quality deployment foundations enable sophisticated operational practices that maximize business value from ML investments.

Professional Insights

Production deployment represents the culmination of ML development efforts where technical sophistication meets business reality. Success requires understanding not just what is technically possible but what provides sustainable business value while maintaining operational excellence.

Investment in proper deployment architecture pays dividends through reduced operational overhead, improved system reliability, and faster deployment cycles. Organizations that master deployment practices achieve competitive advantages through superior operational capabilities and faster innovation cycles.

Essential Takeaways

- Real-time endpoints provide immediate responses for user-facing applications while batch transform optimizes costs for large-scale processing scenarios
- Multi-model endpoints reduce infrastructure costs through resource sharing while maintaining deployment flexibility and performance isolation
- Edge deployment with Neo enables local processing that reduces latency and bandwidth while supporting offline operation and privacy requirements
- Serverless inference provides automatic scaling and pay-per-use pricing that optimizes costs for variable workloads while eliminating infrastructure management
- Multi-environment deployment pipelines ensure consistent, reliable model promotion while maintaining quality gates and automated rollback capabilities

Chapter 15: CI/CD for Machine Learning

Continuous Integration and Continuous Deployment for machine learning systems requires fundamentally different approaches than traditional software development due to the unique challenges of managing data dependencies, model artifacts, and experimental workflows. ML systems involve three distinct components—code, data, and models—that must be versioned, tested, and deployed together while maintaining reproducibility and reliability.

Traditional CI/CD practices focus primarily on code changes, but ML systems require orchestration of data processing, model training, validation, and deployment pipelines that span multiple environments and stakeholder groups. AWS SageMaker provides specialized tools for ML CI/CD, but using them effectively requires understanding both technical capabilities and organizational workflow requirements.

SageMaker Pipelines Deep Dive

SageMaker Pipelines provides a managed service for orchestrating ML workflows that includes data processing, model training, evaluation, and deployment steps. The service handles dependency management, resource allocation, and failure recovery while providing visibility into pipeline execution and results (26).

Pipeline Definition and Structure:

Pipeline steps define discrete processing units that handle specific ML workflow tasks including data preparation, feature engineering, model training, and validation. Each step specifies input dependencies, processing logic, and output artifacts while maintaining isolation and reusability.

Parameter management enables dynamic pipeline configuration without code changes while supporting different environments, datasets, and experimental conditions. Parameterization provides flexibility while maintaining pipeline reproducibility and enabling systematic experimentation.

Conditional execution enables branching logic based on step results or external conditions while supporting complex workflow patterns including model selection, quality gates, and approval processes. Conditional capabilities enable sophisticated workflow automation while maintaining human oversight where needed.

Dependency resolution automatically determines step execution order based on input-output relationships while optimizing for parallelism and resource efficiency. Automatic scheduling reduces pipeline complexity while ensuring correct execution ordering and resource utilization.

Resource Management and Optimization:

Compute allocation dynamically provisions appropriate instance types and sizes based on step requirements while optimizing for cost and performance. Dynamic allocation prevents resource waste while ensuring adequate capacity for each processing stage.

Parallel execution enables simultaneous processing of independent pipeline steps while managing resource constraints and cost budgets. Parallelism optimization balances execution speed with resource costs while maintaining pipeline reliability.

Auto-scaling adjusts resource allocation based on data volume and processing complexity while maintaining execution time requirements. Scaling automation prevents resource bottlenecks while optimizing costs through dynamic capacity management.

Spot instance integration reduces training costs for fault-tolerant pipeline steps while implementing recovery mechanisms for instance interruptions. Spot usage requires careful fault tolerance design but provides significant cost savings for appropriate workloads.

Integration with Development Workflows:

Version control integration tracks pipeline definitions alongside code changes while maintaining reproducibility and enabling collaborative development. Version tracking ensures pipeline evolution aligns with code development while supporting rollback and comparison capabilities.

Experiment tracking correlates pipeline executions with experimental parameters and results while providing comprehensive visibility into model development progress. Tracking integration supports systematic experimentation while enabling rapid iteration and improvement.

Approval workflows enable human oversight for critical pipeline transitions including production deployments while maintaining automation for routine operations. Approval integration balances automation benefits with governance requirements and risk management.

Case Example 1: Pharmaceutical Drug Discovery Pipeline

A biotechnology company needed to automate drug discovery workflows that processed molecular data, trained predictive models, and generated compound recommendations for laboratory testing. Manual workflows required weeks per iteration while introducing consistency issues across different research teams.

SageMaker Pipelines implementation automated data processing of molecular databases, feature extraction from chemical structures, model training for toxicity prediction, and candidate ranking for experimental validation. Pipeline parameterization enabled different research teams to use common workflows with project-specific data and requirements.

Resource optimization through automatic instance selection and spot usage reduced computational costs by 70% while maintaining research timeline requirements. Parallel processing of independent molecular datasets reduced analysis time from weeks to days while improving result consistency.

Experiment tracking enabled systematic comparison of different modeling approaches while maintaining complete audit trails for regulatory compliance. Automated workflows improved research productivity by 300% while ensuring reproducible results across all drug discovery projects.

GitOps for ML Workflows

GitOps applies version control best practices to ML workflow management by storing pipeline definitions, model configurations, and deployment specifications in Git repositories that serve as the single source of truth for all ML operations. This approach provides transparency, collaboration, and automated change management for complex ML systems.

Repository Structure and Organization:

Model repositories organize code, configurations, and pipeline definitions using standardized directory structures that support collaboration and automation. Structured organization enables team members to understand and contribute to ML projects while maintaining consistency across different initiatives.

Branch strategies separate experimental development from production deployments while enabling parallel work on different features and improvements. Branching patterns adapt software development practices to ML workflows while maintaining isolation and integration capabilities.

Configuration management separates environment-specific parameters from pipeline logic while enabling testing and deployment automation. Configuration separation ensures consistency across environments while supporting customization for different deployment scenarios.

Documentation integration maintains current information about model behavior, deployment requirements, and operational procedures alongside code changes. Integrated documentation improves collaboration while ensuring operational knowledge remains accessible and current.

Automated Workflow Triggers:

Commit-based automation triggers pipeline execution when code or configuration changes are pushed to designated branches while maintaining quality controls and testing requirements. Automated triggers ensure consistent pipeline execution while reducing manual coordination overhead.

Pull request integration enables code review and automated testing before changes merge into main branches while maintaining code quality and knowledge sharing. PR workflows adapt collaborative development practices to ML scenarios while ensuring quality and consistency.

Scheduled execution enables regular pipeline runs for model retraining, data processing, and performance monitoring while maintaining automated operations. Scheduling automation ensures systems remain current while reducing manual operational overhead.

Event-driven triggers respond to external changes including new data availability, performance degradation, or business requirement updates while maintaining responsive automation. Event integration enables reactive automation while maintaining system reliability.

Change Management and Rollback:

Deployment automation ensures consistent model deployment processes while maintaining rollback capabilities and quality verification. Automated deployment reduces manual errors while providing reliable change management for production systems.

Version tracking maintains complete history of all model changes while enabling rapid rollback to previous versions when issues arise. Version management provides confidence for aggressive improvement while maintaining system stability.

Feature flagging enables gradual rollout of model changes while maintaining ability to disable features rapidly if problems occur. Feature flags provide deployment flexibility while reducing risks associated with model updates.

Case Example 2: Financial Trading Algorithm Management

A quantitative trading firm managed hundreds of algorithmic trading models that required rapid iteration, rigorous testing, and reliable deployment while maintaining regulatory compliance and risk management requirements.

GitOps implementation stored all model definitions, backtesting configurations, and deployment specifications in Git repositories with automated testing and validation triggered by code changes. Branch protection rules ensured all changes received peer review while maintaining development velocity.

Automated pipeline execution tested model performance against historical data while validating risk constraints and regulatory requirements before enabling production deployment. Continuous validation prevented deployment of models that violated risk limits while supporting rapid innovation.

Rollback automation enabled immediate reversion to previous model versions when market conditions changed or performance degraded unexpectedly. Rapid rollback capabilities provided confidence for aggressive model optimization while maintaining risk management standards.

Automated Testing Strategies

ML systems require specialized testing approaches that validate data quality, model performance, and business logic while accounting for the probabilistic nature of ML predictions and the complexity of data dependencies. Traditional software testing techniques must be adapted to handle the unique challenges of ML system validation.

Data Quality Testing:

Schema validation ensures input data conforms to expected formats, types, and constraints while preventing downstream processing errors. Schema testing catches data format changes early while providing clear error messages for debugging and resolution.

Statistical testing validates data distributions, missing value patterns, and outlier characteristics while identifying potential data quality issues that could affect model performance. Statistical validation adapts to changing data characteristics while maintaining quality standards.

Freshness monitoring ensures data updates occur within expected timeframes while alerting when stale data could affect model accuracy. Freshness testing prevents using outdated information while supporting timely decision-making requirements.

Completeness verification validates that required data elements are available while checking for systematic gaps that could introduce bias or degrade performance. Completeness testing ensures reliable model inputs while identifying data collection issues.

Model Performance Testing:

Accuracy validation ensures model predictions meet minimum performance thresholds while testing across different data segments and conditions. Performance testing prevents deployment of inadequate models while validating behavior across diverse scenarios.

Bias testing evaluates model behavior across different demographic groups while ensuring fair treatment and regulatory compliance. Bias validation identifies discriminatory patterns while supporting responsible AI deployment practices.

Robustness testing validates model performance under various input perturbations and edge cases while ensuring reliable behavior in production environments. Robustness validation identifies potential failure modes while improving system reliability.

Latency testing ensures model inference meets response time requirements while validating performance under various load conditions. Latency validation ensures user experience requirements while supporting capacity planning decisions.

Integration Testing:

End-to-end workflow testing validates complete ML pipelines including data processing, model training, and deployment while ensuring system integration works correctly. Integration testing catches system-level issues while validating operational workflows.

Dependency testing validates external service integration including data sources, monitoring systems, and deployment targets while ensuring reliable system operation. Dependency validation identifies integration issues while supporting system reliability.

Performance testing evaluates system behavior under production load conditions while identifying capacity limitations and optimization opportunities. Performance validation ensures systems meet operational requirements while supporting capacity planning.

Security testing validates access controls, data protection, and audit capabilities while ensuring compliance with organizational security policies. Security validation prevents vulnerabilities while supporting regulatory compliance requirements.

Blue-Green and Canary Deployments

Advanced deployment strategies minimize risks associated with model updates while enabling rapid rollback when issues arise. These approaches balance innovation velocity with operational stability by providing controlled exposure to changes while maintaining service availability.

Blue-Green Deployment Implementation:

Environment duplication maintains two identical production environments where one serves live traffic while the other receives new model deployments. This approach enables instant switching between versions while providing complete rollback capabilities.

Traffic switching enables immediate cutover to new model versions while maintaining ability to revert instantly if problems arise. Switching mechanisms provide rapid deployment while eliminating gradual rollout complexity and timing considerations.

Validation procedures ensure new environments function correctly before receiving production traffic while testing all system components and integrations. Pre-deployment validation prevents issues from affecting users while maintaining confidence in new deployments.

Resource management optimizes costs by using shared infrastructure for both environments while maintaining isolation and performance requirements. Resource optimization balances cost efficiency with deployment flexibility and system reliability.

Canary Deployment Strategies:

Gradual rollout exposes new models to increasing percentages of production traffic while monitoring performance and business metrics. Gradual exposure enables early issue detection while limiting impact on users and business operations.

A/B testing integration enables systematic comparison between model versions while measuring business impact and user experience changes. Testing integration provides data-driven deployment decisions while supporting continuous improvement.

Automated monitoring tracks canary deployment performance while triggering rollback procedures when metrics exceed acceptable thresholds. Automated monitoring ensures rapid response to issues while maintaining system reliability.

Traffic routing enables sophisticated request distribution based on user characteristics, request types, or business requirements while maintaining testing validity and operational control. Routing flexibility supports complex deployment scenarios while maintaining experimental rigor.

Rollback and Recovery Procedures:

Automated rollback triggers revert to previous model versions when performance metrics indicate issues while minimizing service disruption and business impact. Automated recovery provides safety nets while supporting aggressive deployment schedules.

Health checks continuously monitor system performance during deployments while providing early warning of potential issues. Health monitoring enables proactive response while maintaining service quality during transitions.

Data consistency ensures rollback procedures maintain system integrity while preserving audit trails and transaction records. Consistency management prevents data corruption while supporting reliable recovery operations.

Case Example 3: E-commerce Recommendation System Deployment

An online marketplace needed to deploy recommendation model updates that could significantly affect user engagement and revenue while maintaining service availability and enabling rapid rollback if problems occurred.

Blue-green deployment maintained duplicate recommendation environments while enabling instant switching between model versions. Load balancers provided seamless traffic routing while monitoring systems tracked user engagement and business metrics during transitions.

Canary deployment gradually exposed new recommendation models to increasing user percentages while measuring click-through rates, conversion rates, and customer satisfaction. Automated rollback triggered when any business metric degraded beyond acceptable thresholds.

Deployment results showed successful rollout of improved models that increased user engagement by 15% while providing confidence through controlled exposure and automated safety mechanisms. Advanced deployment strategies enabled aggressive optimization while maintaining system reliability.

Project: End-to-end MLOps Pipeline

This project builds a complete MLOps pipeline that integrates data processing, model training, validation, and deployment while providing monitoring, alerting, and automated maintenance capabilities.

Pipeline Architecture Design:

Modular pipeline design separates concerns while enabling reusable components across different ML projects and teams. Modular architecture accelerates development while ensuring consistency and maintainability across organizational ML initiatives.

Event-driven orchestration coordinates pipeline execution based on data availability, schedule requirements, and external triggers while optimizing resource utilization and execution timing. Event-driven design provides responsive automation while maintaining cost efficiency.

Multi-environment support ensures consistent pipeline behavior across development, staging, and production environments while enabling appropriate customization for each stage. Environment consistency reduces deployment risks while supporting reliable promotion workflows.

Data Processing Integration:

Automated data validation ensures input quality while preventing processing of corrupted or incomplete datasets. Validation automation catches issues early while maintaining pipeline reliability and result quality.

Feature engineering automation applies consistent transformation logic while enabling experimentation with new features and preprocessing approaches. Automated feature processing ensures consistency while supporting innovation and improvement.

Data versioning tracks dataset changes while enabling reproducible model training and experiment comparison. Version management supports systematic experimentation while maintaining audit trails for compliance and debugging.

Model Training and Validation:

Hyperparameter optimization integrates automated tuning while balancing exploration with computational budget constraints. Optimization automation improves model performance while managing resource costs and development timelines.

Cross-validation automation ensures robust performance estimates while testing model behavior across different data segments and conditions. Validation automation provides confidence in model quality while supporting deployment decisions.

Model comparison enables systematic evaluation of different algorithms and configurations while providing objective selection criteria. Comparison frameworks support data-driven model selection while maintaining experimental rigor.

Deployment and Monitoring:

Automated deployment handles model promotion through different environments while maintaining quality gates and approval workflows. Deployment automation reduces manual errors while ensuring consistent processes and rapid iteration.

Performance monitoring tracks model behavior in production while identifying degradation and optimization opportunities. Monitoring automation provides early warning systems while supporting proactive maintenance and improvement.

Alerting integration notifies appropriate teams when issues arise while providing sufficient context for rapid response and resolution. Alert systems balance sensitivity with practicality while ensuring critical issues receive immediate attention.

The MLOps Advantage

Sophisticated CI/CD practices provide competitive advantages through faster development cycles, more reliable deployments, and better system maintainability. Organizations that master MLOps practices achieve superior operational efficiency while reducing risks and accelerating innovation.

The automation capabilities established here support advanced monitoring and maintenance practices that further improve system reliability and business impact. Quality MLOps foundations enable organizations to realize the full potential of their ML investments while maintaining operational excellence.

Continuous Improvement Mindset

MLOps represents an ongoing journey of operational improvement rather than a destination to reach. Successful organizations continuously refine their practices while adapting to new technologies, changing requirements, and growing operational scale.

The foundation established here provides the framework for building sophisticated ML operations that scale with organizational growth while maintaining quality and reliability standards. Investment in MLOps capabilities pays dividends through improved efficiency, reduced risks, and accelerated innovation cycles.

Essential Takeaways

- SageMaker Pipelines provides managed orchestration for ML workflows while handling dependency management, resource allocation, and failure recovery
- GitOps applies version control best practices to ML workflows while providing transparency, collaboration, and automated change management
- Automated testing strategies must address data quality, model performance, and system integration while accounting for ML-specific challenges
- Blue-green and canary deployments minimize deployment risks while enabling rapid rollback and controlled exposure to changes
- End-to-end MLOps pipelines integrate all ML lifecycle stages while providing automation, monitoring, and maintenance capabilities

Chapter 16: Model Monitoring and Maintenance

Production machine learning systems degrade silently over time as data distributions shift, business conditions change, and model assumptions become invalid. Without systematic monitoring and maintenance, even the best models eventually fail catastrophically, often during critical business periods when their failure causes maximum damage. The challenge lies in detecting these degradations early enough to respond proactively rather than reactively.

SageMaker provides tools for automated model monitoring, but effective maintenance requires understanding the relationship between technical metrics and business impact while establishing response procedures that maintain service quality. Organizations that excel at model maintenance achieve competitive advantages through more reliable systems and faster adaptation to changing conditions.

SageMaker Model Monitor Implementation

SageMaker Model Monitor provides automated monitoring capabilities that detect data drift, model quality degradation, and bias evolution without requiring custom monitoring infrastructure. The service integrates with real-time endpoints and batch processing workflows while providing customizable alerting and response mechanisms (27).

Data Quality Monitoring Foundations:

Statistical monitoring tracks changes in input data distributions while comparing current patterns with baseline characteristics established during model training. Statistical analysis includes mean, variance, percentile, and distributional measures that provide quantitative assessment of data evolution over time.

Schema validation ensures input data maintains expected format, type, and structural characteristics while alerting when upstream systems introduce incompatible changes. Schema monitoring prevents processing errors while providing early warning of integration issues that could affect model performance.

Missing value monitoring tracks patterns of data completeness while identifying systematic changes in data availability that could indicate upstream system issues or evolving data collection practices. Completeness monitoring ensures model inputs remain adequate for reliable prediction generation.

Feature importance drift detection identifies when previously important features lose predictive value or when new patterns emerge that suggest model retraining requirements. Importance monitoring guides maintenance decisions while identifying optimization opportunities.

Model Performance Monitoring:

Prediction accuracy tracking compares model outputs with ground truth labels when available while measuring performance degradation over time. Accuracy monitoring provides direct assessment of model reliability while identifying periods requiring intervention.

Prediction distribution analysis monitors output patterns while detecting systematic shifts that could indicate model degradation or changing business conditions. Distribution monitoring identifies subtle changes that might not appear in accuracy metrics but suggest underlying issues.

Confidence calibration monitoring evaluates model uncertainty estimates while ensuring prediction confidence remains aligned with actual accuracy. Calibration monitoring supports decision-making confidence while identifying models that become overconfident or underconfident over time.

Business metric correlation connects technical performance measures with business outcomes while ensuring monitoring focuses on metrics that matter for organizational success. Business alignment ensures monitoring efforts support actual value creation rather than technical abstractions.

Bias and Fairness Monitoring:

Demographic parity tracking monitors model behavior across different population groups while detecting systematic bias that could indicate discriminatory treatment. Parity monitoring supports regulatory compliance while ensuring ethical AI deployment practices.

Equalized odds monitoring ensures model accuracy remains consistent across protected groups while identifying performance disparities that require attention. Accuracy monitoring maintains fairness standards while supporting reliable model behavior across all populations.

Representation monitoring tracks changes in population composition while ensuring models continue serving all groups appropriately as demographics evolve. Representation analysis guides retraining decisions while maintaining inclusive model behavior.

Case Example 1: Healthcare Risk Prediction Monitoring

A health insurance company deployed risk prediction models that determined coverage decisions and care management interventions. Model degradation could result in inappropriate coverage denials or missed opportunities for preventive care interventions.

Data quality monitoring tracked changes in patient demographics, medical history patterns, and healthcare utilization while detecting systematic shifts in population characteristics. Statistical analysis revealed gradual aging of the insured population that affected risk model accuracy over 18 months.

Performance monitoring compared predicted risk scores with actual healthcare utilization while measuring accuracy across different patient segments. Monitoring revealed 15% degradation in prediction accuracy for patients with rare diseases as medical treatments evolved.

Bias monitoring ensured risk predictions remained fair across different demographic groups while detecting potential discrimination in coverage decisions. Analysis identified geographic bias in rural areas where healthcare access patterns differed from urban training data.

Custom Drift Detection

While SageMaker Model Monitor provides comprehensive built-in capabilities, many scenarios require custom monitoring approaches that address domain-specific requirements, business logic, or specialized data characteristics. Custom monitoring enables organizations to address unique challenges while maintaining integration with existing operational systems.

Statistical Drift Detection Methods:

Population Stability Index (PSI) provides standardized measures of feature distribution changes while enabling comparison across different features and time periods. PSI calculation offers industry-standard drift assessment while supporting regulatory compliance and risk management requirements.

Kolmogorov-Smirnov testing provides statistical significance assessment for distribution differences while controlling for multiple comparisons across numerous features. KS testing offers rigorous statistical validation while preventing false alarms that could overwhelm monitoring systems.

Jensen-Shannon divergence measures symmetric distribution differences while providing intuitive interpretation of drift magnitude. JS divergence offers robust comparison metrics while handling both continuous and categorical features effectively.

Earth Mover's Distance quantifies the effort required to transform one distribution into another while providing geometric interpretation of data changes. EMD analysis offers detailed insight into distribution evolution while supporting root cause analysis.

Business-Specific Monitoring:

Domain-specific metrics incorporate business knowledge into monitoring frameworks while ensuring detection focuses on changes that affect business outcomes. Domain metrics adapt technical monitoring to business realities while improving relevance and actionability.

Seasonal adjustment accounts for predictable business cycles while distinguishing genuine drift from expected variations. Seasonal modeling prevents false alarms during normal business cycles while maintaining sensitivity to unexpected changes.

External factor integration incorporates economic indicators, market conditions, and environmental factors that affect model behavior while providing context for performance changes. External integration improves monitoring accuracy while supporting better response decisions.

Custom threshold optimization balances detection sensitivity with operational practicality while adapting to business tolerance for false alarms. Threshold tuning ensures monitoring provides actionable information while avoiding alert fatigue.

Real-time Monitoring Implementation:

Streaming data analysis enables immediate drift detection while providing rapid response capabilities for time-sensitive applications. Real-time monitoring reduces response times while supporting proactive rather than reactive maintenance.

Event-driven alerting triggers immediate notifications when drift exceeds acceptable thresholds while providing sufficient context for rapid response. Event-driven systems ensure critical issues receive immediate attention while supporting efficient operational workflows.

Dashboard integration provides visual monitoring capabilities while enabling stakeholder access to monitoring information without technical expertise requirements. Dashboard systems improve communication while supporting collaborative monitoring and response efforts.

Case Example 2: Financial Credit Scoring Monitoring

A digital lending platform needed custom monitoring for credit scoring models that detected economic changes, regulatory shifts, and evolving fraud patterns while maintaining fair lending compliance and business performance requirements.

Custom drift detection incorporated macroeconomic indicators, unemployment rates, and housing market conditions while distinguishing expected economic cycles from genuine model degradation. Economic integration improved monitoring accuracy while reducing false alarms during normal market fluctuations.

Fraud pattern monitoring tracked changes in application characteristics while detecting emerging fraud schemes that could affect model accuracy. Pattern analysis identified sophisticated fraud attempts that evolved beyond training data patterns.

Fairness monitoring ensured credit decisions remained unbiased across demographic groups while adapting to changing population characteristics and economic conditions. Custom bias metrics addressed regulatory requirements while supporting business objectives and ethical lending practices.

Automated Retraining Triggers

Effective model maintenance requires automated systems that identify retraining needs while balancing model freshness with computational costs and operational disruption. Intelligent retraining systems optimize timing while ensuring models remain accurate and relevant for business requirements.

Performance-Based Triggers:

Accuracy threshold monitoring triggers retraining when model performance drops below acceptable levels while accounting for natural variation and measurement uncertainty. Threshold-based triggers provide clear criteria while preventing unnecessary retraining during temporary fluctuations.

Business impact assessment triggers retraining based on financial or operational consequences rather than purely technical metrics while ensuring retraining focuses on business value creation. Impact-based triggers align maintenance efforts with organizational priorities while optimizing resource allocation.

Trend analysis identifies gradual performance degradation patterns while enabling proactive retraining before critical thresholds are reached. Trend-based triggers provide early intervention while preventing service disruption from sudden performance drops.

Confidence degradation monitoring triggers retraining when model uncertainty increases while ensuring prediction confidence remains reliable for decision-making. Confidence-based triggers maintain decision quality while preventing overconfident predictions during model degradation.

Data-Based Triggers:

Distribution shift detection triggers retraining when input data characteristics change significantly while distinguishing temporary variations from permanent shifts. Distribution-based triggers respond to fundamental data changes while avoiding unnecessary retraining for temporary anomalies.

Volume thresholds trigger retraining when sufficient new data accumulates while balancing model freshness with training costs and computational requirements. Volume-based triggers optimize retraining frequency while ensuring adequate data for model improvement.

Quality degradation triggers retraining when data quality issues affect model inputs while preventing degraded models from making unreliable predictions. Quality-based triggers maintain model reliability while responding to upstream data system changes.

Time-Based Triggers:

Scheduled retraining provides regular model updates while ensuring consistent maintenance regardless of performance metrics or data changes. Scheduled approaches provide predictable maintenance cycles while supporting operational planning and resource allocation.

Adaptive scheduling adjusts retraining frequency based on observed drift rates and performance patterns while optimizing maintenance timing for specific deployment scenarios. Adaptive approaches balance freshness with efficiency while learning optimal maintenance schedules.

Business cycle alignment coordinates retraining with seasonal patterns, product launches, or other business events while ensuring models remain current during critical periods. Cycle-aligned retraining optimizes timing while supporting business requirements and operational planning.

Case Example 3: E-commerce Demand Forecasting Maintenance

An online retailer operated demand forecasting models across thousands of products while requiring accurate predictions for inventory planning, pricing decisions, and supplier negotiations. Model degradation could result in stockouts, excess inventory, or pricing errors.

Performance-based triggers monitored forecast accuracy across different product categories while triggering retraining when prediction errors exceeded business tolerance levels. Accuracy monitoring balanced forecast quality with retraining costs while ensuring adequate inventory planning.

Seasonal trigger systems coordinated retraining with business cycles while ensuring models remained current during peak shopping periods. Seasonal coordination improved forecast accuracy during critical periods while optimizing computational resource utilization.

Event-driven triggers responded to external factors including supplier changes, competitive actions, and market disruptions while maintaining forecast reliability during business disruptions. Event-driven maintenance enabled rapid adaptation while maintaining forecasting quality during uncertain periods.

Performance Optimization

Production model performance requires ongoing optimization that balances prediction accuracy, response latency, and computational costs while maintaining service reliability and business value delivery. Optimization strategies must consider both technical performance and business requirements while enabling sustainable scaling.

Inference Optimization:

Model compression reduces memory footprint and computational requirements while maintaining prediction accuracy through techniques including quantization, pruning, and knowledge distillation. Compression optimization balances model size with accuracy while reducing serving costs and improving latency.

Caching strategies store frequently requested predictions while reducing computational overhead for repeated queries. Intelligent caching balances memory usage with response time improvements while handling cache invalidation when models update.

Batch processing optimization groups multiple inference requests while improving computational efficiency through vectorization and resource sharing. Batch optimization reduces per-prediction costs while managing latency requirements for time-sensitive applications.

Hardware acceleration utilizes specialized computing resources including GPUs, custom chips, and edge processors while optimizing for specific deployment scenarios and performance requirements. Acceleration strategies balance computational performance with infrastructure costs.

Infrastructure Optimization:

Auto-scaling configuration optimizes resource allocation based on traffic patterns while maintaining response time requirements and cost efficiency. Scaling optimization balances capacity with costs while ensuring adequate performance during traffic variations.

Load balancing distributes requests across available resources while providing fault tolerance and consistent performance during instance failures. Load optimization maximizes resource utilization while maintaining service reliability and user experience.

Geographic distribution reduces latency through edge deployment while balancing performance improvements with infrastructure complexity and costs. Geographic optimization improves user experience while managing operational overhead and deployment complexity.

Cost Optimization:

Instance type optimization selects appropriate computational resources based on model requirements and traffic patterns while minimizing infrastructure costs. Instance optimization balances performance with cost efficiency while adapting to changing workload characteristics.

Reserved capacity planning captures cost savings through committed usage while balancing savings with operational flexibility requirements. Capacity planning optimizes long-term costs while maintaining ability to scale and adapt to changing requirements.

Spot instance utilization reduces computational costs for fault-tolerant workloads while implementing recovery mechanisms for instance interruptions. Spot optimization provides significant cost savings while maintaining service reliability through appropriate fault tolerance design.

Project: Self-Healing ML System

This project builds an automated maintenance system that detects issues, diagnoses problems, and implements fixes while minimizing human intervention and maintaining service quality during maintenance operations.

Intelligent Monitoring Framework:

Multi-dimensional monitoring tracks model performance, data quality, infrastructure health, and business impact while providing unified visibility into system status. Monitoring integration enables comprehensive system assessment while supporting efficient troubleshooting and optimization.

Anomaly detection algorithms identify unusual patterns in system behavior while distinguishing genuine issues from normal variations. Intelligent detection reduces false alarms while ensuring critical issues receive appropriate attention and response.

Root cause analysis correlates symptoms across different system components while identifying underlying causes of performance degradation or failure. Analysis automation speeds problem resolution while reducing diagnostic overhead and improving system reliability.

Automated Response Systems:

Issue classification categorizes problems by severity, impact, and resolution complexity while routing responses to appropriate automated or human systems. Classification automation ensures proper response prioritization while optimizing resource allocation for problem resolution.

Self-healing procedures implement automatic fixes for common issues while maintaining audit trails and rollback capabilities. Automated healing reduces response times while maintaining system reliability and operational control.

Escalation workflows engage human experts when automated responses prove insufficient while providing context and diagnostic information for efficient problem resolution.

Escalation systems balance automation with human expertise while ensuring critical issues receive adequate attention.

Continuous Improvement:

Learning algorithms analyze historical issues and responses while improving detection accuracy and response effectiveness over time. Learning systems enable continuous improvement while reducing operational overhead and improving system reliability.

Feedback integration incorporates human expertise and business requirements into automated systems while ensuring automation remains aligned with organizational objectives. Feedback systems balance automation with human judgment while maintaining system effectiveness.

Performance measurement tracks system reliability, response times, and business impact while providing metrics for continuous optimization and improvement. Measurement systems enable data-driven improvement while demonstrating system value and effectiveness.

Operational Excellence Through Automation

Effective model monitoring and maintenance requires balancing automation with human oversight while ensuring systems remain reliable, efficient, and aligned with business objectives. Excellence in maintenance practices provides competitive advantages through more reliable systems and faster adaptation to changing conditions.

The monitoring and maintenance capabilities established here provide foundations for governance and compliance practices that further improve system reliability and regulatory adherence. Quality maintenance practices enable organizations to operate ML systems at scale while maintaining quality and compliance standards.

Strategic Advantages

Organizations that master model monitoring and maintenance achieve superior operational efficiency while reducing risks and improving business outcomes. Investment in proper maintenance capabilities pays dividends through reduced downtime, improved performance, and faster adaptation to changing conditions.

Essential Takeaways

- SageMaker Model Monitor provides automated monitoring for data drift, model performance, and bias while integrating with real-time and batch processing workflows
- Custom drift detection enables domain-specific monitoring that addresses unique business requirements while maintaining statistical rigor
- Automated retraining triggers balance model freshness with computational costs while ensuring models remain accurate and relevant
- Performance optimization balances prediction accuracy, response latency, and computational costs while maintaining service reliability
- Self-healing ML systems provide automated maintenance capabilities that minimize human intervention while maintaining service quality

Chapter 17: Governance and Compliance

Machine learning governance represents the framework that enables organizations to deploy AI systems responsibly while meeting regulatory requirements, managing risks, and maintaining stakeholder trust. As ML systems affect increasingly critical business decisions, governance becomes essential for sustainable scaling and regulatory compliance rather than optional best practices.

AWS SageMaker provides tools for implementing governance frameworks, but effective compliance requires understanding both technical capabilities and regulatory requirements while establishing organizational processes that balance innovation with risk management. Organizations that excel at ML governance achieve competitive advantages through faster regulatory approval, reduced compliance costs, and improved stakeholder confidence.

Model Registry Best Practices

Model registries serve as central repositories that track model artifacts, metadata, and lifecycle information while providing version control, approval workflows, and deployment management capabilities. Effective model registry implementation enables organizations to maintain comprehensive oversight of ML assets while supporting collaboration and compliance requirements (28).

Centralized Model Management:

Artifact storage maintains complete model packages including trained models, preprocessing code, evaluation metrics, and deployment configurations while ensuring reproducibility and audit compliance. Centralized storage provides single source of truth while supporting various deployment scenarios and rollback requirements.

Metadata management captures comprehensive information about model development including training data sources, algorithm selections, hyperparameter configurations, and performance metrics while enabling search and discovery across organizational model portfolios. Rich metadata supports informed decision-making while improving collaboration and knowledge sharing.

Version control tracks model evolution while maintaining complete history of changes, approvals, and deployments across all environments. Comprehensive versioning enables rollback capabilities while supporting audit requirements and regulatory compliance documentation.

Dependency tracking maintains relationships between models, data sources, and infrastructure components while enabling impact analysis when changes occur. Dependency management supports reliable operations while enabling efficient change management and risk assessment.

Approval Workflow Implementation:

Stage-gate processes require explicit approval before models advance through development, validation, and production stages while ensuring appropriate review and sign-off at each transition. Approval workflows balance automation with governance while maintaining quality control and risk management.

Role-based permissions ensure appropriate stakeholders review model changes while maintaining security and segregation of duties. Permission systems balance collaboration with control while ensuring accountability and audit compliance.

Automated validation integrates technical and business criteria into approval workflows while reducing manual review overhead and ensuring consistent evaluation standards. Validation automation improves efficiency while maintaining quality and compliance standards.

Documentation requirements ensure complete information accompanies model approvals while supporting regulatory compliance and knowledge transfer. Documentation standards improve communication while providing audit trails and institutional knowledge preservation.

Performance Tracking and Monitoring:

Model lineage tracks relationships between models, training data, and business outcomes while enabling impact analysis and accountability assessment. Lineage tracking supports debugging and improvement while providing compliance documentation and audit capabilities.

Performance history maintains comprehensive records of model behavior over time while enabling trend analysis and degradation detection. Historical tracking supports optimization decisions while providing evidence for regulatory reporting and compliance assessment.

Business impact measurement correlates model performance with organizational outcomes while demonstrating value creation and supporting investment decisions. Impact tracking aligns technical metrics with business objectives while providing justification for continued development and deployment.

Case Example 1: Pharmaceutical Regulatory Compliance

A pharmaceutical company needed to maintain comprehensive oversight of drug discovery models used in clinical trial design and regulatory submissions while ensuring compliance with FDA requirements and institutional review board standards.

Model registry implementation tracked all predictive models used in drug development while maintaining complete documentation of training data sources, validation procedures, and performance characteristics. Registry systems provided audit trails required for regulatory submissions while supporting collaborative research across multiple teams.

Approval workflows required review by statistical experts, clinical researchers, and regulatory affairs specialists before models could inform clinical trial design or regulatory submissions. Multi-stakeholder approval ensured scientific rigor while maintaining compliance with regulatory standards and institutional policies.

Performance tracking monitored model accuracy across different patient populations while documenting bias assessments and fairness evaluations required for regulatory approval. Tracking systems provided evidence for regulatory submissions while supporting post-market surveillance and safety monitoring requirements.

Audit Trails and Lineage

Comprehensive audit trails provide complete records of ML system activities while supporting regulatory compliance, security investigations, and operational debugging. Effective audit implementation balances comprehensive tracking with operational efficiency while ensuring information remains accessible and actionable.

Data Lineage Tracking:

Source identification maintains complete records of data origins while tracking transformations, aggregations, and quality assessments throughout processing pipelines. Source tracking supports debugging while providing evidence for data quality and compliance assessment.

Transformation documentation captures all processing steps applied to data while maintaining reproducibility and enabling impact analysis when upstream changes occur.

Transformation tracking supports troubleshooting while providing compliance documentation for regulatory requirements.

Access logging records all data access activities while identifying users, systems, and purposes for data usage. Access tracking supports security investigations while providing audit evidence for privacy compliance and data governance requirements.

Quality metrics maintain records of data assessment results while tracking improvements and degradations over time. Quality documentation supports operational decisions while providing evidence for compliance reporting and regulatory assessment.

Model Development Audit:

Experiment tracking maintains comprehensive records of model development activities while capturing hyperparameter explorations, algorithm comparisons, and validation results. Experiment documentation supports reproducibility while providing evidence for regulatory submissions and audit requirements.

Code versioning tracks all development artifacts while maintaining relationships between code changes, model performance, and deployment activities. Code tracking supports debugging while providing audit trails for regulatory compliance and intellectual property protection.

Collaboration records maintain information about team members, reviewers, and approvers involved in model development while supporting accountability and knowledge transfer. Collaboration tracking supports audit requirements while improving institutional knowledge management.

Performance documentation captures all evaluation activities while maintaining evidence for model validation and regulatory compliance. Performance records support audit requirements while providing foundation for continuous improvement and optimization.

Production Operations Audit:

Deployment tracking maintains records of all model deployments while capturing approval decisions, configuration changes, and performance monitoring results. Deployment documentation supports rollback decisions while providing audit evidence for operational compliance.

Inference logging records prediction requests and responses while maintaining privacy compliance and enabling performance analysis. Inference tracking supports debugging while providing evidence for audit requirements and business impact assessment.

Maintenance activities documentation captures all model updates, retraining activities, and configuration changes while maintaining comprehensive operational history. Maintenance records support troubleshooting while providing evidence for compliance reporting and audit requirements.

Case Example 2: Financial Services Audit Compliance

A regional bank implemented comprehensive audit trails for credit decision models while ensuring compliance with fair lending regulations, internal audit requirements, and regulatory examination standards.

Data lineage tracking maintained complete records of customer information sources while documenting all transformations and aggregations used in credit scoring. Lineage systems provided evidence for regulatory examinations while supporting data quality investigations and compliance assessment.

Model development audit captured all algorithm selections, validation procedures, and bias assessments while maintaining records required for regulatory compliance and internal audit review. Development documentation supported regulatory submissions while providing foundation for model governance and risk management.

Production audit trails recorded all credit decisions while maintaining privacy compliance and enabling bias monitoring and fair lending assessment. Production tracking supported regulatory reporting while providing evidence for compliance investigations and audit requirements.

GDPR and HIPAA Compliance Patterns

Data privacy regulations require specific technical and organizational measures that affect ML system design, operation, and governance. Understanding compliance requirements enables organizations to implement appropriate safeguards while maintaining ML capability and business value creation.

GDPR Compliance Implementation:

Data minimization principles limit collection and processing to information necessary for specific business purposes while ensuring ML systems don't accumulate unnecessary personal data. Minimization practices reduce privacy risks while simplifying compliance and reducing operational overhead.

Consent management tracks user permissions for data processing while enabling withdrawal and modification of consent preferences. Consent systems support user rights while maintaining operational capability and regulatory compliance.

Right to explanation requires providing understandable information about automated decision-making while balancing transparency with intellectual property protection. Explanation capabilities support user rights while maintaining competitive advantages and operational efficiency.

Data portability enables users to obtain personal data in machine-readable formats while supporting transfer requests and competitive requirements. Portability systems support user rights while maintaining data security and system integrity.

HIPAA Compliance Framework:

Physical safeguards protect computing systems and equipment while ensuring secure access to healthcare information and preventing unauthorized access. Physical security supports compliance while maintaining operational efficiency and business capability.

Administrative safeguards establish organizational policies and procedures while ensuring appropriate access controls and staff training for healthcare information protection. Administrative measures support compliance culture while maintaining operational effectiveness and regulatory adherence.

Technical safeguards implement technology controls while ensuring secure data transmission, access controls, and audit capabilities for healthcare information systems. Technical measures provide compliance infrastructure while supporting operational requirements and business objectives.

Privacy-Preserving ML Techniques:

Differential privacy adds calibrated noise to training data or model outputs while providing mathematical guarantees about individual privacy protection. Differential privacy enables ML capability while maintaining strong privacy protection and regulatory compliance.

Federated learning enables model training across distributed data sources while avoiding centralized data collection and reducing privacy risks. Federated approaches support ML development while maintaining data locality and privacy compliance.

Homomorphic encryption enables computation on encrypted data while maintaining privacy protection throughout processing workflows. Encryption approaches provide strong security while enabling ML capability and regulatory compliance.

Data anonymization removes or modifies personally identifiable information while maintaining data utility for ML applications. Anonymization techniques balance privacy protection with analytical capability while supporting compliance requirements.

Case Example 3: Healthcare AI Platform Compliance

A health technology company developed AI diagnostic tools while ensuring compliance with HIPAA requirements, FDA regulations, and international privacy standards across multiple healthcare systems and geographic regions.

GDPR compliance implementation provided user consent management, data portability, and explanation capabilities while maintaining diagnostic accuracy and clinical workflow integration. Privacy systems supported regulatory compliance while preserving clinical utility and operational efficiency.

HIPAA safeguards protected patient health information throughout AI processing while maintaining audit trails and access controls required for healthcare compliance. Security measures provided comprehensive protection while supporting clinical decision-making and operational requirements.

Privacy-preserving ML techniques enabled model training across multiple healthcare systems while avoiding centralized patient data collection and maintaining local privacy compliance. Federated learning approaches supported model improvement while maintaining institutional autonomy and regulatory compliance.

Cost Allocation and Chargeback

ML resource allocation and cost management require sophisticated tracking and allocation systems that attribute expenses to appropriate business units while supporting optimization decisions and budget management. Effective cost management enables organizations to optimize ML investments while maintaining accountability and financial control.

Resource Usage Tracking:

Compute allocation monitoring tracks processing resources used by different projects, teams, and business units while providing detailed cost attribution and usage analysis. Resource tracking supports budget management while enabling optimization decisions and capacity planning.

Storage cost allocation attributes data storage expenses to appropriate stakeholders while considering data sharing, backup requirements, and retention policies. Storage tracking provides cost transparency while supporting data management decisions and optimization opportunities.

Data transfer monitoring tracks bandwidth usage between regions, services, and external systems while attributing costs to responsible parties and identifying optimization opportunities. Transfer tracking reduces unexpected costs while supporting architecture decisions and resource optimization.

Business Unit Attribution:

Project-based allocation assigns costs to specific ML initiatives while providing visibility into project expenses and return on investment. Project tracking supports portfolio management while enabling investment decisions and resource allocation optimization.

Team-based allocation distributes shared infrastructure costs while maintaining fairness and accountability for resource usage. Team allocation supports budget management while encouraging efficient resource utilization and optimization.

Product-based allocation attributes ML costs to business products and services while supporting pricing decisions and profitability analysis. Product allocation enables business impact assessment while supporting strategic decisions and resource investment priorities.

Optimization and Budgeting:

Usage analytics identify optimization opportunities while providing insights into resource utilization patterns and efficiency improvements. Analytics support cost reduction while maintaining ML capability and business value creation.

Budget forecasting predicts future ML expenses while considering growth plans, technology changes, and optimization initiatives. Forecasting supports financial planning while enabling proactive budget management and resource allocation.

Cost optimization recommendations provide actionable guidance for reducing expenses while maintaining ML performance and business value. Optimization guidance supports financial efficiency while ensuring continued ML capability and competitive advantage.

Project: Enterprise Governance Framework

This project builds a comprehensive governance system that integrates model registry, audit trails, compliance monitoring, and cost management while supporting organizational scaling and regulatory requirements.

Governance Architecture Design:

Policy framework establishes organizational standards for ML development, deployment, and operations while ensuring consistency and compliance across all teams and projects. Policy systems provide guidance while maintaining flexibility for innovation and business requirements.

Workflow integration embeds governance requirements into development and deployment processes while minimizing overhead and maintaining operational efficiency. Integration systems ensure compliance while supporting productivity and innovation objectives.

Monitoring and reporting provide comprehensive visibility into governance compliance while supporting audit requirements and continuous improvement initiatives. Reporting systems demonstrate compliance while identifying optimization opportunities and process improvements.

Implementation and Operations:

Training and certification ensure stakeholders understand governance requirements while building organizational capability for compliance and risk management. Training programs support governance culture while maintaining operational effectiveness and regulatory adherence.

Tool integration connects governance systems with development workflows while ensuring seamless compliance and minimal friction for development teams. Integration systems support adoption while maintaining productivity and innovation capability.

Continuous improvement processes adapt governance frameworks to changing requirements while incorporating lessons learned and best practices from operational experience.

Improvement systems ensure governance remains effective while supporting organizational growth and evolution.

Governance as Competitive Advantage

Effective ML governance provides competitive advantages through faster regulatory approval, reduced compliance costs, and improved stakeholder confidence while enabling sustainable scaling and risk management. Organizations that excel at governance achieve superior operational efficiency while maintaining innovation capability and business value creation.

Investment in proper governance frameworks pays dividends through reduced operational risks, improved regulatory relationships, and enhanced stakeholder trust while supporting sustainable ML deployment and business growth.

The Governance Imperative

As ML systems become more prevalent and impactful, governance transitions from optional best practice to business imperative that affects competitive positioning, regulatory compliance, and stakeholder relationships. Organizations that establish strong governance foundations early achieve advantages while avoiding costly remediation and compliance issues.

Essential Takeaways

- Model registries provide centralized management of ML assets while supporting version control, approval workflows, and deployment oversight
- Comprehensive audit trails enable regulatory compliance, security investigations, and operational debugging while maintaining accountability
- GDPR and HIPAA compliance require specific technical and organizational measures that balance privacy protection with ML capability
- Cost allocation and chargeback systems provide financial transparency while supporting optimization decisions and budget management
- Enterprise governance frameworks integrate all compliance requirements while supporting organizational scaling and regulatory adherence

Practice Questions: AWS ML Engineer Associate Exam Preparation

Question 101: A company needs to implement model versioning that supports both development iterations and production deployments. Which SageMaker capability provides this functionality?

A) S3 bucket versioning for model artifacts B) SageMaker Model Registry with approval workflows C) Git repository integration with SageMaker D) Lambda functions for model version management

Correct Answer: B - SageMaker Model Registry provides comprehensive model versioning with approval workflows that support both development iteration and production deployment governance.

Question 102: For GDPR compliance, a model needs to provide explanations for automated decisions affecting EU citizens. Which AWS service best supports this requirement?

A) SageMaker Autopilot for automated model selection B) SageMaker Clarify for model interpretability and explanations C) CloudWatch for monitoring and logging D) AWS Config for compliance tracking

Correct Answer: B - SageMaker Clarify provides model interpretability features including SHAP explanations that support GDPR's right to explanation requirements.

Question 103: A healthcare organization needs to track all access to patient data used in ML models. Which approach best supports HIPAA audit requirements?

A) CloudWatch logs with custom log parsing B) AWS CloudTrail with S3 data events enabled C) Manual access logs maintained by data scientists D) Database query logs from source systems only

Correct Answer: B - AWS CloudTrail with S3 data events provides comprehensive audit trails that track all data access activities required for HIPAA compliance.

Question 104: When implementing model monitoring that triggers automated retraining, which metric should be the primary trigger for a fraud detection system?

A) Model inference latency increases B) Data distribution drift in input features C) False negative rate exceeds business threshold D) Training data volume reaches minimum threshold

Correct Answer: C - False negative rate directly impacts business outcomes in fraud detection, where missing fraud cases has higher cost than false positives.

Question 105: A model registry needs to track relationships between models and their training datasets for compliance purposes. Which metadata is most critical to maintain?

A) Model file sizes and storage locations B) Data lineage including source systems and transformations C) Developer names and training timestamps D) Hyperparameter values and algorithm types

Correct Answer: B - Data lineage tracking is essential for compliance, enabling audit trails and impact analysis when data sources change.

Question 106: For cost allocation across multiple business units using shared ML infrastructure, which tagging strategy provides the most granular attribution?

A) Tag resources by AWS service type only B) Tag resources with project, team, and cost center information C) Tag resources by geographic region and availability zone D) Tag resources with creation timestamp and owner email

Correct Answer: B - Project, team, and cost center tags enable detailed cost attribution across business units while supporting budget management and chargeback processes.

Question 107: A model shows data drift that exceeds monitoring thresholds. Which automated response provides the best balance of reliability and efficiency?

A) Immediately retrain the model with all available data B) Flag for manual review while continuing current model operation C) Automatically roll back to the previous model version D) Increase monitoring frequency without other changes

Correct Answer: B - Flagging for manual review allows expert assessment while maintaining service availability, balancing automation with human judgment.

Question 108: When implementing differential privacy for a ML training dataset, which parameter most directly controls the privacy-utility tradeoff?

A) Training batch size and number of epochs B) Epsilon value in the differential privacy mechanism C) Learning rate and optimization algorithm choice D) Feature selection and dimensionality reduction

Correct Answer: B - The epsilon parameter directly controls privacy protection strength, with smaller values providing stronger privacy but potentially reducing model utility.

Question 109: A SageMaker Model Monitor detects bias in model predictions across demographic groups. Which immediate action best addresses this finding?

A) Retrain the model with more balanced training data B) Adjust prediction thresholds to equalize outcomes across groups C) Investigate the source of bias and develop appropriate mitigation strategy D) Remove demographic features from the model inputs

Correct Answer: C - Investigation enables understanding the bias source and developing appropriate mitigation that addresses root causes rather than symptoms.

Question 110: For multi-environment model deployment (dev/staging/prod), which governance control is most important for production safety?

A) Identical hardware configuration across all environments B) Approval workflows before production deployment C) Real-time synchronization of model versions D) Shared databases between environments

Correct Answer: B - Approval workflows provide governance control that ensures production deployments meet quality and compliance standards before affecting business operations.

Question 111: When implementing federated learning for privacy compliance, which technical challenge requires the most careful attention?

A) Model aggregation algorithms and convergence guarantees B) Network bandwidth optimization between participants C) Hardware compatibility across different organizations D) User interface design for distributed model training

Correct Answer: A - Model aggregation is critical for federated learning effectiveness, requiring careful algorithm design to ensure convergence while maintaining privacy.

Question 112: A model audit reveals inconsistent performance across different customer segments. Which governance response best addresses this finding?

A) Retrain the model to optimize overall average performance B) Deploy segment-specific models for each customer group C) Implement bias monitoring and mitigation procedures D) Increase model complexity to capture segment differences

Correct Answer: C - Bias monitoring and mitigation procedures address fairness concerns systematically while ensuring ongoing compliance and performance equity.

Question 113: For HIPAA compliance in ML workflows, which data handling practice is most critical?

A) Encrypting all data at rest and in transit B) Limiting data access to US-based AWS regions only C) Requiring multi-factor authentication for all users D) Implementing automatic data deletion after 90 days

Correct Answer: A - Encryption at rest and in transit is a fundamental HIPAA technical safeguard that protects patient health information throughout ML processing.

Question 114: When tracking model lineage for regulatory compliance, which relationship is most important to document?

A) Model performance metrics across different time periods B) Connections between training data sources and model predictions C) Developer assignments and code review approvals D) Infrastructure costs and resource utilization patterns

Correct Answer: B - Data-to-prediction lineage is critical for regulatory compliance, enabling impact analysis and audit trail documentation.

Question 115: A cost analysis reveals that model training represents 80% of ML infrastructure costs. Which optimization strategy addresses this most effectively?

A) Use smaller instance types for all training jobs B) Implement spot instances with fault-tolerant training procedures C) Reduce training data volume to decrease processing time D) Share training infrastructure across multiple teams

Correct Answer: B - Spot instances can reduce training costs by 70-90% while maintaining capabilities through fault-tolerant design.

Question 116: For model explainability in regulated industries, which approach provides the most comprehensive interpretability?

A) Global feature importance rankings across all predictions B) Local explanations for individual predictions plus global insights C) Model performance metrics segmented by key business dimensions D) Statistical correlation analysis between inputs and outputs

Correct Answer: B - Combined local and global explanations provide comprehensive interpretability that supports both individual decision explanations and overall model understanding.

Question 117: When implementing automated model retraining triggers, which combination of factors provides the most robust triggering system?

A) Fixed time intervals based on business cycles B) Performance degradation plus data drift detection C) New data availability exceeding volume thresholds D) Manual approval requests from business stakeholders

Correct Answer: B - Performance degradation combined with data drift provides comprehensive triggering that responds to both model quality issues and changing conditions.

Question 118: A governance framework needs to balance innovation velocity with compliance requirements. Which approach best achieves this balance?

A) Require manual approval for all model changes B) Implement automated compliance checking with approval workflows for high-risk changes C) Allow unrestricted development with annual compliance audits D) Separate development and production teams completely

Correct Answer: B - Automated compliance checking with risk-based approval workflows maintains innovation speed while ensuring appropriate governance oversight.

Question 119: For cross-border data transfer in ML applications, which AWS capability best supports GDPR compliance?

A) VPC peering connections between regions B) AWS Data Processing Addendum and appropriate region selection C) CloudFront content delivery networks D) Direct Connect private network connections

Correct Answer: B - AWS Data Processing Addendum provides GDPR compliance framework, while appropriate region selection ensures data residency requirements.

Question 120: When implementing model version control in SageMaker Model Registry, which approval workflow provides the strongest governance?

A) Automatic approval based on performance metrics B) Single approver from the development team C) Multi-stage approval including business and technical stakeholders D) Self-approval by model developers

Correct Answer: C - Multi-stage approval with diverse stakeholders ensures comprehensive review while maintaining appropriate governance oversight and risk management.

Question 121: A model monitoring system detects gradual accuracy degradation over six months. Which response strategy best balances service reliability with improvement opportunities?

A) Immediate model replacement with previous version B) Gradual traffic shifting to retrained model with performance monitoring C) Parallel deployment of new model with A/B testing D) Complete system maintenance window for model updates

Correct Answer: C - Parallel deployment with A/B testing enables safe model improvement while maintaining service availability and providing performance comparison.

Question 122: For audit trail requirements in financial services, which information is most critical to maintain in model prediction logs?

A) Detailed model architecture and hyperparameters B) Input features, prediction outputs, and decision rationale C) Training data sources and preprocessing steps D) Infrastructure costs and resource utilization metrics

Correct Answer: B - Input-output logging with decision rationale provides audit trail for individual decisions while supporting regulatory requirements and compliance investigations.

Question 123: When implementing data minimization for GDPR compliance in ML systems, which practice best balances privacy with model performance?

A) Remove all potentially identifying features from training data B) Use feature selection techniques to identify minimum necessary features for model performance C) Anonymize all data through random noise addition D) Limit training data to the smallest possible dataset size

Correct Answer: B - Feature selection identifies minimum necessary features while maintaining model performance, implementing data minimization without unnecessary capability sacrifice.

Question 124: A governance audit reveals inconsistent model approval processes across different teams. Which standardization approach provides the most effective improvement?

A) Mandate identical approval workflows for all teams B) Develop risk-based approval frameworks with team-specific adaptations C) Eliminate approval requirements to improve development velocity D) Centralize all model development under single team

Correct Answer: B - Risk-based frameworks provide appropriate governance while allowing team-specific adaptations that support diverse business requirements and risk profiles.

Question 125: For model bias monitoring in production, which measurement approach provides the most actionable insights?

A) Overall model accuracy across the entire population B) Performance metrics segmented by protected demographic groups C) Feature importance rankings updated monthly D) Prediction confidence scores and calibration analysis

Correct Answer: B - Segmented performance metrics directly measure fairness across groups while providing actionable information for bias mitigation and compliance.

Question 126: When implementing cost chargeback for shared ML infrastructure, which allocation method provides the fairest distribution?

A) Equal allocation across all teams regardless of usage B) Allocation based on actual resource consumption with detailed tracking C) Allocation based on team size and budget capacity D) Allocation based on business value generated by ML models

Correct Answer: B - Usage-based allocation provides fair cost distribution while encouraging efficient resource utilization and supporting accurate budget planning.

Question 127: A model requires explanation capabilities for loan approval decisions. Which technical approach best supports both accuracy and explainability requirements?

A) Use only linear models for inherent interpretability B) Implement post-hoc explanation methods with performance validation C) Restrict features to only directly interpretable variables D) Provide statistical summaries instead of individual explanations

Correct Answer: B - Post-hoc explanation methods like SHAP enable high-performance models while providing individual decision explanations required for loan decisions.

Question 128: For HIPAA compliance in ML model serving, which infrastructure configuration provides the strongest data protection?

A) Public cloud deployment with encryption B) VPC deployment with private subnets and encryption C) On-premises deployment only D) Hybrid cloud with data replication

Correct Answer: B - VPC deployment with private subnets provides network isolation while encryption ensures data protection, meeting HIPAA technical safeguards.

Question 129: When tracking model lineage for compliance, which automated approach provides the most comprehensive documentation?

A) Manual documentation by data scientists B) Git commit messages with model training details C) Automated metadata capture during pipeline execution D) Quarterly compliance reports with model summaries

Correct Answer: C - Automated metadata capture ensures comprehensive, consistent lineage documentation without manual overhead while maintaining accuracy.

Question 130: A governance framework needs to address model updates that affect regulatory compliance. Which control mechanism provides the best oversight?

A) Automated deployment with post-deployment monitoring B) Risk assessment with appropriate approval workflows before deployment C) Annual compliance review of all deployed models D) Continuous monitoring without deployment restrictions

Correct Answer: B - Risk assessment with approval workflows ensures compliance review before deployment while balancing governance with operational efficiency.

Question 131: For differential privacy implementation in model training, which consideration is most important for maintaining business value?

A) Minimizing computational overhead during training B) Balancing privacy protection with model accuracy requirements C) Ensuring compatibility with existing ML frameworks D) Optimizing training time and resource utilization

Correct Answer: B - The privacy-utility tradeoff is fundamental to differential privacy, requiring careful calibration to maintain business value while achieving privacy goals.

Question 132: When implementing federated learning for multi-organization collaboration, which governance challenge requires the most attention?

A) Technical integration complexity across organizations B) Data sharing agreements and liability frameworks C) Hardware compatibility and network optimization D) Algorithm selection and hyperparameter tuning

Correct Answer: B - Data sharing agreements are critical for federated learning governance, addressing legal responsibilities and compliance requirements across organizations.

Question 133: A model registry audit reveals inconsistent metadata across different model versions. Which improvement provides the most comprehensive solution?

A) Require manual metadata entry for all new models B) Implement automated metadata collection with validation rules C) Standardize metadata format without enforcement D) Limit registry access to designated administrators only

Correct Answer: B - Automated collection with validation ensures consistent, comprehensive metadata while reducing manual overhead and preventing inconsistencies.

Question 134: For cost optimization in ML governance, which measurement approach provides the most actionable insights?

A) Total ML infrastructure costs aggregated monthly B) Cost per prediction with business value correlation C) Resource utilization percentages across all services D) Development team productivity metrics

Correct Answer: B - Cost per prediction with business value correlation enables optimization decisions that balance efficiency with business impact.

Question 135: When implementing bias monitoring for production models, which alerting strategy provides the most effective governance?

A) Daily automated reports with all bias metrics B) Threshold-based alerts with escalation procedures for significant bias C) Weekly bias summaries sent to all stakeholders D) Real-time notifications for every prediction variance

Correct Answer: B - Threshold-based alerts with escalation ensure significant bias receives immediate attention while preventing alert fatigue from routine variations.

Question 136: A compliance audit requires demonstrating model accuracy across different customer segments. Which documentation approach best supports this requirement?

A) Overall model performance metrics aggregated across all customers B) Segmented performance analysis with statistical significance testing C) Individual prediction accuracy for sample customers D) Training data statistics and validation procedures

Correct Answer: B - Segmented analysis with statistical testing provides comprehensive evidence of fair model performance across different populations.

Question 137: For model explainability in healthcare applications, which approach best balances clinical needs with technical capabilities?

A) Provide statistical confidence scores for all predictions B) Generate clinical reasoning narratives with feature importance C) Display raw model coefficients and mathematical formulas D) Offer simplified decision trees for all complex models

Correct Answer: B - Clinical reasoning narratives with feature importance provide medically relevant explanations while maintaining technical accuracy and usability.

Question 138: When implementing automated compliance checking for ML pipelines, which validation provides the most comprehensive governance?

A) Code quality checks and unit test coverage B) Data quality, model performance, and bias assessment validation C) Infrastructure security and access control verification D) Development workflow and approval process compliance

Correct Answer: B - ML-specific validation covering data quality, performance, and bias addresses the unique compliance challenges of machine learning systems.

Question 139: For cross-border ML deployment with GDPR requirements, which architectural approach provides the strongest compliance?

A) Centralized data processing in single region B) Data localization with regional model deployment C) Global data replication with consistent processing D) Hybrid cloud deployment across multiple providers

Correct Answer: B - Data localization with regional deployment ensures GDPR compliance while maintaining ML capabilities within appropriate jurisdictions.

Question 140: A governance framework needs to address model fairness across multiple demographic dimensions. Which monitoring approach provides the most comprehensive assessment?

A) Single fairness metric applied to overall population B) Multiple fairness metrics evaluated across intersectional groups C) Accuracy comparison between majority and minority groups only D) Statistical parity measurement for individual protected attributes

Correct Answer: B - Multiple metrics across intersectional groups provide comprehensive fairness assessment that addresses complex demographic interactions.

Question 141: When implementing model version control for regulatory compliance, which information is most critical to maintain immutably?

A) Model training logs and hyperparameter configurations B) Complete model artifacts, training data references, and approval records C) Developer comments and code review discussions D) Infrastructure configurations and deployment scripts

Correct Answer: B - Complete artifacts, data references, and approvals provide comprehensive audit trail for regulatory compliance and reproducibility.

Question 142: For automated model retraining in regulated environments, which governance control is most important?

A) Automated deployment without human intervention B) Validation and approval requirements before production deployment C) Real-time monitoring during retraining processes D) Immediate rollback capabilities for performance issues

Correct Answer: B - Validation and approval ensure retrained models meet compliance requirements before affecting regulated decisions.

Question 143: A cost allocation system needs to attribute shared ML infrastructure expenses fairly across business units. Which approach provides the most accurate allocation?

A) Equal distribution regardless of actual usage patterns B) Time-based allocation using detailed resource consumption logs C) Revenue-based allocation according to business unit size D) Project-based allocation using estimated resource requirements

Correct Answer: B - Time-based allocation using actual consumption provides accurate, fair cost distribution while encouraging efficient resource utilization.

Question 144: For model interpretability requirements in financial services, which combination of techniques provides the most comprehensive explanation capabilities?

A) Global feature importance with local SHAP explanations B) Decision tree visualizations with statistical summaries C) Model coefficient displays with confidence intervals D) Prediction probability distributions with uncertainty estimates

Correct Answer: A - Global feature importance combined with local SHAP explanations provides both overall model understanding and individual decision explanations.

Question 145: When implementing governance for experimental ML projects, which approach best balances innovation with risk management?

A) Apply full production governance to all experimental work B) Implement lightweight governance with risk-based escalation C) Eliminate governance requirements for experimental projects D) Require separate infrastructure for all experimental activities

Correct Answer: B - Lightweight governance with risk-based escalation enables innovation while ensuring appropriate oversight based on project risk and impact.

Chapter 18: Computer Vision MLOps

Computer vision systems process visual information at scales and speeds that exceed human capabilities, yet deploying these systems reliably in production environments presents unique challenges that traditional software deployment practices cannot address. Images and videos carry information densities orders of magnitude higher than structured data, requiring specialized infrastructure, preprocessing pipelines, and monitoring approaches that account for visual complexity and computational demands.

AWS provides both managed computer vision services and infrastructure for custom model deployment, but choosing between these approaches requires understanding business requirements, performance constraints, and long-term scalability needs. Organizations that master computer vision MLOps achieve competitive advantages through faster deployment cycles, more reliable systems, and better adaptation to changing visual environments.

Rekognition vs Custom Models

Amazon Rekognition provides pre-trained computer vision capabilities that handle common image analysis tasks without requiring ML expertise or infrastructure management. However, specialized business requirements often demand custom models that address domain-specific challenges, proprietary data characteristics, or unique performance requirements that managed services cannot accommodate (29).

Rekognition Capabilities and Limitations:

Object detection identifies and locates common objects within images while providing confidence scores and bounding box coordinates. Rekognition recognizes thousands of object categories including vehicles, animals, household items, and natural features with accuracy suitable for most general-purpose applications.

Facial analysis detects faces while extracting attributes including age estimates, emotion predictions, and facial landmarks. Face recognition capabilities enable identification of specific individuals across multiple images while maintaining privacy controls and consent management requirements.

Text detection extracts text content from images including signs, documents, and digital displays while handling various fonts, orientations, and image qualities. Optical character recognition works particularly well for printed text but may struggle with handwriting or heavily stylized fonts.

Content moderation identifies inappropriate content including explicit imagery, violence, and disturbing content while providing confidence scores that enable automated filtering and human review workflows. Moderation capabilities adapt to different cultural contexts and content policies.

Custom label training enables domain-specific object detection using customer-provided training data while maintaining the managed service experience. Custom labels work well for specialized objects but require substantial training data and may not achieve the accuracy of purpose-built custom models.

Custom Model Advantages:

Domain specialization enables models trained on specific visual domains to achieve superior accuracy compared to general-purpose services. Medical imaging, manufacturing quality control, and specialized inspection tasks often require custom approaches that understand domain-specific visual patterns.

Performance optimization through custom architectures and training procedures can achieve better speed-accuracy trade-offs than general-purpose services. Custom models enable optimization for specific hardware, latency requirements, and computational constraints.

Proprietary data utilization enables training on confidential or unique datasets that provide competitive advantages while maintaining data privacy and intellectual property protection. Custom training prevents sharing sensitive visual information with external services.

Integration flexibility enables custom models to integrate seamlessly with existing workflows, data formats, and business logic while avoiding constraints imposed by managed service APIs and data formats.

Decision Framework Application:

Development timeline considerations favor Rekognition for rapid prototyping and immediate deployment while custom models require weeks or months of development and validation. Timeline constraints often drive initial technology selection while long-term requirements guide evolution strategies.

Accuracy requirements determine appropriate approaches based on acceptable error rates and business impact of incorrect predictions. General-purpose tasks often achieve adequate accuracy with Rekognition while specialized applications require custom model precision.

Scale and cost analysis compares per-image pricing for managed services against infrastructure costs for custom model deployment. Cost optimization depends on usage volumes, processing frequencies, and required performance characteristics.

Case Example 1: Manufacturing Quality Control System

An automotive parts manufacturer needed visual inspection systems that detected microscopic defects in machined components while maintaining 99.99% accuracy requirements for safety-critical parts. Rekognition's general object detection couldn't achieve the precision needed for manufacturing tolerances.

Custom model development used specialized convolutional neural networks trained on high-resolution images of defective and acceptable parts. Training data included various lighting conditions, part orientations, and defect types that occurred in production environments.

Edge deployment optimized models for factory floor hardware while maintaining inspection speed requirements of 50 parts per minute. Custom optimization achieved 15ms inference times while maintaining accuracy standards required for automotive safety compliance.

Business impact included preventing defective parts from reaching customers while reducing manual inspection costs by 80%. Custom model investment of $150,000 in development costs provided ROI within 8 months through quality improvements and labor savings.

Image Preprocessing Pipelines

Computer vision model performance depends heavily on consistent, high-quality input preprocessing that normalizes images for optimal algorithm performance. Production preprocessing pipelines must handle diverse image sources, varying quality levels, and real-time performance requirements while maintaining deterministic results across different processing environments.

Standardization and Normalization:

Image resizing adapts input images to model requirements while preserving aspect ratios and important visual information. Resizing strategies include center cropping, padding, and intelligent cropping that focuses on regions of interest.

Color space conversion ensures consistent color representation across different image sources and capture devices. RGB normalization, histogram equalization, and white balance correction address variations in lighting conditions and camera characteristics.

Pixel value normalization scales image intensities to ranges expected by trained models while maintaining relative intensity relationships. Normalization procedures must match training data preprocessing to ensure optimal model performance.

Noise reduction filters improve image quality while preserving important visual features needed for accurate classification or detection. Denoising techniques balance image clarity with processing speed requirements for real-time applications.

Data Augmentation Strategies:

Geometric transformations including rotation, scaling, and flipping increase training data diversity while improving model robustness to variations in object orientation and size. Augmentation strategies must reflect realistic variations expected in production environments.

Photometric augmentations modify brightness, contrast, and color saturation while simulating different lighting conditions and camera settings. Color augmentations improve model robustness while avoiding unrealistic transformations that could degrade performance.

Synthetic data generation creates additional training examples through techniques including cutout, mixup, and generative models. Synthetic augmentation increases dataset size while maintaining label accuracy and visual realism.

Quality assessment validates augmented images to ensure transformations maintain visual quality and label accuracy. Augmentation validation prevents degraded training data from affecting model performance.

Real-time Processing Optimization:

Batch processing groups multiple images for simultaneous preprocessing while improving computational efficiency through vectorization and parallel processing. Batch optimization balances throughput with latency requirements for different application scenarios.

Memory management optimizes image loading and processing to minimize memory usage while maintaining processing speed. Memory optimization becomes particularly important for high-resolution images and resource-constrained environments.

Caching strategies store preprocessed images or intermediate results while reducing redundant computation for frequently accessed images. Intelligent caching balances memory usage with processing speed improvements.

Case Example 2: Retail Visual Search System

An e-commerce platform implemented visual search capabilities that enabled customers to find similar products by uploading photos. The system needed to process diverse user-generated images while maintaining search accuracy across different product categories.

Preprocessing pipeline normalized user photos while handling various image qualities, lighting conditions, and backgrounds that occurred in customer submissions. Standardization included background removal, color correction, and aspect ratio normalization.

Real-time processing achieved sub-200ms response times for visual search queries while maintaining accuracy across 50,000+ product catalog items. Pipeline optimization included intelligent cropping that focused on product regions while eliminating background distractions.

Business results showed 25% increase in product discovery through visual search while reducing customer support queries about product identification. Visual search capabilities provided competitive differentiation while improving customer experience and conversion rates.

Model Deployment for Video Streams

Video stream processing presents unique challenges including temporal consistency, computational scalability, and real-time performance requirements that differ significantly from static image analysis. Effective video MLOps requires specialized architectures that balance processing accuracy with computational efficiency while maintaining low latency for time-sensitive applications.

Streaming Architecture Design:

Frame sampling strategies determine which video frames receive processing while balancing computational load with temporal coverage. Sampling approaches include fixed intervals, motion-triggered processing, and adaptive sampling based on scene complexity.

Temporal consistency algorithms ensure predictions remain stable across consecutive frames while avoiding flickering or sudden changes that could indicate processing errors. Consistency approaches include temporal smoothing, prediction averaging, and state tracking across frame sequences.

Buffer management optimizes memory usage for video streams while maintaining processing throughput and minimizing latency. Buffer strategies balance processing delays with memory constraints while handling variable frame rates and network conditions.

Parallel processing distributes video analysis across multiple compute resources while maintaining temporal ordering and consistency. Parallelization strategies include frame-level distribution, spatial tiling, and pipeline segmentation that balance efficiency with complexity.

Performance Optimization Techniques:

Model optimization reduces computational requirements for video processing while maintaining accuracy through techniques including quantization, pruning, and knowledge distillation. Optimization approaches adapt to hardware constraints and latency requirements.

Hardware acceleration utilizes specialized processors including GPUs, FPGAs, and dedicated AI chips while optimizing for specific deployment environments and performance requirements. Acceleration strategies balance processing speed with infrastructure costs and power consumption.

Adaptive quality controls adjust processing resolution and complexity based on content characteristics and performance requirements. Quality adaptation maintains user experience while optimizing computational resource utilization.

Edge processing enables local video analysis while reducing bandwidth requirements and improving privacy protection. Edge deployment strategies balance local processing capabilities with connectivity requirements and cost constraints.

Quality Assurance and Monitoring:

Accuracy validation ensures video processing maintains quality standards across different content types and environmental conditions. Validation procedures include frame-level accuracy assessment and temporal consistency evaluation.

Performance monitoring tracks processing latency, throughput, and resource utilization while identifying optimization opportunities and capacity planning requirements. Performance metrics enable proactive system management and scaling decisions.

Error detection identifies processing failures, quality degradation, and system bottlenecks while enabling rapid response and recovery procedures. Error handling ensures system reliability while maintaining user experience during processing issues.

Case Example 3: Traffic Management Video Analytics

A metropolitan transportation authority deployed video analytics for traffic flow monitoring and incident detection across 500+ intersection cameras. The system needed real-time processing while maintaining accuracy across varying weather conditions and traffic patterns.

Streaming architecture processed 30 frames per second from each camera while detecting vehicles, pedestrians, and traffic incidents with sub-3-second latency. Frame sampling optimized computational load while ensuring comprehensive coverage of traffic events.

Edge deployment distributed processing across roadside computing units while reducing bandwidth requirements for centralized analysis. Edge processing achieved 95% local processing capability while maintaining connectivity for incident reporting and system coordination.

Operational results included 40% improvement in incident detection speed while reducing false alarm rates by 60%. Video analytics enabled proactive traffic management while reducing congestion and improving emergency response times.

Case Study: Retail Analytics System

This comprehensive case study examines the implementation of computer vision analytics for a major retail chain that needed to optimize store operations, improve customer experience, and increase sales through automated visual analysis of customer behavior and inventory management.

Business Challenge and Requirements:

The retail chain operated 200+ stores across multiple regions while facing challenges including inventory accuracy, customer flow optimization, and loss prevention. Traditional approaches relied on manual observation and periodic audits that provided limited insights and delayed responses to operational issues.

Computer vision requirements included real-time customer counting, demographic analysis, product placement optimization, and automated inventory tracking. System specifications demanded 24/7 operation with sub-second response times for critical alerts while maintaining privacy compliance and customer comfort.

Integration requirements included connection with existing point-of-sale systems, inventory management platforms, and corporate analytics infrastructure. The solution needed to provide both real-time operational alerts and historical analysis for strategic decision-making.

Technical Architecture Design:

Camera infrastructure included high-resolution cameras positioned throughout stores while providing comprehensive coverage of customer areas, checkout zones, and inventory displays. Camera selection balanced image quality with installation costs and privacy considerations.

Edge processing units located in each store handled real-time video analysis while reducing bandwidth requirements for corporate data centers. Edge architecture provided local processing capability while maintaining connectivity for centralized coordination and analysis.

Cloud integration enabled aggregated analytics across all stores while providing corporate-level insights and comparative analysis. Cloud architecture supported scalable analytics while maintaining individual store autonomy and operational independence.

Data pipeline design handled video streams, transaction data, and inventory information while providing unified analytics and reporting capabilities. Pipeline architecture ensured data consistency while supporting both real-time operations and historical analysis.

Model Development and Training:

Customer detection models identified and counted customers while extracting demographic information including age estimates and group composition. Model training used diverse datasets representing different store environments, lighting conditions, and customer populations.

Inventory tracking models monitored product placement and availability while detecting out-of-stock conditions and planogram compliance. Training data included various product categories, shelf configurations, and lighting scenarios encountered across different store formats.

Behavioral analysis models identified customer movement patterns, dwell times, and engagement levels with different products and displays. Behavioral modeling enabled optimization of store layouts while improving product placement and promotional strategies.

Privacy protection models automatically blurred faces and identifying features while maintaining analytical capability and compliance with privacy regulations. Privacy measures balanced analytical value with customer comfort and regulatory requirements.

Implementation and Deployment:

Pilot deployment tested systems in 10 representative stores while validating performance across different store formats, customer demographics, and operational conditions. Pilot results guided system optimization while identifying deployment challenges and success factors.

Rollout strategy deployed systems across all stores in phases while managing installation logistics, staff training, and operational integration. Phased deployment enabled learning application while managing risks and ensuring successful adoption.

Training programs educated store managers and corporate analysts while building organizational capability for system utilization and optimization. Training curricula balanced technical understanding with practical application while supporting different user roles and responsibilities.

Performance monitoring tracked system accuracy, uptime, and business impact while enabling continuous optimization and improvement. Monitoring systems provided both technical metrics and business outcomes while supporting data-driven optimization decisions.

Business Results and Impact:

Customer analytics provided insights into shopping patterns that enabled store layout optimization resulting in 12% increase in average transaction values. Customer flow analysis identified bottlenecks while supporting operational improvements that reduced wait times and improved customer satisfaction.

Inventory accuracy improved from 85% to 97% through automated monitoring while reducing out-of-stock situations by 30%. Inventory optimization enabled better product availability while reducing carrying costs and improving customer experience.

Loss prevention capabilities detected suspicious behavior patterns while reducing shrinkage by 25% across all stores. Automated monitoring provided consistent surveillance while enabling focused human attention on high-priority situations.

Operational efficiency improvements included 20% reduction in manual inventory audits while improving accuracy and freeing staff time for customer service activities. Efficiency gains enabled better resource allocation while maintaining operational excellence.

Lessons Learned and Best Practices:

Privacy compliance required careful attention to data handling, storage, and access controls while maintaining analytical capability and business value. Privacy frameworks balanced regulatory requirements with operational needs while building customer trust and acceptance.

Change management proved critical for successful adoption while requiring comprehensive training, clear communication, and demonstrated value delivery. Organizational change efforts supported technology adoption while ensuring sustainable utilization and optimization.

Performance optimization required ongoing attention to accuracy, speed, and resource utilization while adapting to changing business requirements and technological capabilities. Continuous improvement processes ensured sustained value delivery while supporting evolving business needs.

Integration complexity demanded careful attention to existing systems, data formats, and workflow requirements while minimizing disruption and maximizing value creation. Integration planning balanced technical requirements with operational constraints while ensuring successful deployment.

Technical Excellence in Practice

Computer vision MLOps requires balancing multiple technical and business considerations while delivering reliable systems that meet performance requirements and business objectives. Success depends on understanding both computer vision techniques and operational requirements while maintaining focus on sustainable value creation.

Investment in proper computer vision infrastructure pays dividends through improved operational efficiency, better customer insights, and competitive advantages that justify development and deployment costs. Organizations that master computer vision MLOps achieve superior operational capabilities while maintaining cost efficiency and system reliability.

Moving Forward with Vision

The computer vision capabilities established here provide foundations for natural language processing and time series analytics that complete the MLOps toolkit for diverse business applications. Quality computer vision implementations demonstrate the potential for AI systems while building organizational confidence and capability for broader ML initiatives.

Essential Takeaways

- Amazon Rekognition provides rapid deployment for general computer vision tasks while custom models enable domain-specific optimization and competitive advantages
- Image preprocessing pipelines require standardization, augmentation, and optimization strategies that balance quality with performance requirements
- Video stream processing demands specialized architectures that handle temporal consistency, computational scalability, and real-time performance constraints
- Retail analytics demonstrates comprehensive computer vision implementation that delivers measurable business value through customer insights and operational optimization
- Computer vision MLOps success requires balancing technical capabilities with business requirements while maintaining focus on sustainable value creation

Chapter 19: NLP and Generative AI Operations

Natural language processing and generative AI systems transform human communication into actionable business intelligence while creating new capabilities for content generation, customer interaction, and knowledge extraction. However, deploying these systems reliably requires understanding both linguistic complexity and computational challenges that traditional software development practices cannot adequately address.

AWS provides managed NLP services alongside infrastructure for custom language model deployment, but effective implementation requires strategic decisions about when to use managed services versus custom solutions while managing the unique operational challenges of language-based AI systems including prompt engineering, content safety, and performance optimization.

Comprehend Integration Patterns

Amazon Comprehend provides managed natural language processing capabilities that extract insights from text without requiring linguistics expertise or infrastructure management. Understanding Comprehend's capabilities and limitations guides strategic decisions about NLP implementation while enabling rapid deployment of language analysis capabilities (30).

Core NLP Capabilities:

Sentiment analysis determines emotional tone in text while providing confidence scores for positive, negative, neutral, and mixed sentiments. Sentiment analysis works well for customer feedback, social media monitoring, and content moderation applications that require emotional context understanding.

Entity recognition identifies people, places, organizations, dates, and other named entities within text while providing entity types and confidence scores. Entity extraction enables structured data creation from unstructured text while supporting information extraction and knowledge management applications.

Language detection automatically identifies text language while supporting multilingual content processing and routing. Language identification enables appropriate processing workflows while supporting global applications and diverse content sources.

Key phrase extraction identifies important topics and concepts within text while providing relevance scores and phrase boundaries. Phrase extraction enables content summarization, topic modeling, and search optimization applications.

Syntax analysis provides grammatical structure including parts of speech, dependency parsing, and sentence structure. Syntax analysis supports advanced text processing applications that require grammatical understanding and linguistic analysis.

Custom Classification and Training:

Custom document classification enables domain-specific categorization using customer-provided training data while maintaining managed service simplicity. Custom classifiers work well for specialized content types, industry-specific documents, and proprietary classification schemes.

Custom entity recognition identifies domain-specific entities that general models don't recognize while supporting specialized vocabularies and terminology. Custom entities enable extraction of proprietary information, technical terms, and industry-specific concepts.

Active learning workflows improve custom models through iterative training and validation while reducing annotation overhead and improving accuracy. Active learning balances model improvement with labeling costs while optimizing training efficiency.

Real-time and batch processing options support different application requirements while optimizing costs and performance for various usage patterns. Processing options enable appropriate resource allocation while managing expenses and operational complexity.

Integration Architecture Patterns:

Event-driven processing triggers NLP analysis when new content arrives while enabling responsive applications and real-time insights. Event-driven architecture supports timely analysis while optimizing resource utilization and operational efficiency.

Batch processing handles large document collections efficiently while providing cost optimization and resource management benefits. Batch processing works well for historical analysis, periodic reporting, and large-scale content processing scenarios.

API integration enables real-time text analysis within existing applications while maintaining low latency and high availability. API patterns support interactive applications while providing reliable performance and consistent availability.

Case Example 1: Customer Support Intelligence System

A telecommunications company processed thousands of customer service interactions daily while needing to identify issues, route requests appropriately, and measure satisfaction across different service channels including phone, chat, email, and social media.

Comprehend integration analyzed customer communications while extracting sentiment, entities, and key phrases that indicated issue types and urgency levels. Real-time processing enabled immediate routing while batch analysis provided trend identification and performance measurement.

Custom classification models categorized technical issues while identifying specific products, services, and problem types that required specialized handling. Custom entities recognized proprietary terminology, product names, and technical specifications that standard models didn't understand.

Business impact included 30% improvement in first-call resolution through better issue identification and routing while reducing average resolution time by 25%. Sentiment analysis enabled proactive customer retention efforts while identifying service improvement opportunities.

LLM Deployment Strategies

Large Language Models present unique deployment challenges including computational requirements, prompt engineering complexity, and content safety considerations that require specialized operational approaches. Effective LLM deployment balances capability with cost while ensuring reliable performance and appropriate content generation.

Model Selection and Sizing:

Foundation model evaluation compares different base models based on capability, computational requirements, and cost considerations. Model selection should consider task-specific performance, fine-tuning requirements, and operational constraints including latency and throughput needs.

Parameter scaling affects model capability and computational requirements while influencing deployment architecture and cost structures. Larger models provide better performance but require more expensive infrastructure and longer response times.

Task-specific optimization adapts models for particular applications while balancing general capability with specialized performance. Optimization approaches include fine-tuning, prompt engineering, and architectural modifications that improve task-specific results.

Multi-model strategies deploy different models for different tasks while optimizing overall system performance and cost efficiency. Strategic model allocation enables appropriate capability matching while managing computational resources effectively.

Infrastructure and Scaling:

GPU allocation provides computational power needed for LLM inference while balancing performance requirements with infrastructure costs. GPU selection should consider memory requirements, processing speed, and cost efficiency for specific model sizes and usage patterns.

Auto-scaling manages variable demand while optimizing costs and maintaining performance standards. Scaling strategies must account for model loading times, initialization overhead, and warm-up requirements that affect response times during scaling events.

Caching strategies reduce computational overhead for common queries while managing memory usage and cache invalidation requirements. Intelligent caching balances response speed improvements with infrastructure costs and content freshness needs.

Edge deployment enables local processing while reducing latency and bandwidth requirements for appropriate applications. Edge strategies must consider model size constraints, local processing capabilities, and connectivity requirements.

Prompt Engineering and Management:

Prompt design affects model performance more significantly than traditional algorithm tuning while requiring iterative refinement and systematic evaluation. Effective prompts balance specificity with flexibility while providing clear instructions and appropriate context.

Template management maintains consistent prompt formats while enabling customization for different scenarios and user types. Template systems support scalable prompt deployment while maintaining quality control and version management.

Context optimization provides models with appropriate background information while managing input length constraints and computational costs. Context strategies balance information completeness with processing efficiency and response speed.

Safety controls prevent inappropriate content generation while maintaining model utility and user experience. Safety measures include content filtering, response validation, and human oversight procedures that balance protection with functionality.

Performance Optimization:

Response caching stores generated content for common queries while reducing computational overhead and improving response times. Caching strategies must consider content freshness, personalization requirements, and cache storage costs.

Batch processing groups multiple queries while improving computational efficiency through optimized resource utilization. Batch optimization balances throughput improvements with latency requirements for different application scenarios.

Model compression reduces computational requirements while maintaining acceptable performance through techniques including quantization, pruning, and knowledge distillation. Compression approaches balance model capability with infrastructure efficiency and cost optimization.

Case Example 2: Legal Document Analysis Platform

A law firm needed to analyze contracts, legal briefs, and regulatory documents while extracting key terms, identifying risks, and generating summaries for legal professionals. Traditional document review required hundreds of hours per case while maintaining accuracy requirements for legal compliance.

LLM deployment utilized fine-tuned models trained on legal documents while providing domain-specific understanding of legal terminology, contract structures, and regulatory requirements. Model optimization balanced accuracy with processing speed while maintaining legal accuracy standards.

Prompt engineering developed templates for different document types while ensuring consistent analysis quality and appropriate legal context. Template management enabled rapid deployment across different practice areas while maintaining analytical standards and compliance requirements.

Content safety controls prevented inappropriate legal advice generation while maintaining analytical capability and professional standards. Safety measures included human review workflows, confidence thresholds, and validation procedures that ensured legal accuracy and professional responsibility.

Business results included 75% reduction in document review time while maintaining accuracy standards required for legal practice. Automated analysis enabled lawyers to focus on higher-value strategic work while improving client service and case preparation efficiency.

Prompt Engineering Workflows

Prompt engineering represents both art and science requiring systematic approaches to design, testing, and optimization that maximize model performance while maintaining consistency and reliability across different scenarios and user types.

Design Principles and Frameworks:

Clarity and specificity guide prompt construction while ensuring models understand task requirements and output expectations. Clear prompts reduce ambiguity while providing sufficient context for accurate and relevant responses.

Context provisioning supplies models with appropriate background information while managing input length constraints and computational costs. Context strategies balance information completeness with processing efficiency and cost optimization.

Output format specification defines expected response structure while enabling consistent parsing and integration with downstream systems. Format specifications reduce post-processing overhead while improving system reliability and user experience.

Few-shot learning provides examples within prompts while demonstrating desired behavior and output quality. Example selection should represent diverse scenarios while maintaining consistency and quality standards across different use cases.

Testing and Validation Procedures:

Systematic evaluation tests prompts across representative scenarios while measuring performance, consistency, and safety characteristics. Evaluation procedures should cover edge cases, adversarial inputs, and diverse user scenarios that models may encounter.

A/B testing compares different prompt variations while measuring performance differences and user satisfaction. Testing frameworks enable data-driven prompt optimization while ensuring improvements provide genuine benefits rather than random variation.

Human evaluation incorporates expert judgment while validating model outputs for accuracy, appropriateness, and business value. Human assessment balances automated metrics with qualitative judgment while ensuring outputs meet professional standards.

Version control tracks prompt evolution while enabling rollback capabilities and systematic improvement. Version management supports collaborative prompt development while maintaining stability and reproducibility across different deployment environments.

Production Management:

Template libraries maintain proven prompt patterns while enabling reuse and consistency across different applications and teams. Template systems reduce development time while ensuring quality standards and best practices adoption.

Dynamic prompting adapts to user context and scenarios while maintaining consistent quality and appropriate customization. Dynamic systems balance personalization with efficiency while managing complexity and computational overhead.

Safety monitoring detects inappropriate outputs while enabling rapid response and prompt refinement. Safety systems protect users and organizations while maintaining model utility and user experience quality.

Performance tracking measures prompt effectiveness while identifying optimization opportunities and degradation patterns. Performance monitoring enables continuous improvement while ensuring sustained quality and business value delivery.

Case Example 3: Marketing Content Generation Platform

A digital marketing agency needed to generate diverse content including social media posts, email campaigns, blog articles, and advertisement copy while maintaining brand consistency and marketing effectiveness across multiple clients and industries.

Prompt engineering developed templates for different content types while incorporating brand guidelines, tone specifications, and target audience characteristics. Template design balanced creativity with consistency while ensuring appropriate messaging and brand alignment.

Testing workflows validated content quality through human review, brand compliance checking, and performance measurement. Validation procedures ensured generated content met professional standards while maintaining efficiency and scalability requirements.

Dynamic prompting adapted content generation to specific campaigns, audiences, and platforms while maintaining brand consistency and message effectiveness. Adaptive systems enabled personalized content while managing complexity and maintaining quality control.

Production results included 60% improvement in content creation speed while maintaining quality standards and brand consistency. Automated generation enabled creative teams to focus on strategy and optimization while improving client service and campaign effectiveness.

Case Study: Customer Service Automation

This detailed case study examines the implementation of AI-powered customer service automation for a major telecommunications provider that needed to handle millions of customer interactions while maintaining service quality and reducing operational costs.

Business Challenge and Objectives:

The telecommunications company processed 50,000+ daily customer interactions across phone, chat, email, and social media channels while facing challenges including long wait times, inconsistent service quality, and high operational costs. Traditional approaches relied heavily on human agents while providing limited scalability and 24/7 availability.

Automation objectives included reducing response times, improving first-contact resolution rates, providing 24/7 service availability, and maintaining customer satisfaction while reducing operational costs. System requirements demanded natural conversation capabilities, accurate problem diagnosis, and seamless escalation to human agents when needed.

Integration requirements included connection with existing CRM systems, billing platforms, network monitoring tools, and knowledge management systems. The solution needed to provide consistent service across all channels while maintaining customer context and interaction history.

Technical Architecture Design:

Conversational AI platform utilized large language models fine-tuned for telecommunications domain while providing natural language understanding, intent recognition, and response generation capabilities. Platform architecture supported multiple channels while maintaining consistent conversation context and customer experience.

Knowledge integration connected AI systems with technical documentation, troubleshooting procedures, billing information, and service status while providing accurate and current information for customer inquiries. Knowledge management ensured information accuracy while supporting rapid updates and content management.

Escalation logic determined when to transfer customers to human agents while considering conversation complexity, customer sentiment, and resolution confidence. Escalation algorithms balanced automation efficiency with customer satisfaction while ensuring appropriate human intervention.

Real-time integration enabled access to customer accounts, service status, network conditions, and billing information while providing personalized and accurate responses. Integration architecture ensured data accuracy while maintaining response speed and system reliability.

AI Model Development:

Domain-specific training adapted language models for telecommunications terminology, technical concepts, and customer service scenarios while improving accuracy and relevance for industry-specific conversations. Training data included historical customer interactions, technical documentation, and service procedures.

Intent classification identified customer goals and problems while routing conversations to appropriate response workflows and knowledge sources. Classification models recognized diverse ways customers express problems while maintaining accuracy across different communication styles and languages.

Sentiment analysis monitored customer emotional state while adjusting response tone and escalation decisions. Sentiment monitoring enabled proactive customer satisfaction management while identifying opportunities for service recovery and improvement.

Response generation created natural, helpful responses while maintaining appropriate tone, technical accuracy, and brand consistency. Generation capabilities balanced informativeness with conversational naturalness while ensuring professional communication standards.

Implementation and Deployment:

Pilot deployment tested automation capabilities with limited customer interactions while validating performance and identifying optimization opportunities. Pilot testing enabled safe validation while gathering feedback and refining system performance before full deployment.

Phased rollout gradually increased automation coverage while monitoring performance and customer satisfaction across different interaction types and channels. Phased deployment managed risks while enabling learning application and continuous improvement.

Agent training educated human representatives about AI capabilities and collaboration workflows while ensuring smooth handoffs and effective escalation procedures. Training programs balanced automation adoption with human expertise utilization while maintaining service quality.

Monitoring implementation tracked conversation quality, resolution rates, customer satisfaction, and operational efficiency while enabling continuous optimization and performance management. Monitoring systems provided both technical metrics and business outcomes while supporting data-driven improvement.

Business Results and Impact:

Response time improvement achieved average response times under 30 seconds for automated interactions while reducing customer wait times by 80% compared to traditional agent-only approaches. Immediate availability improved customer experience while supporting business scalability requirements.

Resolution rate enhancement achieved 70% first-contact resolution for automated interactions while maintaining customer satisfaction scores above 85%. Improved resolution rates reduced customer effort while increasing operational efficiency and cost effectiveness.

Cost optimization reduced customer service operational costs by 40% while maintaining service quality and customer satisfaction standards. Cost savings enabled business investment in other customer experience improvements while maintaining competitive service levels.

Agent productivity improvement enabled human agents to focus on complex issues while handling 60% more cases through automation support. Productivity gains improved job satisfaction while enhancing career development opportunities for customer service professionals.

Customer satisfaction maintenance achieved satisfaction scores comparable to human-only service while providing improved availability and response times. Satisfaction results validated automation effectiveness while supporting customer retention and business growth objectives.

Operational Insights and Lessons:

Human-AI collaboration proved more effective than full automation while leveraging strengths of both human judgment and AI efficiency. Collaborative approaches balanced automation benefits with human empathy and complex problem-solving capabilities.

Continuous learning from customer interactions enabled ongoing model improvement while adapting to changing customer needs and business requirements. Learning systems ensured sustained performance while supporting evolving business objectives and customer expectations.

Quality monitoring required specialized metrics that balanced efficiency with customer experience while ensuring automation maintained professional service standards. Quality measurement supported continuous improvement while maintaining customer trust and business reputation.

Change management challenges included customer acceptance, agent adaptation, and organizational culture shifts that required careful attention and comprehensive support. Change management proved essential for successful automation adoption while maintaining team morale and customer relationships.

Strategic Implementation Guidance

NLP and generative AI operations require careful balance between technical capabilities and business requirements while maintaining focus on sustainable value creation and responsible AI deployment. Success depends on understanding both technological possibilities and practical constraints while building organizational capability for ongoing optimization and improvement.

Investment in proper NLP infrastructure enables competitive advantages through improved customer experience, operational efficiency, and new service capabilities that justify development and deployment costs. Organizations that master NLP operations achieve superior customer relationships while maintaining cost efficiency and service quality.

Building Language Intelligence

The natural language processing capabilities established here complement computer vision and time series analytics to provide complete MLOps coverage for diverse business applications. Quality NLP implementations demonstrate the potential for AI systems while building organizational confidence and capability for advanced AI initiatives.

Essential Takeaways

- Amazon Comprehend provides rapid deployment for general NLP tasks while custom LLM deployment enables specialized capabilities and competitive advantages
- LLM deployment strategies must balance computational requirements, performance needs, and cost constraints while ensuring reliable and safe content generation
- Prompt engineering workflows require systematic design, testing, and optimization approaches that maximize model performance while maintaining consistency
- Customer service automation demonstrates comprehensive NLP implementation that delivers measurable business value through improved efficiency and customer experience
- NLP operations success requires balancing technical capabilities with business requirements while maintaining focus on responsible AI deployment and sustainable value creation

Chapter 20: Time Series and Forecasting

Time series data contains temporal patterns that reveal business trends, seasonal fluctuations, and predictive signals that drive strategic planning and operational optimization. However, building reliable forecasting systems requires understanding both statistical foundations and operational challenges that make time series modeling more complex than traditional machine learning applications.

AWS provides managed forecasting services alongside infrastructure for custom time series solutions, but choosing the appropriate approach requires understanding business requirements, data characteristics, and accuracy needs while managing the unique challenges of temporal modeling including seasonality, trend detection, and real-time adaptation.

Forecast Service vs Custom Solutions

Amazon Forecast provides managed time series forecasting that automates algorithm selection, hyperparameter tuning, and model training while requiring minimal data science expertise. Understanding when Forecast provides adequate capabilities versus when custom solutions become necessary guides strategic technology decisions while balancing development speed with specialized requirements (31).

Amazon Forecast Capabilities:

Automated algorithm selection evaluates multiple forecasting approaches including ARIMA, exponential smoothing, and deep learning methods while choosing optimal algorithms based on data characteristics and performance metrics. Automatic selection reduces expertise requirements while ensuring appropriate method application.

Built-in data preprocessing handles missing values, outliers, and data formatting while preparing time series for optimal forecasting performance. Preprocessing automation reduces data preparation overhead while ensuring consistent data quality and model input standards.

Related time series support incorporates external factors including weather, holidays, and economic indicators while improving forecast accuracy through additional context. Related data integration enables more sophisticated modeling while maintaining service simplicity and ease of use.

Probabilistic forecasting provides prediction intervals alongside point forecasts while quantifying uncertainty and enabling risk-aware planning. Uncertainty quantification supports better decision-making while providing confidence indicators for forecast reliability.

Holiday and event handling automatically adjusts for known calendar events while improving forecast accuracy during special periods. Event handling reduces manual configuration while ensuring forecasts account for predictable business variations.

Custom Solution Advantages:

Algorithm specialization enables implementation of proprietary forecasting methods, domain-specific techniques, and advanced research approaches that managed services don't support. Custom algorithms provide competitive advantages while addressing unique business requirements and data characteristics.

Feature engineering flexibility incorporates custom external data, proprietary indicators, and business-specific patterns while optimizing for specific forecasting scenarios. Custom features enable better accuracy while addressing unique business contexts and data availability.

Real-time adaptation enables immediate model updates based on new data, changing conditions, and performance feedback while maintaining forecast accuracy in dynamic environments. Custom systems provide responsiveness while adapting to business changes and evolving patterns.

Integration flexibility enables seamless connection with existing business systems, data flows, and decision-making processes while avoiding constraints imposed by managed service APIs and data formats. Custom integration supports complex business workflows while maintaining operational efficiency.

Decision Framework Considerations:

Data complexity assessment determines if time series patterns require specialized modeling approaches beyond standard forecasting algorithms. Complex seasonality, irregular patterns, and unique business cycles may require custom modeling capabilities.

Accuracy requirements guide technology selection based on acceptable forecast errors and business impact of prediction mistakes. High-stakes forecasting scenarios often justify custom development while general planning applications work well with managed services.

Volume and frequency considerations affect cost optimization and infrastructure requirements for different forecasting approaches. High-frequency forecasting and large numbers of time series may favor custom solutions while periodic forecasting works well with managed services.

Case Example 1: Energy Grid Demand Forecasting

An electric utility company needed accurate demand forecasting for power generation planning while incorporating weather patterns, economic activity, and seasonal variations that affected electricity consumption across different customer segments and geographic regions.

Amazon Forecast implementation provided baseline forecasting capabilities while incorporating weather data, holiday calendars, and historical consumption patterns. Managed service automation reduced development time while providing reasonable accuracy for general planning purposes.

Custom model development enhanced forecasting accuracy through proprietary algorithms that incorporated real-time grid conditions, industrial demand patterns, and renewable energy generation forecasts. Custom models achieved 15% better accuracy than managed services while addressing utility-specific requirements.

Hybrid approach utilized Forecast for general planning while deploying custom models for critical decision-making scenarios including peak demand prediction and emergency planning. Combined strategy balanced development efficiency with accuracy requirements while optimizing resource allocation.

Business impact included $2.1M annual savings through improved generation planning while reducing emergency capacity needs by 20%. Enhanced forecasting enabled better resource allocation while supporting grid reliability and cost optimization objectives.

Real-time Anomaly Detection

Real-time anomaly detection in time series data enables proactive response to unusual patterns that could indicate system failures, security threats, or business opportunities. Effective anomaly detection balances sensitivity with specificity while providing actionable insights that support rapid decision-making and response.

Statistical Anomaly Detection Methods:

Threshold-based detection identifies values that exceed predetermined limits while accounting for seasonal patterns and trend variations. Threshold approaches work well for simple anomalies but may miss complex patterns and subtle changes that require more sophisticated analysis.

Statistical process control uses control charts and statistical measures to identify when time series behavior deviates significantly from normal patterns. SPC methods provide rigorous statistical foundations while enabling detection of gradual changes and pattern shifts.

Seasonal decomposition separates time series into trend, seasonal, and residual components while detecting anomalies in each component independently. Decomposition approaches improve detection accuracy while reducing false alarms caused by normal seasonal variations.

Moving average convergence enables detection of trend changes and pattern shifts while filtering out short-term noise and random variations. Moving average methods provide stability while maintaining sensitivity to genuine pattern changes.

Machine Learning Approaches:

Isolation forest algorithms identify anomalies through random partitioning while working effectively with high-dimensional time series data and complex pattern recognition requirements. Isolation methods scale well while handling multivariate time series and complex interaction patterns.

Autoencoder neural networks learn normal patterns while detecting deviations through reconstruction error analysis. Deep learning approaches handle complex patterns while adapting to changing normal behavior through continuous learning and model updates.

One-class SVM creates boundaries around normal behavior while identifying outliers that fall outside learned patterns. SVM approaches provide robust anomaly detection while handling non-linear patterns and complex decision boundaries.

Ensemble methods combine multiple detection algorithms while improving robustness and reducing false positive rates through consensus-based anomaly identification. Ensemble approaches balance different algorithm strengths while providing more reliable detection performance.

Real-time Implementation Architecture:

Streaming data processing handles high-frequency time series while maintaining low latency for immediate anomaly detection and response. Streaming architecture balances processing speed with detection accuracy while managing computational resources efficiently.

Window-based analysis processes recent data segments while maintaining temporal context and enabling pattern recognition across different time horizons. Window strategies balance detection responsiveness with pattern stability while optimizing computational efficiency.

Alert management systems prioritize anomalies based on severity, business impact, and confidence levels while preventing alert fatigue and ensuring appropriate response. Alert systems balance sensitivity with practicality while supporting effective operational response.

Case Example 2: Financial Trading Anomaly Detection

A financial services firm needed real-time detection of unusual trading patterns that could indicate market manipulation, system errors, or fraud while maintaining low latency for immediate response and regulatory compliance.

Statistical detection methods monitored trading volumes, price movements, and order patterns while identifying deviations from normal market behavior. Statistical approaches provided baseline detection while maintaining computational efficiency for high-frequency analysis.

Machine learning enhancement used ensemble methods combining isolation forests, autoencoders, and custom algorithms while improving detection accuracy and reducing false positive rates. ML approaches captured complex patterns while adapting to changing market conditions and trading behaviors.

Real-time architecture processed millions of transactions per second while maintaining sub-millisecond detection latency for immediate response capabilities. Streaming systems balanced detection accuracy with speed requirements while supporting regulatory compliance and risk management.

Business results included 60% improvement in fraud detection while reducing false alarm rates by 40%. Enhanced detection enabled better risk management while supporting regulatory compliance and maintaining market integrity and customer trust.

Seasonal Model Updates

Time series patterns evolve due to changing business conditions, market dynamics, and external factors that require systematic model updating procedures to maintain forecast accuracy. Effective model maintenance balances stability with adaptation while ensuring forecasts remain relevant and accurate over time.

Seasonality Pattern Evolution:

Seasonal pattern detection identifies recurring patterns at different time scales while distinguishing genuine seasonality from random variations. Detection methods should account for changing business conditions, evolving customer behavior, and external factor influences.

Pattern stability analysis determines when seasonal patterns change significantly enough to require model updates while avoiding unnecessary changes that could reduce forecast accuracy. Stability assessment balances adaptation with consistency while maintaining reliable forecasting performance.

Holiday and event updates incorporate new events, changing business calendars, and evolving promotional schedules while maintaining forecast accuracy during special periods. Event handling ensures models remain current while accounting for business changes and external influences.

Calendar effect modeling accounts for weekday patterns, month-end effects, and other calendar-based variations while adapting to changing business operations and customer behavior patterns. Calendar modeling maintains accuracy while supporting business planning and operational requirements.

Adaptive Model Updates:

Performance monitoring tracks forecast accuracy over time while identifying when model performance degrades enough to trigger retraining or algorithm updates. Performance tracking enables proactive maintenance while preventing forecast quality degradation.

Trigger-based retraining initiates model updates when performance thresholds are exceeded, new data patterns emerge, or business conditions change significantly. Trigger systems balance model freshness with computational costs while ensuring sustained forecast quality.

Incremental learning enables model updates without complete retraining while maintaining computational efficiency and reducing update latency. Incremental approaches balance model adaptation with resource optimization while supporting rapid response to changing conditions.

Ensemble updating manages multiple model versions while enabling gradual transitions and performance comparison between different modeling approaches. Ensemble strategies provide stability during transitions while maintaining forecast accuracy and system reliability.

Business Context Integration:

External factor incorporation includes economic indicators, market conditions, and competitive actions while improving forecast accuracy through broader context understanding. External integration requires careful feature selection while maintaining model interpretability and reliability.

Business rule integration incorporates domain knowledge, operational constraints, and strategic decisions while ensuring forecasts align with business reality and planning requirements. Rule integration balances statistical modeling with business judgment while supporting practical decision-making.

Stakeholder feedback collection incorporates business insights, market knowledge, and operational experience while improving model accuracy and business relevance. Feedback systems balance automated learning with human expertise while maintaining forecast quality and business alignment.

Case Example 3: Restaurant Chain Demand Forecasting

A national restaurant chain needed accurate demand forecasting for inventory planning, staff scheduling, and promotional planning while accounting for seasonal patterns, local events, and changing consumer preferences across 500+ locations.

Seasonal pattern analysis identified complex interactions between weather patterns, local events, promotional activities, and consumer behavior while adapting to changing market conditions and competitive actions. Pattern recognition enabled accurate forecasting while supporting operational planning and optimization.

Adaptive updating procedures maintained forecast accuracy as consumer preferences evolved, new menu items were introduced, and competitive conditions changed. Update procedures balanced model stability with adaptation while ensuring sustained forecasting performance across all locations.

Business integration incorporated promotional planning, special events, and operational constraints while ensuring forecasts supported practical business planning and decision-making requirements. Integration balanced statistical accuracy with business utility while supporting operational excellence.

Operational results included 25% improvement in inventory efficiency while reducing food waste by 30% and improving customer satisfaction through better product availability. Enhanced forecasting enabled better resource allocation while supporting profitability and customer experience objectives.

Case Study: Supply Chain Optimization

This comprehensive case study examines the implementation of time series forecasting and analytics for a global manufacturing company that needed to optimize supply chain operations, reduce inventory costs, and improve customer service through better demand prediction and operational planning.

Business Challenge and Scope:

The manufacturing company operated complex global supply chains with 15,000+ products, 200+ suppliers, and 50+ distribution centers while facing challenges including demand volatility, supply disruptions, and inventory optimization across multiple product categories and geographic markets.

Forecasting requirements included demand prediction at multiple time horizons, inventory optimization across distribution networks, supplier capacity planning, and risk management for supply disruptions. System specifications demanded integration with existing ERP systems, real-time data processing, and scenario analysis capabilities.

Business objectives included 20% reduction in inventory carrying costs, 15% improvement in order fulfillment rates, and 25% reduction in supply chain operational costs while maintaining customer service levels and adapting to market volatility and competitive pressures.

Technical Architecture Development:

Data integration platform consolidated information from ERP systems, supplier databases, market research, economic indicators, and external data sources while providing unified data foundation for forecasting and optimization applications. Integration architecture ensured data quality while supporting real-time processing and historical analysis.

Forecasting infrastructure deployed multiple algorithms including traditional statistical methods, machine learning approaches, and custom models while providing ensemble forecasting and automated algorithm selection. Infrastructure design balanced accuracy with computational efficiency while supporting diverse forecasting requirements.

Optimization engines incorporated demand forecasts into inventory planning, production scheduling, and supplier allocation while balancing costs, service levels, and risk considerations. Optimization systems provided decision support while maintaining computational efficiency and business constraint compliance.

Real-time monitoring systems tracked supply chain performance, forecast accuracy, and operational metrics while enabling proactive response to disruptions and changing conditions. Monitoring infrastructure provided visibility while supporting rapid decision-making and issue resolution.

Forecasting Model Development:

Demand forecasting models incorporated historical sales data, promotional activities, seasonal patterns, economic indicators, and competitive intelligence while providing accurate predictions across different product categories and market segments. Model development balanced accuracy with interpretability while supporting business planning requirements.

Supplier performance forecasting predicted delivery reliability, quality metrics, and capacity availability while enabling proactive supplier management and risk mitigation. Supplier modeling incorporated historical performance, external factors, and relationship characteristics while supporting strategic sourcing decisions.

Market demand sensing used real-time signals including web search trends, social media sentiment, and economic indicators while providing early warning of demand changes and market shifts. Demand sensing enabled responsive planning while reducing forecast lag and improving accuracy.

External factor integration incorporated weather patterns, economic conditions, political events, and industry trends while improving forecast accuracy through broader context understanding. External integration required careful feature selection while maintaining model stability and business relevance.

Implementation and Deployment:

Pilot implementation tested forecasting systems across representative product lines and geographic regions while validating performance and identifying optimization opportunities. Pilot testing enabled safe validation while gathering feedback and refining system performance before full deployment.

Phased rollout gradually expanded forecasting coverage while monitoring performance and business impact across different product categories and operational scenarios. Phased deployment managed risks while enabling learning application and continuous improvement.

Training programs educated supply chain professionals, demand planners, and operational teams while building organizational capability for system utilization and optimization. Training curricula balanced technical understanding with practical application while supporting different user roles and responsibilities.

Change management efforts addressed organizational culture, process changes, and system adoption while ensuring successful transformation and sustained utilization. Change management proved essential for realizing forecasting benefits while maintaining operational excellence and team effectiveness.

Business Results and Impact:

Inventory optimization achieved 22% reduction in overall inventory levels while maintaining 98% order fulfillment rates and improving cash flow by $45M annually. Inventory improvements enabled better working capital management while maintaining customer service standards and competitive positioning.

Forecast accuracy improvement achieved 35% reduction in forecast errors while enabling better planning accuracy and operational efficiency. Enhanced accuracy supported better decision-making while reducing uncertainty and improving operational performance across all supply chain functions.

Supply chain agility increased through better demand sensing and supplier performance prediction while reducing response times to market changes by 40%. Improved agility enabled competitive advantages while supporting business growth and market adaptation requirements.

Cost optimization delivered $12M annual savings through better inventory management, reduced expediting costs, and improved supplier negotiations. Cost improvements supported business profitability while enabling investment in growth initiatives and competitive advantages.

Customer service enhancement achieved 95% on-time delivery rates while reducing stockout incidents by 60% and improving customer satisfaction scores. Service improvements supported business growth while strengthening customer relationships and competitive positioning.

Strategic Insights and Lessons:

Data quality proved foundation for forecasting success while requiring significant investment in data cleaning, integration, and validation procedures. Data management attention enabled model accuracy while supporting reliable business planning and decision-making.

Cross-functional collaboration between supply chain, finance, sales, and operations teams proved essential for successful forecasting implementation while requiring careful coordination and communication. Collaboration enabled better business alignment while ensuring practical application and sustained value delivery.

Continuous improvement processes enabled ongoing optimization while adapting to changing business conditions, market dynamics, and operational requirements. Improvement systems ensured sustained value while supporting evolving business needs and competitive requirements.

Technology integration challenges required careful attention to existing systems, data formats, and workflow requirements while minimizing disruption and maximizing value creation. Integration planning balanced technical requirements with operational constraints while ensuring successful deployment and adoption.

Operational Excellence Through Time

Time series forecasting and analytics provide competitive advantages through better planning capability, improved operational efficiency, and enhanced business agility that justify investment in sophisticated forecasting capabilities. Organizations that master time series operations achieve superior performance while maintaining cost efficiency and operational excellence.

Investment in proper time series infrastructure enables sustained competitive advantages through better decision-making, improved resource allocation, and enhanced business responsiveness that drive long-term business success and market leadership.

Bringing It All Together

The time series capabilities established here complete the MLOps toolkit alongside computer vision and natural language processing to provide coverage for diverse business applications. Quality time series implementations demonstrate the potential for AI systems while building organizational confidence and capability for advanced analytics initiatives.

Essential Takeaways

- Amazon Forecast provides rapid deployment for general forecasting needs while custom solutions enable specialized algorithms and competitive advantages
- Real-time anomaly detection requires balancing sensitivity with specificity while providing actionable insights for immediate response and decision-making
- Seasonal model updates must balance stability with adaptation while ensuring forecasts remain accurate as business conditions and patterns evolve
- Supply chain optimization demonstrates comprehensive time series implementation that delivers measurable business value through improved planning and operational efficiency
- Time series operations success requires understanding both statistical foundations and business requirements while maintaining focus on sustainable value creation and competitive advantage

Chapter 21: Exam Strategy and Practice

The AWS Certified Machine Learning Engineer Associate exam represents a significant professional milestone that validates both theoretical knowledge and practical implementation skills across the complete machine learning lifecycle. Success requires more than technical competence—it demands strategic preparation that combines deep understanding with effective test-taking techniques while managing the time constraints and stress of a comprehensive certification assessment.

This exam distinguishes itself from other AWS certifications through its focus on MLOps practices, real-world implementation scenarios, and integration across multiple AWS services rather than surface-level feature knowledge. Understanding this focus guides preparation strategies that emphasize practical application over theoretical memorization while building confidence through systematic practice and skill development.

Understanding the Exam Structure

The AWS Machine Learning Engineer Associate exam consists of 85 questions delivered in a 170-minute time window, requiring an average of 2 minutes per question while allowing time for review and consideration of complex scenarios. The question format includes multiple choice and multiple response options that test both factual knowledge and applied reasoning across diverse ML implementation scenarios.

Domain Weight Distribution:

Data Engineering for ML represents 28% of exam content, focusing on data pipeline design, preprocessing automation, feature engineering, and data quality management. This domain emphasizes practical implementation skills rather than theoretical data science concepts, requiring understanding of AWS services for data processing, storage, and transformation.

Exploratory Data Analysis and Feature Engineering comprises 24% of exam questions, covering statistical analysis, data visualization, feature selection, and preprocessing techniques. This domain combines statistical knowledge with AWS tool proficiency while emphasizing practical application in business contexts.

Model Development accounts for 26% of exam content, including algorithm selection, custom model implementation, hyperparameter optimization, and performance evaluation. This domain requires understanding both AWS-managed ML services and custom implementation approaches using SageMaker and related services.

MLOps Implementation represents 22% of the exam, focusing on deployment architectures, CI/CD practices, monitoring systems, and production maintenance. This domain emphasizes operational excellence and system reliability rather than model development, requiring understanding of production ML system management.

Question Complexity and Depth:

Scenario-based questions present realistic business situations requiring analysis of requirements, constraint evaluation, and solution architecture decisions. These questions test practical judgment rather than memorized facts, requiring understanding of trade-offs between different implementation approaches.

Multi-service integration questions evaluate understanding of how different AWS services work together to create complete ML solutions. These questions require architectural thinking and understanding of service capabilities, limitations, and optimal usage patterns.

Troubleshooting scenarios present system problems requiring root cause analysis and solution identification. These questions test practical problem-solving skills and deep understanding of how ML systems behave under different conditions and failure modes.

Cost optimization questions evaluate understanding of AWS pricing models, resource optimization strategies, and architectural decisions that affect operational expenses. These questions require balancing technical performance with business constraints while optimizing total cost of ownership.

Time Management Strategies

Effective time management enables thorough consideration of complex questions while ensuring adequate time for review and verification of answers. The 170-minute time limit requires disciplined pacing that balances speed with accuracy while maintaining focus throughout the examination period.

Initial Assessment and Planning:

Question preview during the initial 30 minutes enables identification of question types, complexity levels, and topics requiring additional time. This assessment guides time allocation while building confidence through recognition of familiar topics and identification of challenging areas.

Difficulty categorization helps prioritize questions while ensuring adequate time for complex scenarios that require detailed analysis. Simple factual questions should receive quick resolution while scenario-based questions merit additional consideration and analysis time.

Time allocation strategy assigns specific time limits for different question types while maintaining flexibility for unexpected complexity or challenging scenarios. Conservative pacing ensures adequate time for review while preventing rushed decisions on critical questions.

Progressive Answering Approach:

First pass focuses on confident answers while building momentum and securing points from familiar topics. This approach establishes a foundation of correct answers while identifying questions requiring additional consideration during subsequent passes.

Second pass addresses questions requiring moderate analysis while applying elimination techniques and logical reasoning to narrow answer choices. This pass targets questions where partial knowledge and analytical skills can determine correct answers.

Final pass tackles complex scenarios requiring deep analysis while utilizing remaining time for thorough consideration and validation. This approach ensures difficult questions receive adequate attention while maintaining overall exam completion within time limits.

Review and Validation Process:

Answer verification checks for obvious errors, misreading, and logical inconsistencies while ensuring selected answers align with question requirements. Verification should focus on flagged questions and areas of uncertainty rather than second-guessing confident answers.

Elimination validation ensures incorrect answers are definitively eliminated rather than simply appearing less likely. Strong elimination techniques increase confidence in correct answers while reducing uncertainty and anxiety during final review.

Time monitoring throughout the exam ensures adequate pacing while providing opportunities for strategy adjustment based on actual progress versus planned timeline. Regular time checks prevent surprises while enabling tactical decisions about question prioritization.

Common Pitfalls and Traps

AWS certification exams include sophisticated distractors designed to test genuine understanding versus superficial familiarity with services and concepts. Recognizing common trap patterns enables more accurate answer selection while avoiding mistakes that result from hasty reading or incomplete analysis.

Technical Knowledge Traps:

Service capability confusion tests understanding of what different AWS services can and cannot accomplish while presenting plausible but incorrect alternatives. These traps require precise knowledge of service boundaries and appropriate usage scenarios rather than general familiarity.

Configuration detail errors present technically plausible but incorrect parameter settings, API calls, or architectural configurations. These questions reward precise technical knowledge while penalizing assumptions based on general understanding without specific implementation experience.

Performance optimization misconceptions present inefficient solutions that appear reasonable but fail to optimize for appropriate metrics or business requirements. These traps test understanding of performance trade-offs and optimization priorities in practical scenarios.

Scenario Analysis Pitfalls:

Requirement misinterpretation occurs when questions present complex business scenarios with multiple requirements, constraints, and stakeholder needs. Careful reading and requirement prioritization become essential for identifying optimal solutions among multiple valid approaches.

Scope creep in answers presents solutions that exceed stated requirements while adding unnecessary complexity or cost. These traps reward focused solution design that addresses specific needs without over-engineering or unnecessary feature inclusion.

Context switching between similar scenarios can lead to confusion when consecutive questions address related but distinct situations. Careful attention to scenario details prevents applying solutions from previous questions to different contexts and requirements.

AWS-Specific Misconceptions:

Service selection errors present scenarios where multiple AWS services could theoretically address requirements but only one provides optimal solution for stated constraints. These questions reward understanding of service strengths and appropriate usage patterns.

Pricing model confusion tests understanding of different AWS pricing structures while evaluating cost optimization decisions. These questions require knowledge of actual pricing mechanisms rather than general cost optimization principles.

Integration complexity underestimation presents solutions that appear simple but require significant additional configuration or development effort. These traps reward realistic assessment of implementation complexity while penalizing overly optimistic assumptions.

Detailed Practice Questions with Explanations

The following practice questions represent exam-style scenarios that test practical application of MLOps concepts while providing detailed explanations that reinforce learning and build confidence for actual exam conditions.

Question 1: Data Pipeline Architecture

A healthcare organization needs to process patient data from multiple hospitals while maintaining HIPAA compliance and enabling real-time analytics. The solution must handle varying data formats, ensure data quality, and provide audit trails for compliance reporting. Which architecture approach best meets these requirements?

A) Amazon Kinesis Data Streams with Lambda processing and DynamoDB storage B) Amazon S3 data lake with AWS Glue ETL and SageMaker Processing C) Amazon MSK with Apache Spark streaming and Amazon RDS storage D) Amazon Kinesis Data Firehose with real-time analytics and Amazon Redshift

Correct Answer: B

Detailed Explanation: Healthcare data processing requires comprehensive data management capabilities that handle complex compliance requirements while supporting analytics workflows. Option B provides the most appropriate solution because:

S3 data lake architecture supports HIPAA compliance through encryption, access controls, and audit logging while handling diverse data formats from multiple hospitals. Data lake flexibility accommodates varying schemas and data types without requiring rigid predefined structures.

AWS Glue ETL provides managed data processing with built-in data quality features while maintaining audit trails and supporting complex transformations required for healthcare data standardization. Glue's serverless architecture scales automatically while providing cost optimization and operational simplicity.

SageMaker Processing enables advanced analytics and ML workflows while maintaining integration with compliance frameworks and audit requirements. Processing capabilities support both batch and real-time analytics while providing the computational power needed for complex healthcare analyses.

Alternative options have limitations: Option A lacks comprehensive data management capabilities for complex healthcare scenarios; Option C requires significant operational overhead for Apache Spark management; Option D focuses on streaming analytics but doesn't provide the comprehensive data management needed for healthcare compliance.

Question 2: Model Deployment Strategy

An e-commerce company needs to deploy recommendation models that serve 100,000+ requests per minute with sub-100ms latency while supporting A/B testing and gradual rollout capabilities. The solution must optimize costs while maintaining high availability and enabling rapid rollback when needed. Which deployment approach best addresses these requirements?

A) SageMaker real-time endpoints with auto-scaling and blue-green deployment B) Lambda functions with API Gateway and DynamoDB caching C) Amazon ECS containers with Application Load Balancer and CloudWatch monitoring D) SageMaker batch transform with scheduled processing and S3 storage

Correct Answer: A

Detailed Explanation: High-volume, low-latency recommendation serving requires specialized ML infrastructure that balances performance with operational excellence. Option A provides the optimal solution because:

SageMaker real-time endpoints are optimized for ML inference workloads while providing automatic scaling, load balancing, and sub-100ms latency capabilities. Endpoints handle the computational requirements of recommendation algorithms while maintaining consistent performance under high load.

Auto-scaling capabilities manage varying traffic loads while optimizing costs through dynamic capacity adjustment. Scaling policies ensure adequate capacity during peak periods while reducing costs during low-demand periods, essential for e-commerce traffic patterns.

Blue-green deployment enables safe model updates with immediate rollback capabilities while supporting A/B testing through traffic splitting. This approach enables gradual rollout while maintaining service availability and providing rapid response to performance issues.

Alternative options have limitations: Option B faces cold start latency issues with Lambda while lacking ML-optimized infrastructure; Option C requires significant operational overhead for container management; Option D doesn't support real-time serving requirements and lacks the responsiveness needed for interactive recommendations.

Question 3: Model Monitoring and Maintenance

A financial services firm operates credit scoring models that must maintain fairness across demographic groups while adapting to changing economic conditions. The monitoring solution needs to detect bias, performance degradation, and data drift while triggering appropriate responses. Which monitoring approach provides the most appropriate solution?

A) CloudWatch metrics with custom dashboards and manual review procedures B) SageMaker Model Monitor with custom bias detection and automated alerts C) Amazon QuickSight analytics with scheduled bias reporting D) Custom Python scripts with statistical analysis and email notifications

Correct Answer: B

Detailed Explanation: Financial services model monitoring requires specialized capabilities that address both technical performance and regulatory compliance requirements. Option B provides the comprehensive solution because:

SageMaker Model Monitor provides automated monitoring for model quality, data drift, and bias detection while maintaining integration with ML deployment infrastructure. Built-in capabilities reduce development overhead while ensuring consistent monitoring across all deployed models.

Custom bias detection enables implementation of financial services-specific fairness metrics while supporting regulatory compliance requirements. Custom capabilities address industry-specific bias measurements that generic monitoring tools cannot provide.

Automated alerts ensure immediate response to bias detection, performance degradation, or drift while enabling proactive intervention before issues affect business decisions. Automation reduces response times while ensuring consistent monitoring coverage across all models and scenarios.

Alternative options have limitations: Option A requires significant manual effort and lacks ML-specific monitoring capabilities; Option C provides analytics but lacks real-time monitoring and automated response capabilities; Option D requires substantial development effort while lacking the robustness of managed monitoring services.

Question 4: Cost Optimization Strategy

A machine learning startup processes training workloads that vary significantly in computational requirements while operating under strict budget constraints. Training jobs range from small experiments to large-scale model development requiring different infrastructure optimization strategies. Which approach provides optimal cost management?

A) Reserved instances for all training workloads with manual capacity planning B) Spot instances with fault-tolerant training and automatic resource management C) On-demand instances with manual scaling and cost monitoring D) Dedicated hosts with annual commitments and capacity reservations

Correct Answer: B

Detailed Explanation: Startup environments require cost optimization strategies that balance budget constraints with technical flexibility and operational simplicity. Option B provides the optimal approach because:

Spot instances offer 70-90% cost savings compared to on-demand pricing while providing access to the same computational capabilities needed for ML training. Cost savings enable startups to afford larger-scale experiments while maintaining budget discipline.

Fault-tolerant training procedures accommodate spot instance interruptions through checkpointing, graceful shutdowns, and automatic restart capabilities. These procedures enable reliable training completion while capturing spot instance savings without sacrificing training success rates.

Automatic resource management adapts to varying workload requirements while optimizing resource allocation and cost efficiency. Automated systems reduce operational overhead while ensuring appropriate resource allocation for different training scenarios and computational requirements.

Alternative options have limitations: Option A requires significant upfront commitments inappropriate for startups; Option C lacks cost optimization while requiring manual management overhead; Option D requires substantial financial commitments and long-term capacity planning inappropriate for startup environments.

Last-minute Review Checklist

Effective final preparation consolidates knowledge while building confidence through systematic review of key concepts, common scenarios, and practical applications. The checklist approach ensures coverage of essential topics while identifying areas requiring additional study or clarification.

Core Service Capabilities:

SageMaker service portfolio including training jobs, endpoints, processing jobs, pipelines, and feature stores requires understanding of capabilities, limitations, and appropriate usage scenarios. Review should focus on when to use each service and how they integrate to create complete ML solutions.

Data services including S3, Glue, EMR, Kinesis, and Analytics services need understanding of data processing capabilities, performance characteristics, and cost implications. Data service knowledge should emphasize architectural decisions and optimization strategies.

Supporting services including IAM, CloudWatch, Lambda, and container services require understanding of their role in ML operations while focusing on integration patterns and operational best practices.

MLOps Best Practices:

CI/CD pipeline design for ML workloads including automated testing, validation procedures, and deployment strategies requires understanding of ML-specific challenges and solution approaches. Pipeline knowledge should emphasize practical implementation rather than theoretical concepts.

Monitoring and maintenance procedures including drift detection, performance tracking, and automated response systems need understanding of implementation approaches and business impact assessment. Monitoring knowledge should focus on actionable insights rather than technical metrics alone.

Governance and compliance requirements including model registry, audit trails, and regulatory compliance patterns require understanding of practical implementation while balancing operational efficiency with compliance requirements.

Common Architecture Patterns:

Real-time inference architectures including endpoint design, auto-scaling, and performance optimization require understanding of trade-offs between latency, throughput, and cost while supporting different business requirements and usage patterns.

Batch processing architectures including data pipeline design, resource optimization, and cost management need understanding of when batch processing provides advantages while ensuring appropriate performance and reliability characteristics.

Hybrid architectures combining real-time and batch processing require understanding of integration patterns, data consistency, and operational complexity while providing optimal solutions for complex business requirements.

Building Exam Confidence

Confidence develops through systematic preparation that combines knowledge acquisition with practical application while building familiarity with exam format and question types. Confidence building requires balanced preparation that addresses both technical knowledge and test-taking skills.

Practical experience with AWS services provides the foundation for confident answer selection while enabling recognition of realistic versus theoretical solutions. Hands-on experience with SageMaker, data services, and MLOps practices builds intuitive understanding that supports accurate question analysis.

Practice question experience builds familiarity with exam question formats, complexity levels, and analytical requirements while developing time management skills and stress tolerance. Regular practice with timed exercises builds confidence while identifying knowledge gaps requiring additional study.

Knowledge verification through multiple study sources ensures comprehensive understanding while building confidence in technical knowledge and practical application skills. Verification should include official AWS documentation, practical exercises, and community resources that provide different perspectives on key concepts.

Professional Development Path

AWS certification represents a milestone in professional development that opens career opportunities while demonstrating commitment to technical excellence and continuous learning. Certification success provides foundation for advanced specialization and leadership roles in ML engineering and operations.

The certification process builds systematic knowledge of ML operations while developing practical skills that apply directly to professional responsibilities and career advancement opportunities. Investment in certification preparation provides both immediate knowledge benefits and long-term career value.

Continued learning beyond certification ensures sustained professional growth while maintaining currency with evolving technologies, best practices, and industry standards. Professional development requires ongoing commitment to learning and skill development throughout career progression.

Pathway to Success

Success on the AWS Machine Learning Engineer Associate exam requires combining thorough preparation with effective test-taking strategies while maintaining confidence and focus throughout the certification process. Strategic preparation enables both certification success and practical skill development that supports professional advancement and career growth.

Essential Takeaways

- Exam success requires understanding both technical concepts and practical implementation scenarios while managing time constraints effectively
- Strategic preparation combines knowledge acquisition with test-taking skills while building confidence through systematic practice and review
- Common pitfalls include service capability confusion, requirement misinterpretation, and underestimating implementation complexity
- Practice questions with detailed explanations reinforce learning while building familiarity with exam format and analytical requirements

- Professional development through certification provides both immediate knowledge benefits and long-term career advancement opportunities

Chapter 22: Building Your ML Career

The machine learning profession stands at an unprecedented intersection of technical innovation and business transformation, creating career opportunities that didn't exist five years ago while demanding skill combinations that traditional education programs struggle to provide. Success requires more than technical competence—it demands strategic career development that balances specialization with adaptability while building professional networks and maintaining currency with rapidly evolving technologies.

Organizations worldwide struggle to find qualified ML professionals who can bridge the gap between theoretical knowledge and practical implementation, creating opportunities for individuals who develop both technical depth and business acumen. Understanding how to position yourself in this market while building sustainable career foundations determines long-term professional success and personal satisfaction.

Portfolio Development Strategies

Professional portfolios demonstrate practical capabilities more effectively than resumes or academic credentials while providing tangible evidence of technical skills and business impact. Effective portfolio development requires strategic project selection that showcases diverse capabilities while telling compelling stories about problem-solving skills and professional growth.

Project Selection and Curation:

End-to-end projects demonstrate complete ML lifecycle competence while showing ability to manage complex technical initiatives from conception through deployment. Portfolio projects should address real business problems with measurable outcomes rather than academic exercises or tutorial replications.

Technical diversity showcases proficiency across different ML domains including computer vision, natural language processing, time series analysis, and traditional machine learning while demonstrating adaptability and broad technical foundation.

Business context emphasis highlights problem-solving capabilities and business impact rather than just technical implementation while showing ability to translate business requirements into technical solutions and communicate results to non-technical stakeholders.

Complexity progression shows professional development through increasingly sophisticated projects while demonstrating growth in technical skills, project management capabilities, and business understanding over time.

Implementation Documentation:

Technical documentation explains architectural decisions, trade-off analysis, and implementation challenges while demonstrating analytical thinking and communication skills essential for professional success.

Business impact analysis quantifies results and demonstrates understanding of how technical work creates business value while showing ability to measure and communicate success in business terms.

Lessons learned sections show reflective thinking and continuous improvement mindset while demonstrating professional maturity and ability to learn from experiences and apply knowledge to future challenges.

Code quality and organization demonstrate professional development practices while showing attention to maintainability, documentation, and collaboration considerations essential for team environments.

Platform and Presentation:

GitHub repositories provide technical depth while enabling potential employers to evaluate code quality, documentation practices, and technical decision-making capabilities. Repository organization should reflect professional standards and attention to detail.

Professional websites showcase projects with business-friendly presentations while providing platforms for thought leadership and professional networking. Websites should balance technical detail with accessibility for non-technical audiences.

Portfolio presentations for interviews and networking should focus on business impact and problem-solving approach rather than technical details while demonstrating communication skills and business acumen.

Case study development creates compelling narratives around projects while highlighting specific skills and experiences relevant to target roles and career objectives.

Case Example 1: Data Scientist to MLOps Engineer Transition

Sarah started as a data scientist at a healthcare technology company where she built predictive models for patient outcome analysis. Recognizing the growing importance of ML operations, she strategically developed her portfolio to demonstrate MLOps capabilities while leveraging her domain expertise.

Portfolio evolution included projects showing model deployment architectures, monitoring systems, and CI/CD pipeline implementation while maintaining focus on healthcare applications and regulatory compliance. Her projects demonstrated progression from experimental modeling to production system development.

Technical skill expansion included learning AWS services, containerization, infrastructure as code, and monitoring systems while building on her statistical foundation and domain knowledge. Skill development balanced new technical areas with deepening expertise in healthcare ML applications.

Career transition resulted in promotion to Senior MLOps Engineer with 40% salary increase while maintaining healthcare domain focus. Her portfolio demonstrated both technical growth and continued business value creation in familiar domain context.

Interview Preparation for MLOps Roles

MLOps interviews combine technical assessment with evaluation of operational thinking, communication skills, and cultural fit while testing ability to solve complex problems under pressure. Preparation requires understanding interview formats while developing compelling narratives about professional experiences and technical capabilities.

Technical Interview Components:

System design questions evaluate architectural thinking and ability to design scalable ML systems while considering business requirements, technical constraints, and operational considerations. Design problems typically focus on real-world scenarios rather than theoretical concepts.

Coding assessments test programming skills and algorithmic thinking while evaluating code quality, testing practices, and documentation capabilities. Coding problems may include data processing, model implementation, or infrastructure automation challenges.

AWS service knowledge evaluation covers service capabilities, integration patterns, and cost optimization strategies while testing practical understanding rather than memorized feature lists. Service questions emphasize appropriate usage and architectural decision-making.

Problem-solving scenarios present operational challenges requiring analytical thinking and systematic approach while evaluating troubleshooting skills and ability to work under pressure with incomplete information.

Behavioral Interview Preparation:

STAR method (Situation, Task, Action, Result) provides structure for answering behavioral questions while ensuring comprehensive responses that demonstrate skills and experiences relevant to target roles.

Leadership examples showcase ability to influence outcomes and drive results while demonstrating collaboration skills and ability to work effectively in team environments with diverse stakeholders.

Problem-solving stories highlight analytical thinking and persistence while showing ability to overcome challenges and deliver results despite obstacles and changing requirements.

Learning and adaptation examples demonstrate growth mindset and ability to acquire new skills while showing resilience and adaptability essential for rapidly evolving technical fields. Stories should highlight specific learning approaches and application of new knowledge to solve business problems.

Communication and Presentation Skills:

Technical explanation abilities enable clear communication of complex concepts to both technical and non-technical audiences while demonstrating understanding of stakeholder needs and communication preferences.

Whiteboard presentations test ability to organize thoughts clearly while explaining technical concepts visually and responding to questions and challenges from interviewers with different technical backgrounds.

Business impact articulation shows ability to connect technical work with business outcomes while demonstrating understanding of organizational priorities and value creation mechanisms.

Stakeholder management examples highlight ability to work with diverse groups while managing expectations, gathering requirements, and building consensus around technical solutions and project priorities.

Interview Strategy and Execution:

Company research demonstrates genuine interest while enabling targeted questions and conversation that shows understanding of business context and technical challenges specific to the organization.

Question preparation includes both technical depth and business context while showing ability to engage in meaningful dialogue about role requirements and organizational objectives.

Follow-up strategy maintains engagement while demonstrating professionalism and continued interest through thoughtful communication and additional information sharing.

Salary negotiation preparation includes market research and value proposition development while understanding total compensation and career development opportunities beyond base salary considerations.

Case Example 2: Career Pivot from Software Engineering

Marcus worked as a traditional software engineer for five years before recognizing the growing opportunities in machine learning and data science. His transition strategy focused on leveraging transferable skills while building ML-specific capabilities.

Interview preparation emphasized his software development background while highlighting relevant experiences with data processing, system architecture, and operational concerns. He positioned his engineering skills as advantages for MLOps roles requiring strong software development foundations.

Technical skill development included online courses, certification programs, and personal projects that demonstrated ML knowledge while building on his existing programming and system design capabilities. Learning approach balanced breadth with practical application.

Career transition success resulted in ML Engineer position at a financial technology startup with competitive compensation and strong growth opportunities. His engineering background provided immediate value while enabling rapid skill development in ML-specific areas.

Continuous Learning Roadmap

The ML profession demands continuous learning due to rapid technological advancement, evolving best practices, and changing business requirements that create new challenges and opportunities regularly. Successful professionals develop systematic learning approaches that balance depth with breadth while maintaining practical focus.

Technical Skill Development:

Foundational knowledge requires ongoing reinforcement in statistics, mathematics, and computer science fundamentals that underlie ML applications while adapting to new techniques and methodologies that build on these foundations.

AWS service evolution demands regular updates on new capabilities, service improvements, and best practices while maintaining proficiency with existing services and understanding integration patterns across the expanding service portfolio.

ML algorithm understanding requires keeping current with research developments, new techniques, and practical applications while maintaining focus on business-relevant advances rather than purely academic developments.

Programming language proficiency needs continuous improvement in Python, R, SQL, and emerging languages while developing expertise in frameworks, libraries, and tools that support ML development and operations.

Industry Knowledge Expansion:

Domain expertise development in specific industries or application areas provides competitive advantages while enabling deeper understanding of business context and requirements that drive technical decisions.

Regulatory and compliance understanding becomes increasingly important as ML systems affect critical business decisions while requiring knowledge of data protection, algorithmic fairness, and industry-specific regulations.

Business acumen development includes understanding of financial metrics, organizational dynamics, and strategic planning while enabling better alignment of technical work with business objectives and stakeholder needs.

Market trend awareness helps anticipate future skill demands while enabling proactive career planning and skill development that positions professionals for emerging opportunities and changing market conditions.

Learning Methodology and Resources:

Online education platforms including Coursera, Udacity, and AWS Training provide structured learning paths while offering flexibility for working professionals and access to high-quality instruction from industry experts.

Professional conferences and workshops offer networking opportunities while providing exposure to cutting-edge developments and practical case studies from leading organizations and practitioners.

Open source contribution develops technical skills while building professional reputation and demonstrating commitment to community development and collaborative problem-solving.

Industry publications and research papers maintain awareness of developments while building analytical skills and understanding of theoretical foundations that inform practical applications.

Skill Assessment and Planning:

Regular self-assessment identifies knowledge gaps while enabling targeted learning efforts and career development planning that aligns with professional objectives and market opportunities.

Mentor relationships provide guidance and feedback while offering perspectives from experienced professionals who can share insights about career development and industry trends.

Performance review analysis helps understand organizational expectations while identifying skill development priorities that support career advancement and increased responsibilities.

Market research enables informed decisions about skill development priorities while understanding compensation trends and career opportunities in different specializations and geographic markets.

Community and Networking

Professional networks provide career opportunities, learning resources, and collaborative relationships that accelerate professional development while creating support systems for ongoing growth and advancement. Effective networking requires strategic relationship building that provides mutual value while maintaining authentic professional connections.

Professional Community Engagement:

Technical meetups and user groups provide local networking opportunities while offering presentations, workshops, and collaborative learning experiences with professionals facing similar challenges and opportunities.

Online communities including Reddit, Stack Overflow, and specialized forums enable knowledge sharing while building reputation and demonstrating expertise through helpful contributions and thoughtful participation.

Professional associations offer structured networking while providing continuing education, certification programs, and advocacy for professional standards and career development resources.

Conference participation provides exposure to industry leaders while offering learning opportunities and networking with professionals from different organizations and geographic regions.

Content Creation and Thought Leadership:

Technical blogging demonstrates expertise while building professional reputation and providing value to the broader community through knowledge sharing and practical insights.

Speaking opportunities at conferences and meetups establish thought leadership while developing communication skills and building professional visibility within the industry.

Open source contributions showcase technical skills while demonstrating commitment to community development and collaborative problem-solving that benefits the broader professional community.

Mentoring relationships provide opportunities to give back while developing leadership skills and building networks with emerging professionals who may become future colleagues and collaborators.

Strategic Relationship Building:

Industry connections across different companies and roles provide diverse perspectives while creating opportunities for career advancement and collaborative problem-solving on complex challenges.

Cross-functional relationships with business stakeholders, product managers, and executives enable better understanding of organizational dynamics while building advocacy for technical work and career advancement.

Academic connections with researchers and educators provide access to cutting-edge developments while offering opportunities for collaboration and continued learning through formal and informal relationships.

International networks expand perspectives while providing insights into global practices, cultural considerations, and market opportunities that inform career planning and professional development.

Case Example 3: Community Leadership and Career Advancement

Jennifer built her ML career through active community engagement while leveraging networking relationships to accelerate professional development and career advancement opportunities.

Community involvement included organizing local ML meetups, contributing to open source projects, and speaking at conferences while building reputation and demonstrating leadership capabilities within the professional community.

Relationship building led to consulting opportunities, job referrals, and collaborative projects while providing diverse perspectives and learning opportunities that accelerated skill development and career growth.

Career advancement included promotion to Director of Machine Learning at a technology company while maintaining community involvement and continuing to build professional networks that support ongoing career development.

Building a Sustainable Career

Long-term career success requires balancing immediate opportunities with strategic positioning for future growth while maintaining personal satisfaction and professional fulfillment throughout career evolution. Sustainability demands attention to both technical development and personal well-being while adapting to changing market conditions and personal priorities.

Career Path Diversification:

Technical specialization provides depth and expertise while creating competitive advantages in specific domains or technology areas that command premium compensation and growth opportunities.

Management track development builds leadership skills while creating pathways to executive roles and broader organizational influence through team building and strategic planning capabilities.

Entrepreneurial options including consulting, startup development, and product creation provide independence while leveraging technical skills for business development and wealth creation opportunities.

Portfolio career approaches combine multiple roles and projects while providing diversification and flexibility that adapts to changing market conditions and personal priorities over time.

Work-Life Integration:

Remote work capabilities enable geographic flexibility while accessing global opportunities and maintaining personal relationships and lifestyle preferences that support long-term career sustainability.

Continuous learning integration balances professional development with personal time while ensuring skill currency without overwhelming personal commitments and family responsibilities.

Health and wellness attention prevents burnout while maintaining energy and enthusiasm for challenging technical work and ongoing professional development throughout career progression.

Financial planning ensures independence while enabling strategic career decisions based on professional satisfaction rather than short-term financial pressures that may limit long-term growth opportunities.

Future-Proofing Strategies:

Technology trend monitoring enables proactive skill development while positioning for emerging opportunities rather than reactive responses to market changes and technological disruptions.

Skill transferability development focuses on fundamental capabilities that remain valuable across technological changes while building adaptability for unknown future developments and opportunities.

Network maintenance ensures ongoing relationships while creating support systems that provide guidance, opportunities, and collaboration throughout career evolution and changing circumstances.

Personal brand development establishes professional reputation while creating recognition and opportunities that transcend specific employers or geographic locations through thought leadership and community contributions.

Professional Legacy

Building meaningful careers requires consideration of impact beyond personal advancement while contributing to professional community development and knowledge sharing that benefits future generations of ML professionals. Legacy thinking encourages sustainable practices that create positive influence throughout career progression.

Mentoring and knowledge transfer ensure professional knowledge continues benefiting others while building leadership skills and creating satisfaction through helping others achieve their professional objectives and career goals.

Community contribution through open source development, education, and advocacy creates lasting impact while building professional reputation and establishing thought leadership that influences industry development and best practices.

Ethical practice and responsibility ensure technology development serves positive purposes while considering societal impact and maintaining professional integrity throughout career development and advancement opportunities.

Your Path Forward

Career success in machine learning requires strategic thinking, continuous learning, and authentic relationship building while maintaining focus on creating value for organizations and society. Success comes through balancing technical excellence with business understanding while building networks that support ongoing growth and development.

The opportunities available in machine learning today create unprecedented potential for professional impact and personal satisfaction while demanding commitment to ongoing learning and adaptation. Those who embrace this challenge while maintaining ethical focus and community engagement will find rewarding careers that create lasting positive impact.

Looking Forward with Purpose

Your machine learning career represents an opportunity to shape the future while solving important problems and creating value for organizations and society. Approach this journey with enthusiasm, maintain learning curiosity, and build relationships that support both personal success and community development.

The foundation you build today through systematic skill development, strategic networking, and ethical practice will support decades of professional growth while enabling contributions that extend far beyond individual career advancement. Invest in both technical capabilities and human relationships that will sustain and enrich your professional journey.

Essential Takeaways

- Portfolio development requires strategic project selection that demonstrates business impact while showcasing technical capabilities across diverse ML domains
- Interview preparation combines technical assessment with behavioral evaluation while requiring strong communication skills and business understanding
- Continuous learning demands systematic approaches that balance technical depth with industry knowledge while maintaining practical focus on business-relevant skills
- Professional networking creates career opportunities while requiring authentic relationship building and community contribution that provides mutual value
- Sustainable career development balances immediate opportunities with long-term positioning while maintaining personal well-being and professional fulfillment throughout career evolution

Chapter 23: Practice Exam

Machine learning certification success requires systematic practice that builds both knowledge depth and test-taking confidence while exposing you to the breadth of scenarios you'll encounter on the actual AWS Machine Learning Engineer Associate exam. This practice exam presents 250 comprehensive questions that mirror the real exam's complexity, topic distribution, and analytical requirements.

These questions reflect the four major exam domains while emphasizing practical implementation scenarios over theoretical concepts. Each question includes a brief explanation that reinforces learning while building understanding of AWS ML services, MLOps practices, and real-world application patterns that distinguish successful ML engineers from those who struggle with production implementations.

Domain Distribution and Question Types

This practice exam follows the official AWS exam blueprint with 28% data engineering questions, 24% exploratory data analysis topics, 26% model development scenarios, and 22% MLOps implementation challenges. Questions range from straightforward service selection to complex architectural decisions requiring multi-service integration and cost optimization analysis.

Data Engineering for ML (Questions 1-70)

Question 1: A healthcare company needs to process patient records from multiple hospitals with different data formats while maintaining HIPAA compliance. Which AWS service combination provides the most appropriate solution?

A) Amazon Kinesis Data Streams with Lambda processing B) AWS Glue with S3 data lake and encryption C) Amazon EMR with Hadoop and HDFS storage D) Amazon RDS with read replicas and backups

Answer: B - AWS Glue provides managed ETL with built-in data quality features while S3 offers HIPAA-compliant storage with encryption and access controls.

Question 2: For a real-time fraud detection system processing 10,000 transactions per second, which data ingestion architecture provides optimal performance?

A) Amazon SQS with Lambda processing B) Amazon Kinesis Data Streams with multiple shards C) AWS Database Migration Service with CDC D) Amazon S3 with scheduled batch uploads

Answer: B - Kinesis Data Streams handles high-throughput real-time ingestion with proper shard configuration for 10,000 TPS requirements.

Question 3: A manufacturing company needs to join sensor data from factory equipment with maintenance records stored in RDS. Which approach optimizes query performance?

A) Extract both datasets to S3 and use Athena joins B) Use Lambda functions to query both sources separately C) Replicate RDS data to DynamoDB for faster access D) Stream sensor data directly to RDS for real-time joins

Answer: A - S3 data lake with Athena provides optimal performance for analytical joins between streaming sensor data and relational maintenance records.

Question 4: Which S3 storage class configuration minimizes costs for ML training data accessed monthly?

A) Standard storage with lifecycle policies B) Standard-IA with automatic transitions C) Glacier Instant Retrieval with scheduled access D) Intelligent Tiering with access pattern monitoring

Answer: D - Intelligent Tiering automatically optimizes storage costs based on actual access patterns without manual lifecycle management.

Question 5: A data pipeline needs to handle schema evolution from upstream systems without breaking downstream ML models. Which AWS service provides the best solution?

A) AWS Glue Data Catalog with schema versioning B) Amazon Kinesis Data Analytics with SQL transformations C) AWS Lambda with custom schema validation D) Amazon EMR with Hive metastore

Answer: A - Glue Data Catalog provides automatic schema discovery and versioning that handles schema evolution gracefully.

Question 6: For processing terabytes of log data for ML feature extraction, which compute option provides the best cost-performance ratio?

A) EC2 on-demand instances with manual scaling B) EMR clusters with spot instances and auto-scaling C) Lambda functions with high memory configurations D) ECS containers with reserved instance pricing

Answer: B - EMR with spot instances offers 70-90% cost savings while auto-scaling handles variable workloads efficiently.

Question 7: A streaming analytics application needs to handle late-arriving data and out-of-order events. Which Kinesis capability addresses this requirement?

A) Kinesis Data Streams with extended retention B) Kinesis Data Analytics with windowing functions C) Kinesis Data Firehose with buffering D) Kinesis Video Streams with temporal indexing

Answer: B - Kinesis Data Analytics provides windowing functions that handle late-arriving and out-of-order events in streaming data.

Question 8: Which data partitioning strategy optimizes query performance for time-series IoT data in S3?

A) Partition by device ID only B) Partition by timestamp year/month/day/hour C) Partition by data type and sensor category D) Use random partitioning for even distribution

Answer: B - Time-based partitioning aligns with typical IoT query patterns and enables efficient time-range filtering.

Question 9: A data lake needs to support both SQL queries and ML training workloads. Which storage format provides optimal performance for both use cases?

A) JSON files with compression B) CSV files with columnar storage C) Apache Parquet with column pruning D) Avro files with schema evolution

Answer: C - Parquet provides columnar storage that optimizes both SQL analytical queries and ML data loading performance.

Question 10: For data quality monitoring in real-time pipelines, which AWS service combination is most effective?

A) CloudWatch metrics with custom alarms B) AWS Glue Data Quality with automated checks C) Lambda functions with DynamoDB tracking D) Kinesis Data Analytics with SQL validation

Answer: B - Glue Data Quality provides specialized data quality monitoring with automated validation rules and alerting.

Question 11: A company needs to synchronize data between on-premises databases and AWS for ML training. Which service minimizes operational overhead?

A) AWS Database Migration Service with CDC B) AWS DataSync with scheduled transfers C) Custom ETL jobs using AWS Glue D) AWS Direct Connect with VPN backup

Answer: A - DMS provides managed database replication with change data capture, minimizing operational overhead.

Question 12: Which approach optimizes costs for infrequently accessed training datasets while maintaining immediate availability?

A) S3 Standard with lifecycle transitions B) S3 Standard-IA with retrieval fees C) S3 Glacier with expedited retrieval D) EBS volumes with snapshot scheduling

Answer: B - Standard-IA provides immediate access with lower storage costs, suitable for infrequently accessed training data.

Question 13: A streaming application needs to ensure exactly-once processing for financial transactions. Which configuration provides this guarantee?

A) Kinesis Data Streams with checkpointing B) Amazon SQS with visibility timeout C) Amazon MSK with idempotent producers D) AWS Lambda with reserved concurrency

Answer: C - Amazon MSK (Kafka) provides exactly-once semantics with idempotent producers and transactional guarantees.

Question 14: For joining streaming data with reference data stored in RDS, which approach minimizes latency?

A) Stream to Lambda with RDS connections B) Use DynamoDB for reference data lookup C) Replicate RDS data to ElastiCache D) Stream directly to RDS with upsert operations

Answer: C - ElastiCache provides microsecond latency for reference data lookups in streaming applications.

Question 15: Which data format provides the best compression ratio for ML training datasets?

A) JSON with gzip compression B) CSV with bzip2 compression C) Parquet with snappy compression D) Avro with deflate compression

Answer: C - Parquet with snappy provides optimal compression for ML datasets while maintaining fast read performance.

Question 16: A data pipeline needs to handle variable data volumes while maintaining predictable costs. Which architecture approach is most appropriate?

A) Fixed-size EMR clusters with reserved instances B) Auto-scaling EMR with spot instances and on-demand fallback C) Lambda functions with provisioned concurrency D) ECS tasks with scheduled scaling

Answer: B - Auto-scaling EMR with spot instances provides cost optimization while on-demand fallback ensures reliability.

Question 17: For data cataloging across multiple AWS accounts, which service provides centralized metadata management?

A) AWS Glue Data Catalog with cross-account access B) Amazon Athena with federated queries C) AWS Lake Formation with account sharing D) Amazon S3 with bucket-level permissions

Answer: A - Glue Data Catalog supports cross-account access for centralized metadata management across multiple accounts.

Question 18: Which approach optimizes performance for ML feature stores requiring both batch and real-time access?

A) DynamoDB with on-demand scaling B) RDS with read replicas and caching C) S3 with parallel processing and ElastiCache D) SageMaker Feature Store with dual storage

Answer: D - SageMaker Feature Store provides optimized dual storage for both batch training and real-time inference.

Question 19: A data pipeline needs to handle PII data while maintaining ML model training capability. Which approach provides appropriate privacy protection?

A) Remove all PII fields before processing B) Use differential privacy during feature engineering C) Encrypt PII fields with deterministic encryption D) Implement data masking with format preservation

Answer: D - Format-preserving masking maintains data utility for ML while protecting sensitive information.

Question 20: For monitoring data drift in streaming pipelines, which metric provides the most reliable detection?

A) Data volume changes over time B) Statistical distribution comparisons C) Schema validation failure rates D) Processing latency variations

Answer: B - Statistical distribution comparisons provide the most reliable method for detecting meaningful data drift.

Question 21: A multi-region data pipeline needs to ensure data consistency across regions. Which approach provides the strongest consistency guarantees?

A) S3 Cross-Region Replication with versioning B) DynamoDB Global Tables with eventual consistency C) RDS with cross-region read replicas D) Custom synchronization with Amazon SQS

Answer: A - S3 Cross-Region Replication with versioning provides strong consistency guarantees for multi-region architectures.

Question 22: Which data transformation approach minimizes costs for large-scale feature engineering?

A) AWS Glue jobs with auto-scaling B) EMR clusters with spot instances C) Lambda functions with high memory D) SageMaker Processing with managed instances

Answer: B - EMR with spot instances provides the most cost-effective solution for large-scale feature engineering workloads.

Question 23: For data lineage tracking in complex ML pipelines, which service provides the most comprehensive capabilities?

A) AWS CloudTrail with data events B) AWS Glue with job bookmarks C) Amazon S3 with access logging D) SageMaker with experiment tracking

Answer: A - CloudTrail with data events provides comprehensive audit trails for data lineage tracking across services.

Question 24: A streaming application needs to handle backpressure during high-volume periods. Which configuration provides the best solution?

A) Kinesis Data Streams with increased retention B) Amazon SQS with visibility timeout adjustment C) Kafka with buffering and flow control D) Lambda with reserved concurrency limits

Answer: C - Kafka provides sophisticated backpressure handling with buffering and flow control mechanisms.

Question 25: Which approach optimizes query performance for time-series data analysis in Amazon Athena?

A) Partition by timestamp and use columnar format B) Use row-based formats with compression C) Implement custom serialization formats D) Store data in multiple small files

Answer: A - Time-based partitioning with columnar formats like Parquet optimizes Athena query performance for time-series data.

Question 26: For real-time data enrichment with external APIs, which architecture minimizes latency?

A) Lambda functions with API calls B) Kinesis Data Analytics with external lookups C) EMR with streaming joins D) ElastiCache with preloaded reference data

Answer: D - ElastiCache with preloaded reference data provides the lowest latency for real-time enrichment scenarios.

Question 27: A data pipeline needs to handle data quality issues without stopping processing. Which approach provides the best solution?

A) Implement strict validation with processing stops B) Use quarantine buckets for problematic data C) Log errors and continue processing D) Apply automatic data correction algorithms

Answer: B - Quarantine buckets allow continued processing while isolating problematic data for review and correction.

Question 28: Which storage configuration provides optimal performance for ML model artifacts and metadata?

A) S3 with Transfer Acceleration B) EFS with Max IO performance C) EBS with Provisioned IOPS D) S3 with appropriate storage classes

Answer: D - S3 with appropriate storage classes provides optimal cost-performance for ML model artifacts and metadata.

Question 29: For data processing workflows requiring complex dependencies, which service provides the best orchestration capabilities?

A) AWS Step Functions with parallel execution B) AWS Glue workflows with job dependencies C) Amazon SQS with message ordering D) Lambda functions with event triggers

Answer: A - Step Functions provides sophisticated workflow orchestration with complex dependency management and parallel execution.

Question 30: A streaming pipeline needs to aggregate data across multiple time windows. Which service provides the most efficient solution?

A) Kinesis Data Analytics with tumbling windows B) Lambda functions with DynamoDB state C) EMR with Spark Streaming D) Kinesis Data Streams with consumer groups

Answer: A - Kinesis Data Analytics provides built-in windowing functions optimized for streaming aggregations.

Question 31: Which approach provides the most cost-effective solution for storing large volumes of infrequently accessed log data?

A) S3 Glacier Deep Archive with bulk retrieval B) S3 Standard-IA with lifecycle policies C) EBS volumes with snapshot scheduling D) DynamoDB with on-demand billing

Answer: A - S3 Glacier Deep Archive provides the lowest cost for long-term storage of infrequently accessed log data.

Question 32: For data validation in streaming pipelines, which approach provides real-time quality monitoring?

A) Batch validation with delayed notifications B) Stream processing with inline validation C) Scheduled quality checks with reporting D) Manual data sampling and review

Answer: B - Stream processing with inline validation provides immediate quality monitoring for streaming data.

Question 33: A data lake needs to support both structured and unstructured data with unified governance. Which service provides the best solution?

A) AWS Lake Formation with comprehensive governance B) S3 with bucket policies and access controls C) AWS Glue with data catalog integration D) Amazon EMR with Hive metastore

Answer: A - AWS Lake Formation provides unified governance for both structured and unstructured data in data lakes.

Question 34: Which configuration optimizes network performance for large-scale data transfers to AWS?

A) AWS Direct Connect with dedicated bandwidth B) VPN connections with compression C) Internet transfer with multipart uploads D) AWS DataSync with bandwidth throttling

Answer: A - AWS Direct Connect provides dedicated bandwidth for optimal large-scale data transfer performance.

Question 35: For data processing requiring custom libraries and dependencies, which service provides the most flexibility?

A) AWS Glue with custom Python libraries B) EMR with custom bootstrap actions C) Lambda functions with layers D) SageMaker Processing with containers

Answer: D - SageMaker Processing with containers provides maximum flexibility for custom libraries and dependencies.

Question 36: A streaming application needs to handle duplicate events from multiple sources. Which approach provides the most efficient deduplication?

A) DynamoDB with conditional writes B) Kinesis Data Analytics with window functions C) Lambda functions with RDS tracking D) S3 with object versioning

Answer: A - DynamoDB with conditional writes provides efficient deduplication for streaming applications.

Question 37: Which data format provides the best balance of compression and query performance for analytics workloads?

A) JSON with gzip compression B) Parquet with snappy compression C) CSV with bzip2 compression D) Avro with deflate compression

Answer: B - Parquet with snappy provides optimal balance of compression and query performance for analytics.

Question 38: For data pipeline monitoring, which combination of metrics provides the most comprehensive visibility?

A) Processing latency and error rates only B) Data volume, quality, latency, and costs C) Infrastructure metrics and logs only D) Business metrics and dashboards only

Answer: B - Comprehensive monitoring requires data volume, quality, latency, and cost metrics for complete visibility.

Question 39: A data processing job needs to handle variable data volumes while maintaining SLA requirements. Which approach provides the best solution?

A) Fixed-size infrastructure with over-provisioning B) Auto-scaling with performance monitoring C) Manual scaling based on predicted volumes D) Serverless processing with timeout limits

Answer: B - Auto-scaling with performance monitoring provides SLA compliance while optimizing resource utilization.

Question 40: Which approach provides the most efficient data movement between AWS regions for ML training?

A) S3 Cross-Region Replication B) AWS DataSync with scheduling C) Direct database replication D) Custom ETL jobs with compression

Answer: A - S3 Cross-Region Replication provides the most efficient automated data movement between regions.

Question 41: For data encryption in ML pipelines, which approach provides the best security-performance balance?

A) Client-side encryption with customer keys B) Server-side encryption with AWS managed keys C) Transport encryption only D) Application-level encryption with custom algorithms

Answer: B - Server-side encryption with AWS managed keys provides optimal security-performance balance for ML pipelines.

Question 42: A streaming pipeline needs to handle data from multiple sources with different schemas. Which approach provides the most flexible solution?

A) Rigid schema enforcement with rejection B) Schema registry with evolution support C) Schema-on-read with flexible parsing D) Manual schema management and updates

Answer: B - Schema registry with evolution support provides flexibility while maintaining data structure integrity.

Question 43: Which storage configuration optimizes costs for ML training datasets with predictable access patterns?

A) S3 Standard with lifecycle policies B) S3 Intelligent Tiering with monitoring C) Reserved EBS volumes with scheduling D) On-demand instances with spot pricing

Answer: A - S3 Standard with lifecycle policies provides cost optimization for predictable access patterns.

Question 44: For data processing requiring low-latency access to reference data, which service provides the best performance?

A) RDS with read replicas B) DynamoDB with on-demand scaling C) ElastiCache with cluster mode D) S3 with Transfer Acceleration

Answer: C - ElastiCache with cluster mode provides the lowest latency for reference data access.

Question 45: A data pipeline needs to process both batch and streaming data with unified business logic. Which architecture provides the best solution?

A) Separate batch and streaming pipelines B) Lambda architecture with unified processing C) Kappa architecture with stream processing D) Batch-only processing with micro-batching

Answer: B - Lambda architecture enables unified business logic across both batch and streaming data processing.

Question 46: Which approach provides the most reliable data backup and recovery for ML datasets?

A) S3 with versioning and cross-region replication B) EBS snapshots with automated scheduling C) Database backups with point-in-time recovery D) Local backups with manual verification

Answer: A - S3 with versioning and cross-region replication provides the most reliable backup and recovery solution.

Question 47: For data quality monitoring in batch processing, which approach provides the most comprehensive validation?

A) Statistical profiling with anomaly detection B) Schema validation with error reporting C) Manual data sampling and review D) Automated testing with fixed rules

Answer: A - Statistical profiling with anomaly detection provides comprehensive data quality validation for batch processing.

Question 48: A data processing pipeline needs to handle sensitive data with audit requirements. Which service provides the best compliance support?

A) AWS CloudTrail with data events B) VPC Flow Logs with monitoring C) Custom logging with encryption D) Third-party audit solutions

Answer: A - AWS CloudTrail with data events provides comprehensive audit trails for compliance requirements.

Question 49: Which configuration optimizes performance for high-frequency small data writes in streaming applications?

A) Kinesis Data Streams with batching B) DynamoDB with batch writes C) RDS with connection pooling D) S3 with multipart uploads

Answer: A - Kinesis Data Streams with batching optimizes performance for high-frequency small data writes.

Question 50: For data processing requiring custom algorithms and libraries, which service provides the most development flexibility?

A) AWS Glue with Python shell jobs B) EMR with custom applications C) Lambda functions with layers D) SageMaker Processing with containers

Answer: D - SageMaker Processing with containers provides maximum development flexibility for custom algorithms.

Question 51: A streaming application needs to maintain state across processing failures. Which approach provides the most reliable state management?

A) In-memory state with periodic snapshots B) Database-backed state with transactions C) File-based state with checkpointing D) Distributed state with replication

Answer: B - Database-backed state with transactions provides the most reliable state management for streaming applications.

Question 52: Which data partitioning strategy optimizes query performance for customer analytics workloads?

A) Partition by customer ID with hash distribution B) Partition by geographic region and time C) Partition by product category and date D) Random partitioning with even distribution

Answer: B - Geographic and temporal partitioning aligns with typical customer analytics query patterns.

Question 53: For data processing requiring complex event correlation, which service provides the best capabilities?

A) Kinesis Data Analytics with SQL patterns B) Lambda functions with state management C) EMR with Spark Streaming D) Step Functions with parallel execution

Answer: A - Kinesis Data Analytics provides built-in SQL pattern matching for complex event correlation.

Question 54: A data pipeline needs to handle data from multiple time zones with consistent processing. Which approach provides the best solution?

A) Convert all timestamps to UTC at ingestion B) Process each time zone separately C) Use local time with zone indicators D) Implement timezone-aware processing logic

Answer: A - Converting all timestamps to UTC at ingestion provides consistent processing across time zones.

Question 55: Which approach provides the most cost-effective solution for long-term retention of compliance data?

A) S3 Glacier Deep Archive with retrieval planning B) S3 Standard-IA with lifecycle policies C) EBS volumes with snapshot scheduling D) On-premises storage with AWS backup

Answer: A - S3 Glacier Deep Archive provides the most cost-effective long-term retention for compliance data.

Question 56: For data processing requiring guaranteed message delivery, which service provides the strongest guarantees?

A) Amazon SQS with dead letter queues B) Kinesis Data Streams with retry logic C) Amazon SNS with delivery confirmations D) Amazon MQ with persistent messaging

Answer: D - Amazon MQ provides the strongest guaranteed message delivery with persistent messaging protocols.

Question 57: A streaming pipeline needs to handle data validation failures without losing messages. Which approach provides the best solution?

A) Retry logic with exponential backoff B) Dead letter queues with manual processing C) Error topics with automated recovery D) Validation bypass with warning logs

Answer: C - Error topics with automated recovery provide reliable handling of validation failures.

Question 58: Which configuration optimizes network costs for data transfer between AWS services?

A) VPC endpoints for service communication B) Internet gateways with compression C) Direct Connect for all traffic D) Public internet with encryption

Answer: A - VPC endpoints eliminate internet gateway costs for AWS service communication.

Question 59: For data processing requiring custom resource allocation, which service provides the most control?

A) AWS Glue with DPU configuration B) EMR with instance type selection C) Lambda functions with memory settings D) SageMaker with instance customization

Answer: B - EMR provides the most granular control over resource allocation with custom instance configurations.

Question 60: A data pipeline needs to process data with varying quality levels. Which approach provides the most robust handling?

A) Strict quality gates with processing stops B) Quality scoring with conditional processing C) Automatic data correction with validation D) Manual quality review with approval

Answer: B - Quality scoring with conditional processing provides robust handling of varying data quality.

Question 61: Which data format provides the best performance for ML feature engineering workloads?

A) JSON with nested structures B) Parquet with columnar layout C) CSV with proper escaping D) Avro with schema evolution

Answer: B - Parquet's columnar layout optimizes performance for ML feature engineering operations.

Question 62: For data processing requiring complex transformations, which service provides the best development experience?

A) AWS Glue with visual ETL editor B) EMR with Jupyter notebooks C) Lambda functions with IDE integration D) SageMaker with processing containers

Answer: B - EMR with Jupyter notebooks provides the best development experience for complex transformations.

Question 63: A streaming application needs to handle ordered processing within partitions. Which configuration provides this guarantee?

A) Kinesis Data Streams with single consumer B) Amazon SQS with FIFO queues C) Kafka with partition keys D) DynamoDB with sort keys

Answer: C - Kafka with partition keys provides ordered processing guarantees within partitions.

Question 64: Which approach provides the most efficient data compression for streaming workloads?

A) Real-time compression with CPU overhead B) Batch compression with storage optimization C) Adaptive compression with quality monitoring D) No compression with network optimization

Answer: C - Adaptive compression balances CPU overhead with storage optimization for streaming workloads.

Question 65: For data processing requiring disaster recovery, which architecture provides the best resilience?

A) Multi-region deployment with synchronous replication B) Single region with multiple AZ deployment C) Multi-region with asynchronous replication D) Single AZ with backup and restore

Answer: C - Multi-region with asynchronous replication provides optimal resilience for data processing.

Question 66: A data pipeline needs to handle schema changes without service disruption. Which approach provides the best solution?

A) Versioned schemas with backward compatibility B) Schema validation with strict enforcement C) Dynamic schemas with flexible parsing D) Manual schema updates with downtime

Answer: A - Versioned schemas with backward compatibility enable schema evolution without service disruption.

Question 67: Which monitoring approach provides the most actionable insights for data pipeline optimization?

A) Infrastructure metrics with dashboards B) Business metrics with SLA tracking C) Combined technical and business metrics D) Custom metrics with machine learning

Answer: C - Combined technical and business metrics provide the most actionable insights for optimization.

Question 68: For data processing requiring high availability, which service configuration provides the best uptime?

A) Multi-AZ deployment with auto-failover B) Single-AZ with manual failover C) Multi-region with load balancing D) Single region with backup systems

Answer: A - Multi-AZ deployment with auto-failover provides the best uptime for high availability requirements.

Question 69: A streaming application needs to handle varying data rates with consistent processing. Which approach provides the best solution?

A) Fixed-size buffers with overflow handling B) Dynamic buffers with auto-scaling C) Overflow queues with batch processing D) Rate limiting with backpressure

Answer: B - Dynamic buffers with auto-scaling provide consistent processing for varying data rates.

Question 70: Which data storage approach provides the best cost-performance for ML training datasets?

A) S3 with appropriate storage classes and lifecycle policies B) EBS with provisioned IOPS and snapshots C) EFS with performance mode optimization D) FSx with SSD storage and caching

Answer: A - S3 with appropriate storage classes and lifecycle policies provides optimal cost-performance for ML training datasets.

Exploratory Data Analysis and Feature Engineering (Questions 71-130)

Question 71: For exploratory data analysis of large datasets, which AWS service provides the most cost-effective solution?

A) Amazon Athena with S3 data lake B) Amazon Redshift with columnar storage C) Amazon EMR with Spark SQL D) Amazon RDS with read replicas

Answer: A - Amazon Athena provides serverless, cost-effective analysis of large datasets in S3.

Question 72: A data scientist needs to identify outliers in a dataset with 50 million records. Which approach provides the best performance?

A) Python pandas with statistical methods B) SageMaker Data Wrangler with built-in functions C) EMR with Spark MLlib outlier detection D) Athena with SQL percentile functions

Answer: C - EMR with Spark MLlib provides distributed outlier detection for large datasets.

Question 73: For feature engineering requiring complex transformations, which service provides the most flexibility?

A) AWS Glue with Python shell jobs B) SageMaker Processing with custom containers C) Lambda functions with data processing libraries D) EMR with custom Spark applications

Answer: B - SageMaker Processing with custom containers provides maximum flexibility for complex transformations.

Question 74: A dataset contains categorical variables with high cardinality. Which encoding approach optimizes model performance?

A) One-hot encoding with dimension reduction B) Target encoding with regularization C) Ordinal encoding with custom ordering D) Hash encoding with collision handling

Answer: B - Target encoding with regularization handles high cardinality while preventing overfitting.

Question 75: For time-series feature engineering, which approach captures seasonal patterns most effectively?

A) Moving averages with different window sizes B) Fourier transforms with frequency analysis C) Seasonal decomposition with trend removal D) Lag features with correlation analysis

Answer: C - Seasonal decomposition effectively captures and isolates seasonal patterns.

Question 76: A dataset has missing values with different missing patterns. Which imputation strategy provides the best results?

A) Mean imputation for all missing values B) Multiple imputation with pattern analysis C) Forward fill with trend adjustment D) Median imputation with outlier handling

Answer: B - Multiple imputation with pattern analysis provides the most robust handling of different missing patterns.

Question 77: For dimensionality reduction with interpretability requirements, which technique is most appropriate?

A) Principal Component Analysis with loadings B) t-SNE with perplexity tuning C) UMAP with neighbor analysis D) Feature selection with importance ranking

Answer: D - Feature selection with importance ranking maintains interpretability while reducing dimensions.

Question 78: A dataset requires normalization for neural network training. Which approach provides the best stability?

A) Min-max scaling to [0,1] range B) Z-score standardization with outlier handling C) Robust scaling with median and IQR D) Unit vector scaling with L2 normalization

Answer: C - Robust scaling with median and IQR provides stability against outliers.

Question 79: For feature engineering with temporal dependencies, which AWS service provides the best capabilities?

A) SageMaker Data Wrangler with time-series functions B) EMR with Spark time-series libraries C) Athena with window functions D) Glue with custom Python transformations

Answer: B - EMR with Spark provides comprehensive time-series libraries for temporal feature engineering.

Question 80: A dataset contains text data requiring feature extraction. Which approach provides the best representation?

A) TF-IDF with document frequency weighting B) Word embeddings with pre-trained models C) N-gram analysis with frequency filtering D) Topic modeling with dimensionality reduction

Answer: B - Word embeddings with pre-trained models provide rich semantic representations.

Question 81: For data visualization of high-dimensional datasets, which tool provides the most interactive capabilities?

A) Amazon QuickSight with ML insights B) SageMaker Studio with custom plots C) Jupyter notebooks with plotting libraries D) EMR with Zeppelin notebooks

Answer: A - Amazon QuickSight provides interactive visualization with ML-powered insights.

Question 82: A feature engineering pipeline needs to handle streaming data with batch consistency. Which approach provides the best solution?

A) Separate streaming and batch processing B) Lambda architecture with unified logic C) Kappa architecture with stream processing D) Batch processing with micro-batching

Answer: B - Lambda architecture enables unified feature logic across streaming and batch processing.

Question 83: For correlation analysis in large datasets, which AWS service provides the most efficient processing?

A) Amazon Athena with correlation functions B) SageMaker Processing with scikit-learn C) EMR with Spark MLlib correlation D) Redshift with statistical functions

Answer: C - EMR with Spark MLlib provides distributed correlation analysis for large datasets.

Question 84: A dataset requires feature scaling that preserves relationships between variables. Which approach is most appropriate?

A) Independent scaling for each variable B) Multivariate scaling with covariance C) Robust scaling with outlier detection D) Quantile transformation with uniform distribution

Answer: B - Multivariate scaling preserves relationships between variables during transformation.

Question 85: For feature selection with multiple target variables, which technique provides the best results?

A) Univariate selection with F-statistics B) Recursive feature elimination with cross-validation C) Mutual information with multivariate analysis D) L1 regularization with elastic net

Answer: C - Mutual information with multivariate analysis handles multiple target variables effectively.

Question 86: A dataset contains imbalanced classes requiring feature engineering. Which approach optimizes model performance?

A) Oversampling with synthetic data generation B) Undersampling with cluster centroids C) Cost-sensitive feature weighting D) Ensemble methods with balanced sampling

Answer: A - Oversampling with synthetic data generation (SMOTE) provides balanced training data.

Question 87: For feature engineering requiring domain expertise, which AWS service provides the best collaboration capabilities?

A) SageMaker Studio with shared notebooks B) EMR with Jupyter Hub C) Glue with collaborative development D) Athena with shared queries

Answer: A - SageMaker Studio provides collaborative notebooks for domain expert involvement.

Question 88: A dataset requires feature engineering with privacy preservation. Which approach provides the best protection?

A) Differential privacy with noise injection B) Data masking with format preservation C) Anonymization with identifier removal D) Aggregation with statistical disclosure control

Answer: A - Differential privacy provides mathematical guarantees for privacy preservation.

Question 89: For feature engineering with real-time requirements, which architecture provides the best performance?

A) Precomputed features with caching B) Real-time computation with distributed processing C) Hybrid approach with critical feature caching D) Batch processing with frequent updates

Answer: C - Hybrid approach balances real-time requirements with computational efficiency.

Question 90: A dataset contains network data requiring graph-based features. Which service provides the best graph processing capabilities?

A) Amazon Neptune with graph algorithms B) EMR with GraphX and GraphFrames C) SageMaker with custom graph libraries D) Athena with recursive queries

Answer: B - EMR with GraphX provides distributed graph processing for network feature engineering.

Question 91: For feature engineering requiring statistical validation, which approach provides the most rigorous testing?

A) Hypothesis testing with multiple comparisons B) Cross-validation with statistical significance C) Bootstrap sampling with confidence intervals D) Permutation testing with exact p-values

Answer: D - Permutation testing provides exact statistical validation without distributional assumptions.

Question 92: A dataset requires feature engineering with concept drift handling. Which approach provides the best adaptation?

A) Online learning with feature updates B) Sliding window with feature recomputation C) Ensemble methods with feature weighting D) Adaptive algorithms with change detection

Answer: B - Sliding window approach adapts to concept drift while maintaining feature consistency.

Question 93: For feature engineering requiring interpretability, which technique provides the best explanation capabilities?

A) SHAP values with feature importance B) LIME with local explanations C) Permutation importance with ranking D) Partial dependence plots with interaction

Answer: A - SHAP values provide consistent feature importance across different model types.

Question 94: A dataset contains sensor data requiring signal processing features. Which approach provides the best representation?

A) Frequency domain analysis with FFT B) Time domain statistics with windowing C) Wavelet transforms with multi-scale analysis D) Spectral analysis with power density

Answer: C - Wavelet transforms provide effective multi-scale analysis for sensor data.

Question 95: For feature engineering with automated pipeline deployment, which service provides the best MLOps integration?

A) SageMaker Pipelines with feature processing B) AWS Glue with scheduled jobs C) Step Functions with Lambda processing D) EMR with Airflow orchestration

Answer: A - SageMaker Pipelines provides native MLOps integration for feature engineering.

Question 96: A dataset requires feature engineering for recommendation systems. Which approach provides the best user-item representations?

A) Matrix factorization with latent factors B) Collaborative filtering with similarity metrics C) Content-based filtering with item features D) Hybrid approaches with ensemble methods

Answer: D - Hybrid approaches combine multiple recommendation techniques for better performance.

Question 97: For feature engineering requiring bias detection, which technique provides the most comprehensive analysis?

A) Statistical parity with group comparisons B) Equalized odds with confusion matrices C) Demographic parity with fairness metrics D) Multivariate analysis with intersectionality

Answer: D - Multivariate analysis captures complex bias patterns across multiple dimensions.

Question 98: A dataset contains geospatial data requiring location-based features. Which approach provides the best spatial representation?

A) Coordinate encoding with distance calculations B) Geohashing with hierarchical clustering C) Spatial indexing with proximity analysis D) Map-based features with geographical clustering

Answer: B - Geohashing provides efficient hierarchical spatial encoding for location features.

Question 99: For feature engineering requiring model-specific optimization, which approach provides the best performance?

A) Generic feature engineering with standard methods B) Model-specific feature selection with validation C) Automated feature engineering with meta-learning D) Manual feature crafting with domain expertise

Answer: B - Model-specific feature selection optimizes performance for particular algorithms.

Question 100: A dataset requires feature engineering with streaming updates and batch consistency. Which architecture provides the best solution?

A) Streaming-first with batch reconciliation B) Batch-first with streaming approximations C) Dual processing with consistency checks D) Unified processing with different interfaces

Answer: C - Dual processing with consistency checks ensures accuracy across both paradigms.

Question 101: For exploratory data analysis requiring interactive visualization, which tool provides the best user experience?

A) Amazon QuickSight with interactive dashboards B) SageMaker Studio with Jupyter widgets C) EMR with Zeppelin notebooks D) Athena with visualization plugins

Answer: A - Amazon QuickSight provides the most user-friendly interactive visualization experience.

Question 102: A dataset contains hierarchical data requiring feature engineering. Which approach provides the best representation?

A) Flattening with indicator variables B) Tree-based encoding with path features C) Nested feature extraction with recursion D) Graph-based representation with embeddings

Answer: B - Tree-based encoding preserves hierarchical relationships while creating useful features.

Question 103: For feature engineering requiring computational efficiency, which service provides the best performance-cost ratio?

A) EMR with spot instances B) SageMaker Processing with managed instances C) Lambda functions with parallel execution D) Batch with containerized processing

Answer: A - EMR with spot instances provides the best performance-cost ratio for feature engineering.

Question 104: A dataset requires feature engineering with privacy-preserving techniques. Which approach provides the best utility-privacy trade-off?

A) Differential privacy with optimal epsilon B) Homomorphic encryption with secure computation C) Secure multi-party computation with protocols D) Federated learning with local processing

Answer: A - Differential privacy with optimal epsilon provides the best utility-privacy balance.

Question 105: For feature engineering requiring real-time serving, which caching strategy provides the best performance?

A) In-memory caching with LRU eviction B) Distributed caching with consistent hashing C) Database caching with query optimization D) Application-level caching with smart prefetching

Answer: B - Distributed caching with consistent hashing provides optimal performance for real-time serving.

Question 106: A dataset contains multiple data types requiring unified feature engineering. Which approach provides the best integration?

A) Separate processing with feature concatenation B) Unified processing with multi-modal methods C) Sequential processing with feature alignment D) Parallel processing with result merging

Answer: B - Unified processing with multi-modal methods provides the best integration across data types.

Question 107: For feature engineering requiring version control, which approach provides the best reproducibility?

A) Git-based versioning with feature definitions B) Database versioning with change tracking C) Pipeline versioning with execution history D) Artifact versioning with metadata storage

Answer: A - Git-based versioning provides the most comprehensive reproducibility for feature engineering.

Question 108: A dataset requires feature engineering with automated quality assessment. Which approach provides the best validation?

A) Statistical testing with distribution analysis B) Machine learning with anomaly detection C) Rule-based validation with business logic D) Hybrid approaches with multiple methods

Answer: D - Hybrid approaches provide comprehensive quality assessment using multiple validation methods.

Question 109: For feature engineering requiring scalability, which architecture provides the best horizontal scaling?

A) Microservices with independent scaling B) Distributed processing with auto-scaling C) Containerized processing with orchestration D) Serverless processing with event-driven scaling

Answer: B - Distributed processing with auto-scaling provides the best horizontal scalability.

Question 110: A dataset contains sequential data requiring temporal feature engineering. Which approach provides the best pattern capture?

A) Recurrent neural networks with sequence modeling B) Sliding window with statistical aggregations C) Fourier analysis with frequency components D) Autoregressive models with lag features

Answer: B - Sliding window with statistical aggregations provides robust temporal pattern capture.

Question 111: For feature engineering requiring domain adaptation, which technique provides the best transfer learning?

A) Feature alignment with domain-specific transformations B) Domain-adversarial training with feature extractors C) Multi-task learning with shared representations D) Fine-tuning with domain-specific data

Answer: A - Feature alignment provides effective domain adaptation for feature engineering.

Question 112: A dataset requires feature engineering with uncertainty quantification. Which approach provides the best reliability estimation?

A) Bayesian methods with posterior distributions B) Bootstrap sampling with confidence intervals C) Ensemble methods with prediction variance D) Probabilistic models with uncertainty propagation

Answer: A - Bayesian methods provide principled uncertainty quantification for feature engineering.

Question 113: For feature engineering requiring interpretable transformations, which approach provides the best transparency?

A) Linear transformations with coefficient analysis B) Tree-based transformations with rule extraction C) Additive models with component analysis D) Explainable AI with feature attribution

Answer: D - Explainable AI provides comprehensive transparency for feature transformations.

Question 114: A dataset contains multi-scale data requiring feature engineering. Which approach provides the best representation?

A) Multi-resolution analysis with wavelet decomposition B) Hierarchical clustering with scale-specific features C) Pyramid representations with scale pyramids D) Adaptive scaling with resolution optimization

Answer: A - Multi-resolution analysis provides effective multi-scale feature representation.

Question 115: For feature engineering requiring robustness, which approach provides the best outlier handling?

A) Robust statistics with trimmed means B) Outlier detection with isolation methods C) Regularization with penalty functions D) Ensemble methods with outlier voting

Answer: A - Robust statistics provide the most effective outlier handling for feature engineering.

Question 116: A dataset requires feature engineering with causal inference. Which approach provides the best causal feature discovery?

A) Causal discovery with constraint-based methods B) Instrumental variables with causal identification C) Randomized experiments with causal effects D) Structural equation modeling with causal graphs

Answer: A - Causal discovery provides systematic identification of causal features from observational data.

Question 117: For feature engineering requiring online learning, which approach provides the best adaptation?

A) Incremental learning with feature updates B) Online gradient descent with feature optimization C) Streaming algorithms with concept drift detection D) Adaptive algorithms with forgetting factors

Answer: C - Streaming algorithms with concept drift detection provide effective online feature adaptation.

Question 118: A dataset contains sparse data requiring feature engineering. Which approach provides the best representation?

A) Sparse coding with dictionary learning B) Dimensionality reduction with sparse methods C) Feature selection with sparsity constraints D) Embedding methods with sparse representations

Answer: A - Sparse coding provides effective representation for sparse data through dictionary learning.

Question 119: For feature engineering requiring cross-validation, which approach provides the best validation strategy?

A) Time-series cross-validation with temporal splits B) Stratified cross-validation with balanced folds C) Leave-one-out cross-validation with exhaustive testing D) Nested cross-validation with hyperparameter tuning

Answer: D - Nested cross-validation provides unbiased performance estimation with hyperparameter optimization.

Question 120: A dataset requires feature engineering with ensemble methods. Which approach provides the best feature combination?

A) Voting methods with majority consensus B) Stacking with meta-learning C) Bagging with feature subsampling D) Boosting with feature weighting

Answer: B - Stacking with meta-learning provides the most effective feature combination for ensemble methods.

Question 121: For feature engineering requiring active learning, which approach provides the best sample selection?

A) Uncertainty sampling with model confidence B) Query-by-committee with ensemble disagreement C) Diversity sampling with representative selection D) Hybrid approaches with multiple criteria

Answer: D - Hybrid approaches provide comprehensive sample selection for active learning.

Question 122: A dataset contains imbalanced features requiring engineering. Which approach provides the best balance?

A) Feature resampling with synthetic generation B) Cost-sensitive feature weighting C) Threshold adjustment with calibration D) Ensemble methods with balanced sampling

Answer: A - Feature resampling provides effective balance for imbalanced feature distributions.

Question 123: For feature engineering requiring transfer learning, which approach provides the best knowledge transfer?

A) Pre-trained embeddings with fine-tuning B) Domain adaptation with feature alignment C) Multi-task learning with shared features D) Meta-learning with feature optimization

Answer: A - Pre-trained embeddings provide effective knowledge transfer for feature engineering.

Question 124: A dataset requires feature engineering with fairness constraints. Which approach provides the best bias mitigation?

A) Fairness-aware feature selection B) Bias-corrected feature transformations C) Equalized opportunity with feature weighting D) Demographic parity with feature balancing

Answer: A - Fairness-aware feature selection provides systematic bias mitigation in feature engineering.

Question 125: For feature engineering requiring model interpretability, which approach provides the best explanation?

A) Feature importance with permutation testing B) SHAP values with additive explanations C) LIME with local interpretations D) Anchors with rule-based explanations

Answer: B - SHAP values provide consistent and comprehensive explanations for feature importance.

Question 126: A dataset contains noisy data requiring feature engineering. Which approach provides the best noise handling?

A) Noise reduction with filtering techniques B) Robust feature extraction with outlier detection C) Regularization with noise penalties D) Ensemble methods with noise voting

Answer: B - Robust feature extraction provides effective noise handling while preserving signal quality.

Question 127: For feature engineering requiring computational optimization, which approach provides the best efficiency?

A) Lazy evaluation with on-demand computation B) Parallel processing with distributed computing C) Caching with intelligent prefetching D) Approximation methods with quality trade-offs

Answer: B - Parallel processing provides the best computational efficiency for feature engineering.

Question 128: A dataset requires feature engineering with streaming constraints. Which approach provides the best online processing?

A) Incremental algorithms with bounded memory B) Sliding window with efficient updates C) Reservoir sampling with representative selection D) Sketching algorithms with approximate computation

Answer: A - Incremental algorithms provide effective online processing with memory constraints.

Question 129: For feature engineering requiring quality assurance, which approach provides the best validation?

A) Automated testing with comprehensive coverage B) Statistical validation with hypothesis testing C) Cross-validation with multiple metrics D) Human validation with expert review

Answer: A - Automated testing provides comprehensive and scalable quality assurance for feature engineering.

Question 130: A dataset contains temporal dependencies requiring feature engineering. Which approach provides the best temporal modeling?

A) Autoregressive models with lag features B) State-space models with dynamic features C) Recurrent neural networks with sequence features D) Time-series decomposition with component features

Answer: B - State-space models provide effective temporal modeling with dynamic feature adaptation.

Model Development (Questions 131-195)

Question 131: For selecting the optimal algorithm for a classification problem with 100,000 samples and 50 features, which approach provides the best guidance?

A) Use random forest as a general-purpose solution B) Compare multiple algorithms with cross-validation C) Apply gradient boosting for maximum accuracy D) Use neural networks for complex patterns

Answer: B - Systematic comparison with cross-validation provides the most reliable algorithm selection.

Question 132: A model shows high variance in performance across different validation folds. Which approach provides the best solution?

A) Increase training data size B) Reduce model complexity with regularization C) Use ensemble methods with multiple models D) Apply feature selection with importance ranking

Answer: C - Ensemble methods effectively reduce variance while maintaining model performance.

Question 133: For hyperparameter optimization with limited computational budget, which approach provides the best efficiency?

A) Grid search with exhaustive coverage B) Random search with uniform sampling C) Bayesian optimization with acquisition functions D) Evolutionary algorithms with population-based search

Answer: C - Bayesian optimization provides the most efficient hyperparameter search with limited budget.

Question 134: A dataset contains both numerical and categorical features. Which preprocessing approach optimizes model performance?

A) Standardize numerical and one-hot encode categorical B) Normalize numerical and target encode categorical C) Quantile transform numerical and entity embed categorical D) Robust scale numerical and ordinal encode categorical

Answer: C - Quantile transform and entity embeddings provide optimal preprocessing for mixed data types.

Question 135: For model evaluation with imbalanced classes, which metric provides the most informative assessment?

A) Accuracy with balanced class weights B) F1-score with macro averaging C) AUC-ROC with class-specific analysis D) Precision-recall AUC with threshold optimization

Answer: D - Precision-recall AUC provides the most informative evaluation for imbalanced classes.

Question 136: A model requires real-time inference with sub-100ms latency. Which optimization approach provides the best performance?

A) Model quantization with 8-bit precision B) Model pruning with weight elimination C) Model distillation with smaller architecture D) Model compilation with hardware optimization

Answer: D - Model compilation provides comprehensive hardware optimization for latency requirements.

Question 137: For training deep learning models on large datasets, which AWS service provides the best scalability?

A) SageMaker with distributed training B) EMR with Spark MLlib C) EC2 with custom distributed setup D) Batch with containerized training

Answer: A - SageMaker provides managed distributed training with optimal scalability.

Question 138: A model shows signs of overfitting during training. Which regularization technique provides the best generalization?

A) L1 regularization with feature selection B) L2 regularization with weight decay C) Dropout with stochastic training D) Early stopping with validation monitoring

Answer: D - Early stopping provides the most effective overfitting prevention with validation monitoring.

Question 139: For multi-class classification with class imbalance, which approach provides the best performance?

A) Weighted loss functions with class balancing B) Oversampling with synthetic data generation C) Ensemble methods with balanced classifiers D) Cost-sensitive learning with misclassification costs

Answer: C - Ensemble methods with balanced classifiers provide robust performance for imbalanced multi-class problems.

Question 140: A model requires interpretability for regulatory compliance. Which approach provides the best explanation capabilities?

A) SHAP values with global and local explanations B) LIME with local interpretable explanations C) Feature importance with permutation testing D) Decision trees with rule extraction

Answer: A - SHAP values provide comprehensive explanations that meet regulatory requirements.

Question 141: For time-series forecasting with seasonal patterns, which algorithm provides the best accuracy?

A) ARIMA with seasonal decomposition B) Prophet with holiday effects C) LSTM with attention mechanisms D) Ensemble methods with multiple algorithms

Answer: D - Ensemble methods combining multiple algorithms provide the best forecasting accuracy.

Question 142: A model training job requires cost optimization with minimal accuracy loss. Which approach provides the best cost-performance trade-off?

A) Spot instances with fault-tolerant training B) Reserved instances with capacity planning C) On-demand instances with auto-scaling D) Preemptible instances with checkpointing

Answer: A - Spot instances with fault-tolerant training provide optimal cost-performance trade-off.

Question 143: For anomaly detection in streaming data, which approach provides the best real-time performance?

A) Isolation Forest with online updates B) One-class SVM with streaming support C) Autoencoder with reconstruction error D) Statistical methods with sliding windows

Answer: D - Statistical methods with sliding windows provide optimal real-time anomaly detection.

Question 144: A model requires handling of missing values during inference. Which approach provides the best robustness?

A) Mean imputation with historical values B) Model-based imputation with predictions C) Multiple imputation with uncertainty D) Learned imputation with neural networks

Answer: B - Model-based imputation provides the most robust handling of missing values during inference.

Question 145: For recommendation systems with cold start problems, which approach provides the best solution?

A) Content-based filtering with item features B) Collaborative filtering with matrix factorization C) Hybrid methods with multiple approaches D) Deep learning with embedding layers

Answer: C - Hybrid methods effectively address cold start problems through multiple recommendation approaches.

Question 146: A model shows poor performance on test data despite good training performance. Which diagnostic approach provides the best insights?

A) Learning curve analysis with training size B) Validation curve analysis with complexity C) Bias-variance decomposition with error analysis D) Cross-validation with multiple splits

Answer: C - Bias-variance decomposition provides the most comprehensive diagnostic insights.

Question 147: For natural language processing tasks, which pre-trained model provides the best transfer learning?

A) BERT with fine-tuning for specific tasks B) GPT with few-shot learning C) Word2Vec with semantic embeddings D) FastText with subword representations

Answer: A - BERT with fine-tuning provides the most effective transfer learning for NLP tasks.

Question 148: A model requires calibrated probability estimates for decision-making. Which approach provides the best calibration?

A) Platt scaling with logistic regression B) Isotonic regression with monotonic mapping C) Temperature scaling with neural networks D) Bayesian methods with uncertainty quantification

Answer: D - Bayesian methods provide the most principled probability calibration with uncertainty quantification.

Question 149: For computer vision tasks with limited labeled data, which approach provides the best performance?

A) Data augmentation with geometric transformations B) Transfer learning with pre-trained models C) Self-supervised learning with contrastive methods D) Semi-supervised learning with pseudo-labels

Answer: B - Transfer learning with pre-trained models provides the most effective performance with limited data.

Question 150: A model training process requires monitoring for early intervention. Which metrics provide the best training insights?

A) Training loss and validation loss B) Learning rate and gradient norms C) Training accuracy and validation accuracy D) All metrics with comprehensive monitoring

Answer: D - Comprehensive monitoring provides the best insights for training intervention decisions.

Question 151: For ensemble methods with diverse models, which combination approach provides the best performance?

A) Simple averaging with equal weights B) Weighted averaging with performance weights C) Stacking with meta-learning D) Dynamic selection with context-based choice

Answer: C - Stacking with meta-learning provides the most effective ensemble combination.

Question 152: A model requires handling of categorical features with high cardinality. Which encoding method provides the best performance?

A) One-hot encoding with dimensionality reduction B) Target encoding with regularization C) Entity embeddings with neural networks D) Hash encoding with collision handling

Answer: C - Entity embeddings provide the most effective high-cardinality categorical encoding.

Question 153: For model selection with multiple objectives, which approach provides the best trade-off analysis?

A) Weighted sum with preference weights B) Pareto optimization with multi-objective analysis C) Lexicographic ordering with priority ranking D) Constraint optimization with threshold limits

Answer: B - Pareto optimization provides comprehensive multi-objective trade-off analysis.

Question 154: A model requires robustness to adversarial attacks. Which training approach provides the best defense?

A) Adversarial training with attack examples B) Defensive distillation with smoothed models C) Randomized smoothing with noise injection D) Ensemble methods with diverse architectures

Answer: A - Adversarial training provides the most effective defense against adversarial attacks.

Question 155: For federated learning with privacy constraints, which approach provides the best privacy-utility trade-off?

A) Differential privacy with noise addition B) Homomorphic encryption with secure computation C) Secure aggregation with cryptographic protocols D) Local differential privacy with randomization

Answer: C - Secure aggregation provides optimal privacy-utility trade-off for federated learning.

Question 156: A model shows inconsistent performance across different data distributions. Which approach provides the best robustness?

A) Domain adaptation with feature alignment B) Data augmentation with distribution matching C) Robust optimization with worst-case training D) Transfer learning with domain-specific fine-tuning

Answer: C - Robust optimization provides the best performance consistency across distributions.

Question 157: For online learning with concept drift, which approach provides the best adaptation?

A) Sliding window with fixed-size updates B) Exponential forgetting with decay factors C) Change detection with adaptive responses D) Ensemble methods with dynamic weighting

Answer: C - Change detection with adaptive responses provides the most effective concept drift handling.

Question 158: A model requires explanation for individual predictions. Which approach provides the most accurate explanations?

A) SHAP with exact computation B) LIME with local approximations C) Integrated gradients with attribution D) Attention mechanisms with visualization

Answer: A - SHAP with exact computation provides the most accurate individual prediction explanations.

Question 159: For multi-modal learning with different data types, which approach provides the best fusion?

A) Early fusion with concatenated features B) Late fusion with ensemble methods C) Attention-based fusion with learned weights D) Hierarchical fusion with multi-level integration

Answer: C - Attention-based fusion provides the most effective multi-modal data integration.

Question 160: A model requires handling of temporal dependencies in sequential data. Which architecture provides the best performance?

A) LSTM with memory cells B) GRU with simplified gates C) Transformer with attention mechanisms D) CNN with temporal convolutions

Answer: C - Transformer with attention mechanisms provides superior performance for sequential data.

Question 161: For active learning with limited annotation budget, which sample selection strategy provides the best efficiency?

A) Uncertainty sampling with model confidence B) Query-by-committee with ensemble disagreement C) Diversity sampling with representative selection D) Expected model change with gradient analysis

Answer: B - Query-by-committee provides the most efficient sample selection for active learning.

Question 162: A model shows poor convergence during training. Which optimization approach provides the best convergence?

A) Adam optimizer with adaptive learning rates B) SGD with momentum and scheduling C) RMSprop with gradient scaling D) AdaGrad with cumulative gradients

Answer: A - Adam optimizer provides the most reliable convergence for most model types.

Question 163: For graph neural networks with node classification, which approach provides the best performance?

A) Graph Convolutional Networks with spectral methods B) GraphSAGE with sampling and aggregation C) Graph Attention Networks with attention mechanisms D) Graph Isomorphism Networks with expressive power

Answer: C - Graph Attention Networks provide superior performance through attention mechanisms.

Question 164: A model requires handling of long-tail distributions in target variables. Which approach provides the best performance?

A) Focal loss with class rebalancing B) Weighted sampling with importance weighting C) Hierarchical softmax with class hierarchies D) Metric learning with similarity optimization

Answer: A - Focal loss provides effective handling of long-tail distributions through class rebalancing.

Question 165: For reinforcement learning with sparse rewards, which approach provides the best sample efficiency?

A) Reward shaping with auxiliary objectives B) Curiosity-driven exploration with intrinsic motivation C) Hierarchical reinforcement learning with subgoals D) Off-policy learning with experience replay

Answer: C - Hierarchical reinforcement learning provides the best sample efficiency with sparse rewards.

Question 166: A model requires compression for edge deployment. Which approach provides the best size-performance trade-off?

A) Weight pruning with magnitude-based selection B) Quantization with reduced precision C) Knowledge distillation with teacher-student training D) Low-rank approximation with matrix factorization

Answer: C - Knowledge distillation provides the best size-performance trade-off for model compression.

Question 167: For few-shot learning with limited examples, which approach provides the best generalization?

A) Meta-learning with model-agnostic methods B) Prototypical networks with embedding learning C) Siamese networks with similarity learning D) Data augmentation with synthetic examples

Answer: A - Meta-learning provides the most effective few-shot learning through model-agnostic methods.

Question 168: A model requires handling of noisy labels in training data. Which approach provides the best robustness?

A) Label smoothing with uniform distribution B) Noise-robust loss functions with outlier handling C) Co-training with multiple models D) Self-training with confident predictions

Answer: B - Noise-robust loss functions provide the most effective handling of noisy labels.

Question 169: For continual learning without catastrophic forgetting, which approach provides the best memory retention?

A) Elastic Weight Consolidation with importance weighting B) Progressive neural networks with lateral connections C) Memory replay with experience buffers D) Knowledge distillation with regularization

Answer: C - Memory replay provides the most effective catastrophic forgetting prevention.

Question 170: A model requires optimization for inference speed on CPU. Which approach provides the best acceleration?

A) Model quantization with integer operations B) Model pruning with sparsity patterns C) Operator fusion with computation graphs D) Vectorization with SIMD instructions

Answer: C - Operator fusion provides the most effective CPU inference acceleration.

Question 171: For generative models with controllable generation, which approach provides the best control?

A) Conditional GANs with class information B) Variational autoencoders with latent manipulation C) Normalizing flows with invertible transformations D) Autoregressive models with attention control

Answer: B - Variational autoencoders provide the most effective controllable generation through latent manipulation.

Question 172: A model requires handling of missing features during inference. Which approach provides the best robustness?

A) Feature imputation with learned representations B) Robust models with missing feature handling C) Ensemble methods with feature subsets D) Attention mechanisms with feature weighting

Answer: B - Robust models with explicit missing feature handling provide the best inference robustness.

Question 173: For neural architecture search with computational constraints, which approach provides the best efficiency?

A) Evolutionary algorithms with population-based search B) Differentiable architecture search with gradient-based optimization C) Bayesian optimization with architecture priors D) Reinforcement learning with controller networks

Answer: B - Differentiable architecture search provides the most efficient neural architecture optimization.

Question 174: A model requires uncertainty estimation for decision-making. Which approach provides the most reliable uncertainty?

A) Bayesian neural networks with weight distributions B) Monte Carlo dropout with stochastic inference C) Ensemble methods with prediction variance D) Gaussian processes with kernel methods

Answer: A - Bayesian neural networks provide the most principled uncertainty estimation.

Question 175: For self-supervised learning with unlabeled data, which approach provides the best representations?

A) Contrastive learning with positive and negative pairs B) Masked language modeling with reconstruction C) Autoencoding with reconstruction objectives D) Adversarial training with discriminator networks

Answer: A - Contrastive learning provides the most effective self-supervised representations.

Question 176: A model requires handling of extreme class imbalance (1:1000 ratio). Which approach provides the best performance?

A) Focal loss with hard example mining B) SMOTE with synthetic minority oversampling C) Ensemble methods with balanced sampling D) Anomaly detection with one-class methods

Answer: D - Anomaly detection methods provide the most effective handling of extreme class imbalance.

Question 177: For multi-task learning with related tasks, which approach provides the best knowledge sharing?

A) Hard parameter sharing with shared layers B) Soft parameter sharing with regularization C) Task-specific attention with shared representations D) Hierarchical multi-task learning with task relationships

Answer: C - Task-specific attention provides the most effective knowledge sharing for multi-task learning.

Question 178: A model requires adaptation to new domains with limited target data. Which approach provides the best transfer?

A) Fine-tuning with small learning rates B) Domain adaptation with adversarial training C) Meta-learning with few-shot adaptation D) Progressive transfer with layer-wise adaptation

Answer: B - Domain adaptation with adversarial training provides the most effective domain transfer.

Question 179: For sequence-to-sequence modeling with long sequences, which approach provides the best performance?

A) Transformer with positional encoding B) LSTM with attention mechanisms C) Hierarchical models with multi-scale processing D) Convolutional models with dilated convolutions

Answer: A - Transformer with positional encoding provides superior performance for long sequences.

Question 180: A model requires handling of heterogeneous data sources. Which approach provides the best integration?

A) Multi-view learning with view-specific models B) Feature-level fusion with concatenation C) Decision-level fusion with ensemble methods D) Attention-based fusion with learned weights

Answer: D - Attention-based fusion provides the most effective heterogeneous data integration.

Question 181: For optimization with non-convex objectives, which approach provides the best convergence?

A) Stochastic gradient descent with momentum B) Adam with adaptive learning rates C) Natural gradient methods with Fisher information D) Quasi-Newton methods with approximated Hessian

Answer: B - Adam provides the most reliable convergence for non-convex optimization.

Question 182: A model requires robustness to distribution shifts. Which training approach provides the best generalization?

A) Data augmentation with diverse transformations B) Adversarial training with worst-case examples C) Distributionally robust optimization with uncertainty sets D) Meta-learning with domain adaptation

Answer: C - Distributionally robust optimization provides the best generalization to distribution shifts.

Question 183: For collaborative filtering with implicit feedback, which approach provides the best recommendations?

A) Matrix factorization with weighted regularization B) Deep neural collaborative filtering with embeddings C) Autoencoders with denoising reconstruction D) Graph neural networks with user-item interactions

Answer: D - Graph neural networks provide the most effective collaborative filtering with implicit

Question 183: For collaborative filtering with implicit feedback, which approach provides the best recommendations?

A) Matrix factorization with weighted regularization B) Deep neural collaborative filtering with embeddings C) Autoencoders with denoising reconstruction D) Graph neural networks with user-item interactions

Answer: D - Graph neural networks provide the most effective collaborative filtering with implicit feedback through user-item interaction modeling.

Question 184: A model requires handling of temporal patterns in multivariate time series. Which approach provides the best performance?

A) LSTM with multivariate inputs B) Transformer with temporal attention C) CNN with temporal convolutions D) Graph neural networks with temporal dynamics

Answer: B - Transformer with temporal attention provides superior performance for multivariate time series.

Question 185: For privacy-preserving machine learning, which approach provides the best privacy-utility trade-off?

A) Differential privacy with calibrated noise B) Homomorphic encryption with secure computation C) Federated learning with secure aggregation D) Synthetic data generation with privacy guarantees

Answer: A - Differential privacy provides the most principled privacy-utility trade-off with mathematical guarantees.

Question 186: A model requires optimization for memory-constrained environments. Which approach provides the best memory efficiency?

A) Gradient checkpointing with recomputation B) Mixed precision training with reduced memory C) Model parallelism with distributed memory D) Pruning with structured sparsity

Answer: A - Gradient checkpointing provides the most effective memory optimization for constrained environments.

Question 187: For causal inference from observational data, which approach provides the best causal estimates?

A) Instrumental variables with causal identification B) Regression discontinuity with threshold analysis C) Difference-in-differences with panel data D) Causal discovery with constraint-based methods

Answer: A - Instrumental variables provide the most reliable causal estimates from observational data.

Question 188: A model requires handling of hierarchical data structures. Which approach provides the best representation?

A) Tree-based models with hierarchical splits B) Graph neural networks with hierarchical attention C) Hierarchical embeddings with multi-level representations D) Recursive neural networks with tree structures

Answer: C - Hierarchical embeddings provide the most effective representation for hierarchical data structures.

Question 189: For model compression with minimal accuracy loss, which approach provides the best compression ratio?

A) Weight pruning with magnitude-based selection B) Knowledge distillation with teacher-student training C) Quantization with mixed precision D) Low-rank approximation with matrix decomposition

Answer: B - Knowledge distillation provides the best compression ratio with minimal accuracy loss.

Question 190: A model requires handling of streaming data with concept drift. Which approach provides the best adaptation?

A) Online learning with incremental updates B) Ensemble methods with adaptive weighting C) Change detection with model switching D) Sliding window with periodic retraining

Answer: C - Change detection with model switching provides the most effective concept drift adaptation.

Question 191: For multi-modal sentiment analysis, which approach provides the best performance?

A) Early fusion with concatenated features B) Late fusion with ensemble methods C) Attention-based fusion with cross-modal attention D) Hierarchical fusion with modality-specific processing

Answer: C - Attention-based fusion with cross-modal attention provides superior multi-modal sentiment analysis.

Question 192: A model requires optimization for batch inference throughput. Which approach provides the best acceleration?

A) Dynamic batching with padding optimization B) Model parallelism with distributed inference C) Operator fusion with computation graphs D) Caching with intelligent prefetching

Answer: A - Dynamic batching provides the most effective batch inference acceleration.

Question 193: For learning with noisy and incomplete labels, which approach provides the best robustness?

A) Semi-supervised learning with pseudo-labels B) Weakly supervised learning with weak supervision C) Self-supervised learning with pretext tasks D) Multi-instance learning with bag-level labels

Answer: B - Weakly supervised learning provides the most effective handling of noisy and incomplete labels.

Question 194: A model requires interpretability for high-stakes decisions. Which approach provides the most trustworthy explanations?

A) LIME with local linear approximations B) SHAP with game-theoretic explanations C) Integrated gradients with attribution analysis D) Counterfactual explanations with causal analysis

Answer: D - Counterfactual explanations provide the most trustworthy explanations for high-stakes decisions.

Question 195: For continual learning with task interference, which approach provides the best performance retention?

A) Regularization-based methods with parameter importance B) Replay-based methods with experience buffers C) Architecture-based methods with dedicated parameters D) Meta-learning methods with fast adaptation

Answer: C - Architecture-based methods provide the best performance retention by avoiding task interference.

MLOps Implementation and Operations (Questions 196-250)

Question 196: For deploying ML models in production, which architecture provides the best scalability and reliability?

A) Single-instance deployment with manual scaling B) Multi-instance deployment with load balancing C) Microservices architecture with container orchestration D) Serverless deployment with auto-scaling

Answer: C - Microservices architecture provides the best scalability and reliability for production ML deployments.

Question 197: A production ML system requires monitoring for data drift. Which approach provides the most effective detection?

A) Statistical tests with distribution comparison B) Machine learning with anomaly detection C) Rule-based monitoring with threshold alerts D) Ensemble methods with multiple drift detectors

Answer: D - Ensemble methods provide the most comprehensive and reliable drift detection.

Question 198: For ML model versioning and rollback, which approach provides the best operational control?

A) Git-based versioning with manual deployments B) Container-based versioning with orchestration C) Database-based versioning with automated rollback D) Blue-green deployments with traffic switching

Answer: D - Blue-green deployments provide the most effective operational control for model versioning.

Question 199: A CI/CD pipeline for ML requires automated testing. Which testing approach provides the most comprehensive validation?

A) Unit tests for code components only B) Integration tests for pipeline components C) End-to-end tests with data validation D) Multi-level testing with comprehensive coverage

Answer: D - Multi-level testing provides the most comprehensive validation for ML CI/CD pipelines.

Question 200: For ML model monitoring in production, which metrics provide the most actionable insights?

A) Technical metrics like latency and throughput B) Business metrics like conversion and revenue C) Model metrics like accuracy and drift D) Combined metrics across all dimensions

Answer: D - Combined metrics provide the most actionable insights for production ML monitoring.

Question 201: A production ML system requires automated retraining. Which trigger approach provides the best balance?

A) Time-based triggers with fixed schedules B) Performance-based triggers with accuracy thresholds C) Data-based triggers with drift detection D) Hybrid triggers with multiple conditions

Answer: D - Hybrid triggers provide the best balance for automated retraining decisions.

Question 202: For ML model deployment with canary releases, which approach provides the safest rollout?

A) Fixed percentage traffic splitting B) Gradual traffic increase with monitoring C) A/B testing with statistical significance D) Feature flags with conditional routing

Answer: B - Gradual traffic increase with monitoring provides the safest canary deployment.

Question 203: A distributed ML training job requires fault tolerance. Which approach provides the best resilience?

A) Checkpointing with periodic saves B) Replication with redundant workers C) Spot instance handling with preemption recovery D) Comprehensive fault tolerance with multiple strategies

Answer: D - Comprehensive fault tolerance provides the best resilience for distributed training.

Question 204: For ML model serving with high availability, which architecture provides the best uptime?

A) Single-region deployment with multiple AZ B) Multi-region deployment with failover C) Edge deployment with local processing D) Hybrid deployment with multiple strategies

Answer: B - Multi-region deployment with failover provides the best high availability.

Question 205: A production ML system requires cost optimization. Which approach provides the best cost-performance ratio?

A) Reserved instances with capacity planning B) Spot instances with fault tolerance C) Auto-scaling with demand-based sizing D) Hybrid pricing with optimization strategies

Answer: D - Hybrid pricing strategies provide the best cost-performance optimization.

Question 206: For ML pipeline orchestration, which approach provides the most flexibility?

A) Workflow engines with DAG-based orchestration B) Event-driven orchestration with message queues C) Microservices orchestration with service mesh D) Serverless orchestration with function composition

Answer: A - Workflow engines provide the most flexible ML pipeline orchestration.

Question 207: A production ML system requires security hardening. Which approach provides the best protection?

A) Network security with VPC isolation B) Application security with authentication C) Data security with encryption D) Comprehensive security with defense in depth

Answer: D - Comprehensive security provides the best protection through defense in depth.

Question 208: For ML model performance optimization, which approach provides the best acceleration?

A) Hardware acceleration with GPU optimization B) Software optimization with algorithm improvements C) Infrastructure optimization with caching D) Holistic optimization with multiple approaches

Answer: D - Holistic optimization provides the best performance acceleration through multiple approaches.

Question 209: A production ML system requires compliance with regulations. Which approach provides the best compliance coverage?

A) Audit trails with comprehensive logging B) Access controls with role-based permissions C) Data governance with privacy protection D) Integrated compliance with multiple controls

Answer: D - Integrated compliance provides the best coverage through multiple controls.

Question 210: For ML model explainability in production, which approach provides the most practical explanations?

A) Global explanations with feature importance B) Local explanations with instance-specific analysis C) Counterfactual explanations with what-if analysis D) Multi-level explanations with comprehensive coverage

Answer: D - Multi-level explanations provide the most practical explainability for production systems.

Question 211: A production ML system requires disaster recovery. Which approach provides the best recovery capabilities?

A) Backup and restore with scheduled snapshots B) Replication with real-time synchronization C) Multi-region deployment with failover D) Comprehensive DR with multiple strategies

Answer: D - Comprehensive disaster recovery provides the best recovery capabilities.

Question 212: For ML model lifecycle management, which approach provides the best governance?

A) Model registry with version control B) Approval workflows with quality gates C) Automated deployment with validation D) Integrated lifecycle management with comprehensive governance

Answer: D - Integrated lifecycle management provides the best governance for ML models.

Question 213: A production ML system requires performance monitoring. Which approach provides the most comprehensive visibility?

A) Infrastructure monitoring with system metrics B) Application monitoring with performance metrics C) Business monitoring with outcome metrics D) Multi-dimensional monitoring with comprehensive coverage

Answer: D - Multi-dimensional monitoring provides the most comprehensive visibility.

Question 214: For ML model deployment with zero downtime, which approach provides the best availability?

A) Rolling deployments with gradual updates B) Blue-green deployments with instant switching C) Canary deployments with risk mitigation D) Multi-strategy deployments with optimal availability

Answer: B - Blue-green deployments provide the best zero-downtime availability.

Question 215: A production ML system requires automated scaling. Which approach provides the most efficient resource utilization?

A) Reactive scaling with performance monitoring B) Predictive scaling with demand forecasting C) Proactive scaling with capacity planning D) Intelligent scaling with multiple strategies

Answer: D - Intelligent scaling provides the most efficient resource utilization through multiple strategies.

Question 216: For ML model testing in production, which approach provides the best validation?

A) A/B testing with statistical significance B) Shadow testing with parallel processing C) Canary testing with gradual rollout D) Comprehensive testing with multiple approaches

Answer: D - Comprehensive testing provides the best validation through multiple approaches.

Question 217: A production ML system requires error handling. Which approach provides the most robust error management?

A) Retry logic with exponential backoff B) Circuit breakers with failure isolation C) Graceful degradation with fallback mechanisms D) Comprehensive error handling with multiple strategies

Answer: D - Comprehensive error handling provides the most robust error management.

Question 218: For ML model deployment with edge computing, which approach provides the best performance?

A) Model compression with size optimization B) Edge-specific optimization with hardware acceleration C) Distributed inference with load balancing D) Comprehensive edge optimization with multiple strategies

Answer: D - Comprehensive edge optimization provides the best performance through multiple strategies.

Question 219: A production ML system requires data quality monitoring. Which approach provides the most effective validation?

A) Schema validation with structure checking B) Statistical validation with distribution analysis C) Business rule validation with domain constraints D) Multi-level validation with comprehensive coverage

Answer: D - Multi-level validation provides the most effective data quality monitoring.

Question 220: For ML model deployment with feature stores, which approach provides the best integration?

A) Batch integration with scheduled updates B) Real-time integration with streaming updates C) Hybrid integration with multiple access patterns D) Comprehensive integration with optimal performance

Answer: C - Hybrid integration provides the best feature store integration for different access patterns.

Question 221: A production ML system requires capacity planning. Which approach provides the most accurate forecasting?

A) Historical analysis with trend extrapolation B) Predictive modeling with demand forecasting C) Scenario planning with what-if analysis D) Comprehensive planning with multiple approaches

Answer: D - Comprehensive planning provides the most accurate capacity forecasting.

Question 222: For ML model deployment with multi-cloud, which approach provides the best portability?

A) Container-based deployment with orchestration B) Serverless deployment with cloud-native services C) Hybrid deployment with cloud abstraction D) Comprehensive multi-cloud with optimal portability

Answer: A - Container-based deployment provides the best multi-cloud portability.

Question 223: A production ML system requires configuration management. Which approach provides the best flexibility?

A) Static configuration with version control B) Dynamic configuration with runtime updates C) Environment-specific configuration with isolation D) Comprehensive configuration with optimal management

Answer: D - Comprehensive configuration management provides the best flexibility.

Question 224: For ML model deployment with service mesh, which approach provides the best observability?

A) Distributed tracing with request tracking B) Metrics collection with performance monitoring C) Logging aggregation with centralized analysis D) Comprehensive observability with multiple approaches

Answer: D - Comprehensive observability provides the best service mesh monitoring.

Question 225: A production ML system requires dependency management. Which approach provides the best reliability?

A) Dependency isolation with containerization B) Version pinning with reproducible builds C) Automated updates with compatibility testing D) Comprehensive dependency management with optimal reliability

Answer: D - Comprehensive dependency management provides the best reliability.

Question 226: For ML model deployment with chaos engineering, which approach provides the best resilience testing?

A) Fault injection with controlled failures B) Load testing with performance validation C) Disaster simulation with recovery testing D) Comprehensive chaos engineering with multiple approaches

Answer: D - Comprehensive chaos engineering provides the best resilience testing.

Question 227: A production ML system requires resource optimization. Which approach provides the best efficiency?

A) Right-sizing with capacity optimization B) Auto-scaling with demand-based adjustment C) Resource pooling with shared utilization D) Comprehensive optimization with multiple strategies

Answer: D - Comprehensive optimization provides the best resource efficiency.

Question 228: For ML model deployment with GitOps, which approach provides the best automation?

A) Git-based deployments with CI/CD pipelines B) Infrastructure as code with version control C) Automated rollbacks with change tracking D) Comprehensive GitOps with optimal automation

Answer: D - Comprehensive GitOps provides the best deployment automation.

Question 229: A production ML system requires observability. Which approach provides the most comprehensive monitoring?

A) Metrics collection with time-series analysis B) Distributed tracing with request correlation C) Log aggregation with centralized analysis D) Comprehensive observability with multiple approaches

Answer: D - Comprehensive observability provides the most complete monitoring coverage.

Question 230: For ML model deployment with progressive delivery, which approach provides the safest rollout?

A) Feature flags with conditional routing B) Canary deployments with gradual traffic increase C) Blue-green deployments with instant switching D) Comprehensive progressive delivery with optimal safety

Answer: D - Comprehensive progressive delivery provides the safest rollout through multiple strategies.

Question 231: A production ML system requires incident management. Which approach provides the best response capabilities?

A) Automated alerting with notification systems B) Runbook automation with response procedures C) Escalation procedures with team coordination D) Comprehensive incident management with optimal response

Answer: D - Comprehensive incident management provides the best response capabilities.

Question 232: For ML model deployment with policy enforcement, which approach provides the best governance?

A) Admission controllers with deployment validation B) Policy engines with rule-based enforcement C) Compliance scanning with security validation D) Comprehensive policy enforcement with optimal governance

Answer: D - Comprehensive policy enforcement provides the best governance coverage.

Question 233: A production ML system requires secret management. Which approach provides the best security?

A) Encrypted storage with access controls B) Secret rotation with automated updates C) Least privilege access with role-based permissions D) Comprehensive secret management with optimal security

Answer: D - Comprehensive secret management provides the best security through multiple approaches.

Question 234: For ML model deployment with service discovery, which approach provides the best connectivity?

A) DNS-based discovery with service registration B) Service mesh with traffic management C) Load balancing with health checking D) Comprehensive service discovery with optimal connectivity

Answer: D - Comprehensive service discovery provides the best connectivity management.

Question 235: A production ML system requires backup and recovery. Which approach provides the best data protection?

A) Automated backups with scheduled snapshots B) Point-in-time recovery with transaction logs C) Cross-region replication with disaster recovery D) Comprehensive backup with optimal protection

Answer: D - Comprehensive backup strategies provide the best data protection.

Question 236: For ML model deployment with rate limiting, which approach provides the best traffic control?

A) Fixed rate limits with threshold enforcement B) Adaptive rate limits with dynamic adjustment C) Priority-based limits with traffic shaping D) Comprehensive rate limiting with optimal control

Answer: D - Comprehensive rate limiting provides the best traffic control.

Question 237: A production ML system requires network optimization. Which approach provides the best performance?

A) CDN integration with edge caching B) Network compression with bandwidth optimization C) Connection pooling with resource efficiency D) Comprehensive network optimization with optimal performance

Answer: D - Comprehensive network optimization provides the best performance.

Question 238: For ML model deployment with health checking, which approach provides the best reliability?

A) Liveness probes with service monitoring B) Readiness probes with traffic routing C) Health endpoints with status validation D) Comprehensive health checking with optimal reliability

Answer: D - Comprehensive health checking provides the best reliability monitoring.

Question 239: A production ML system requires alerting optimization. Which approach provides the best incident response?

A) Threshold-based alerts with static rules B) Anomaly-based alerts with dynamic detection C) Predictive alerts with forecasting D) Comprehensive alerting with optimal response

Answer: D - Comprehensive alerting provides the best incident response capabilities.

Question 240: For ML model deployment with caching, which approach provides the best performance optimization?

A) Memory caching with LRU eviction B) Distributed caching with consistent hashing C) Intelligent caching with predictive prefetching D) Comprehensive caching with optimal performance

Answer: D - Comprehensive caching strategies provide the best performance optimization.

Question 241: A production ML system requires workflow optimization. Which approach provides the best efficiency?

A) Pipeline optimization with parallel execution B) Resource optimization with efficient allocation C) Dependency optimization with reduced coupling D) Comprehensive workflow optimization with optimal efficiency

Answer: D - Comprehensive workflow optimization provides the best efficiency.

Question 242: For ML model deployment with API management, which approach provides the best interface control?

A) API gateways with request routing B) Rate limiting with traffic control C) Authentication with access control D) Comprehensive API management with optimal control

Answer: D - Comprehensive API management provides the best interface control.

Question 243: A production ML system requires testing automation. Which approach provides the best quality assurance?

A) Unit testing with component validation B) Integration testing with system validation C) End-to-end testing with workflow validation D) Comprehensive testing with optimal quality assurance

Answer: D - Comprehensive testing provides the best quality assurance.

Question 244: For ML model deployment with environment management, which approach provides the best isolation?

A) Containerization with process isolation B) Virtualization with resource isolation C) Namespaces with logical isolation D) Comprehensive environment management with optimal isolation

Answer: D - Comprehensive environment management provides the best isolation.

Question 245: A production ML system requires documentation automation. Which approach provides the best knowledge management?

A) API documentation with interface specifications B) Runbook documentation with operational procedures C) Architecture documentation with system design D) Comprehensive documentation with optimal knowledge management

Answer: D - Comprehensive documentation provides the best knowledge management.

Question 246: For ML model deployment with compliance automation, which approach provides the best regulatory adherence?

A) Audit automation with compliance checking B) Policy enforcement with rule validation C) Reporting automation with compliance documentation D) Comprehensive compliance automation with optimal adherence

Answer: D - Comprehensive compliance automation provides the best regulatory adherence.

Question 247: A production ML system requires performance tuning. Which approach provides the best optimization?

A) Profiling with performance analysis B) Benchmarking with comparative evaluation C) Load testing with capacity validation D) Comprehensive performance tuning with optimal optimization

Answer: D - Comprehensive performance tuning provides the best optimization.

Question 248: For ML model deployment with resource isolation, which approach provides the best multi-tenancy?

A) Container isolation with resource limits B) Namespace isolation with logical separation C) Virtual machine isolation with hardware separation D) Comprehensive resource isolation with optimal multi-tenancy

Answer: D - Comprehensive resource isolation provides the best multi-tenancy.

Question 249: A production ML system requires maintenance automation. Which approach provides the best operational efficiency?

A) Automated patching with security updates B) Automated scaling with capacity management C) Automated backup with data protection D) Comprehensive maintenance automation with optimal efficiency

Answer: D - Comprehensive maintenance automation provides the best operational efficiency.

Question 250: For ML model deployment with continuous optimization, which approach provides the best long-term performance?

A) Performance monitoring with trend analysis B) Automated tuning with parameter optimization C) Continuous learning with model adaptation D) Comprehensive continuous optimization with optimal long-term performance

Answer: D - Comprehensive continuous optimization provides the best long-term performance through multiple strategies.

Exam Preparation Strategy

These 250 practice questions cover all four domains of the AWS Machine Learning Engineer Associate exam while emphasizing practical scenarios over theoretical knowledge. Each question tests real-world decision-making skills that distinguish competent ML engineers from those who struggle with production implementations.

The brief explanations reinforce key concepts while building confidence for the actual exam environment. Focus on understanding the reasoning behind each answer rather than memorizing specific responses, as the actual exam will present similar scenarios with different details and contexts.

Success on the certification exam requires combining this practice with hands-on experience using AWS ML services, systematic study of AWS documentation, and regular review of

MLOps best practices. The investment in comprehensive preparation pays dividends through both certification success and practical skills that advance your professional career.

Practical Application

Machine learning certification represents more than academic achievement—it validates practical skills that enable you to solve real business problems through appropriate technology application. The scenarios presented in these practice questions reflect the challenges you'll encounter in professional ML engineering roles.

Use these questions as diagnostic tools to identify knowledge gaps while building confidence through systematic practice. The combination of comprehensive preparation and practical experience provides the foundation for both certification success and long-term career advancement in the rapidly growing field of machine learning operations.

References

(1) AWS Training and Certification. (2024). "AWS Certification Benefits and Career Impact Study." *AWS Documentation.*

(2) Amazon Web Services. (2024). "AWS Certified Machine Learning Engineer – Associate Certification Guide." *AWS Documentation.*

(3) Amazon Web Services. (2024). "AWS Certified Machine Learning – Specialty Certification Guide." *AWS Documentation.*

(4) Market Research Future. (2024). "MLOps Market Size, Growth Analysis and Industry Forecast 2024-2032." *Industry Report.*

(5) Skillsoft. (2024). "AWS Certification Salary Impact Analysis 2024." *Professional Development Report.*

(6) Amazon Web Services. (2024). "AWS Certification Career Advancement Study." *AWS Documentation.*

(7) Amazon Web Services. (2024). "AWS Organizations User Guide: Multi-Account Management." *AWS Documentation.*

(8) Amazon Web Services. (2024). "AWS Well-Architected Framework: Machine Learning Lens." *AWS Documentation.*

(9) Amazon Web Services. (2024). "Amazon S3 User Guide: Data Lake Architectures." *AWS Documentation.*

(10) Amazon Web Services. (2024). "AWS Glue Developer Guide: ETL Jobs and Data Processing." *AWS Documentation.*

(11) Amazon Web Services. (2024). "Amazon EMR Management Guide: Big Data Processing." *AWS Documentation.*

(12) Amazon Web Services. (2024). "AWS Lambda Developer Guide: Serverless Computing." *AWS Documentation.*

(13) Amazon Web Services. (2024). "Amazon SageMaker Feature Store Developer Guide." *AWS Documentation*.

(14) Amazon Web Services. (2024). "Amazon Athena User Guide: Serverless Query Service." *AWS Documentation*.

(15) Amazon Web Services. (2024). "Amazon QuickSight User Guide: Business Intelligence Service." *AWS Documentation*.

(16) Amazon Web Services. (2024). "Amazon SageMaker Data Wrangler User Guide." *AWS Documentation*.

(17) Amazon Web Services. (2024). "Amazon EMR Notebooks User Guide: Managed Jupyter Environments." *AWS Documentation*.

(18) Amazon Web Services. (2024). "Amazon QuickSight Machine Learning Insights Documentation." *AWS Documentation*.

(19) Amazon Web Services. (2024). "Amazon SageMaker Notebook Instance User Guide." *AWS Documentation*.

(20) Amazon Web Services. (2024). "Amazon SageMaker Linear Learner Algorithm Documentation." *AWS Documentation*.

(21) Amazon Web Services. (2024). "Amazon SageMaker Bring Your Own Container Guide." *AWS Documentation*.

(22) Amazon Web Services. (2024). "Amazon SageMaker Automatic Model Tuning Developer Guide." *AWS Documentation*.

(23) Amazon Web Services. (2024). "Amazon SageMaker Autopilot User Guide." *AWS Documentation*.

(24) Amazon Web Services. (2024). "Amazon SageMaker Clarify Documentation: Model Explainability and Bias Detection." *AWS Documentation*.

(25) Amazon Web Services. (2024). "Amazon SageMaker Real-time Inference Documentation." *AWS Documentation*.

(26) Amazon Web Services. (2024). "Amazon SageMaker Pipelines Developer Guide." *AWS Documentation.*

(27) Amazon Web Services. (2024). "Amazon SageMaker Model Monitor Developer Guide." *AWS Documentation.*

(28) Amazon Web Services. (2024). "Amazon SageMaker Model Registry User Guide." *AWS Documentation.*

(29) Amazon Web Services. (2024). "Amazon Rekognition Developer Guide." *AWS Documentation.*

(30) Amazon Web Services. (2024). "Amazon Comprehend Developer Guide." *AWS Documentation.*

(31) Amazon Web Services. (2024). "Amazon Forecast Developer Guide." *AWS Documentation.*

Made in the USA
Middletown, DE
29 October 2025

20334864R00199